2/60

2000 BLUES Licks That Rock!

by Lawrence Fritts

ISBN 978-1-57424-285-0
SAN 683-8022

Cover by James Creative Group

Copyright © 2012 CENTERSTREAM Publishing, LLC
P.O. Box 17878 - Anaheim Hills, CA 92817

www.centerstream-usa.com

Table of Contents

Backing Track CDs

The book is accompanied by three CDs containing 43 blues backing tracks recorded live by John Klinkowitz—guitar; Nate Basinger—organ, electric piano; Drew Morton—bass; and Justin LeDuc—drums.

CD 1

1. BABY TALK BLUES in G ....(4:46)
2. BACKDOOR BUZZER BLUES in D...(3:53)
3. BIG DADDY'S PLACE BLUES in F...(4:23)
4. BIG TIPPER BLUES in G...(4:40)
5. BLIND OYSTER BLUES in E..(3:28)
6. BODY LANGUAGE BLUES in F ....(4:17)
7. BROWN SHOES BLUES in C ....(4:22)
8. BUBBLE GUM BLUES in A...(5:29)
9. BUMPER TO BUMBER BLUES in G ....(5:30)
10. CAFETERIA BLUES in D..(5:05)
11. CALL ME A CAB BLUES in A ....(5:10)
12. CAT BARF BLUES in C...(4:19)
13. CLASS A BLUES in D ....(4:07)
14. COLD CALL BLUES in F ....(5:06)

CD 2

1. CUPCAKE BLUES in G ....(4:30)
2. CUT MY GRASS BLUES in Bb..(4:37)
3. DOOR TO DOOR BLUES in F ....(4:36)
4. DUMB DOG BLUES in E...(3:47)
5. EAST CHICAGO BLUES in D...(4:02)
6. EXPIRED TAGS BLUES in F ....(5:11)
7. EXTRA SENSORY BLUES in C ....(4:39)
8. FACE TIME BLUES in F ....(4:24)
9. HOLY GHOST BLUES in Bb..(4:45)
10. HOPPED UP BLUES in D..(4:22)
11. LAST EL STOP BLUES in G ....(4:29)
12. MAKE ME TARDY BLUES in Bb ....(3:30)
13. MORON BLUES in A..(4:25)
14. MR. GOECKE BLUES in D ....(4:20)

CD 3

1. NEANDERTHAL BLUES in G...(3:48)
2. NON-COMPLIANT BLUES in A..(3:58)
3. POST MODERN BLUES in G...(3:45)
4. RESPECT MY CAT BLUES in A ....(4:23)
5. SIDE EYE BLUES in E...(4:27)
6. SNORING CAT BLUES in D ....(4:01)
7. STOMP AND BAWL BLUES in A ....(4:53)
8. SUCKER PUNCH BLUES in A ....(4:13)
9. TOO GOOD FOR ME BLUES in Bb ....(4:08)
10. TRANSCENDENTAL BLUES in C..(5:14)
11. USUAL BLUES in E...(4:46)
12. WALK THAT POODLE Blues in F..(4:23)
13. WE NEED TO TALK BLUES in F...(4:39)
14. WHERE'S MY PANTS BLUES in C...(3:47)
15. WHOSE BEER BLUES in C...(4:23)

Introduction

The 2,000+ licks in this book are organized into 36 chapters. These chapters explore the different pitches, rhythms, techniques, and methods of phrasing found in blues and blues-infuenced guitar solos and fills. These may be played along with the accompanying 43 backing tracks included on 3 CDs that come with the book. The licks in the book are all written in the key of a C blues, while the backing tracks are played in the keys of E, A, D, G, C, F, and Bb. The table below shows how to transpose up or down from C to other blues keys.

Key	Transposed Up	Transposed Down
C	0 frets higher	0 frets lower
C# or Db	1 fret higher	11 frets lower
D	2 frets higher	10 frets lower
Eb	3 frets higher	9 frets lower
E	4 frets higher	8 frets lower
F	5 frets higher	7 frets lower
F# or Gb	6 frets higher	6 frets lower
G	7 frets higher	5 frets lower
Ab	8 frets higher	4 frets lower
A	9 frets higher	3 frets lower
Bb	10 frets higher	2 frets lower
B	11 frets higher	1 fret lower

The backing tracks are all in the 12-bar blues form. However, most of the licks in the book do not necessarily have to be played over specific chords in the progression. Because the harmonic system of the blues treats dissonance differently than other styles, chords in a blues song exert a much weaker influence over which notes should be emphasized in a melody or solo. As an example, consider the backing on CD 1, "Cold Call Blues," which is in F. Since the licks in the book are written in C, to play one of them, say, Lick 8, along with "Cold Call Blues," one must finger it 7 frets higher, as the chart above indicates. The lick may be played in any bar of the song that suites your ear and feeling that you wish to create. The theory behind this is something that can be studied with a good teacher.

Acknowledgements

I am deeply grateful to the members and moderators of the TDPRI Forum, at http://www.tdpri.com/ for their support of this project. Ken Lasaine, Tim Bowen, Jeff Matz, and Stevie Gurr were especially helpful and generous. I would also like to thank my wife Sue Hettmansperger for all of her help and support. This book would not have been possible without my friend Gene Swift, to whom the work is dedicated.

About the author

Lawrence Fritts has played guitar in blues, rock, country, and jazz groups since 1968. He is member of the blues trio, Larry and the Belief System, and for over 40 years, a member of the Dog Years along with Gary Harmon and Gene Swift. He earned his PhD in Composition from the University of Chicago, and is currently Associate Professor of Composition and Theory at the University of Iowa, where he has directed the Electronic Music Studios since 1994. He is a founding editorial board member of the *Journal of Mathematics and Music,* and his compositions for instruments and electronics are recorded on CDs and DVD on the Albany, Centaur, Innova, SEAMUS, Frog Peak, and Tempo Primo labels. More information on Dr. Fritts can be found on his website, www.lawrence-fritts.com.

Chapter 1:
C Eb F G Bb

The licks in this chapter are made up of the notes C Eb F G Bb. These are most commonly known as a C minor pentatonic scale. These notes form the backbone of most blues vocal melodies and guitar solos. Most of Muddy Waters', Howlin' Wolf's, and Willie Dixon's songs use the minor pentatonic exclusively. The note C is called the tonic, and it creates a feeling of stability, resolution, and finality. The note Eb is one of the so-called *blue notes*. It can express sadness, anger, and aggression. The note F is often used as a *passing tone* between Eb and G. When it is emphasized by being held for a beat or more, it often resolves downward to Eb. The note G has a dual purpose, creating a feeling of stability or a need to resolve to the note C, depending on context. The note Bb is another blues note, expressing sadness, longing, and rootlessness.

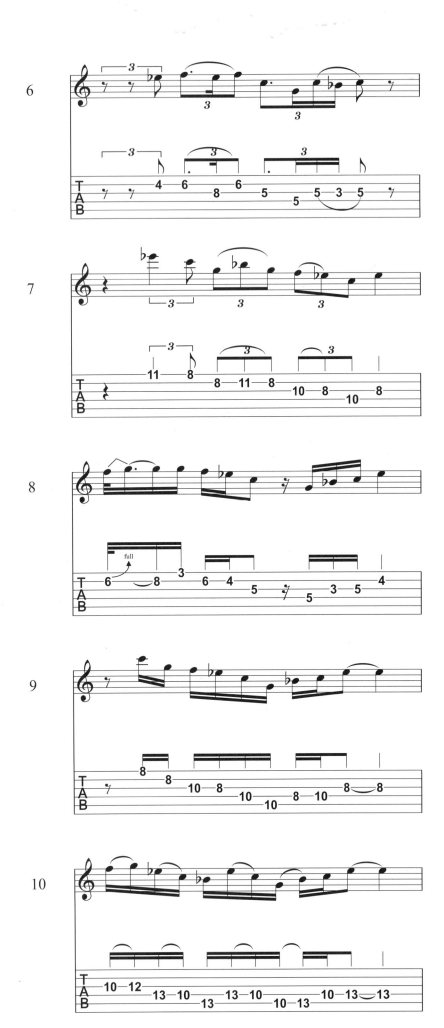

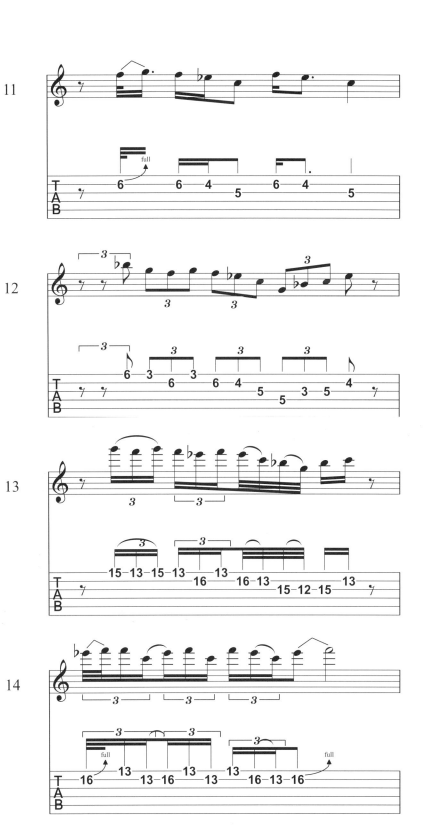

Dorian Michael

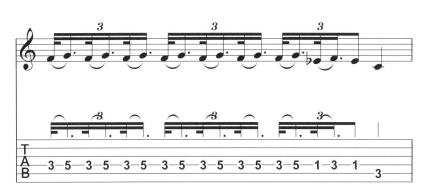

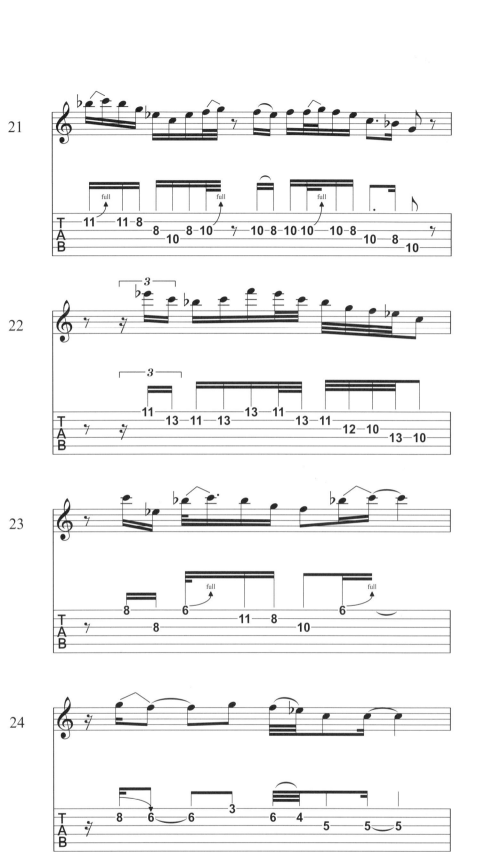
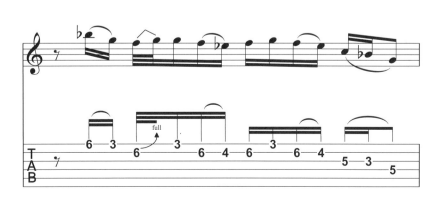

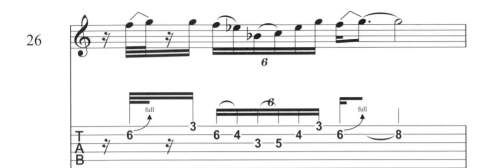

Chuck Berry

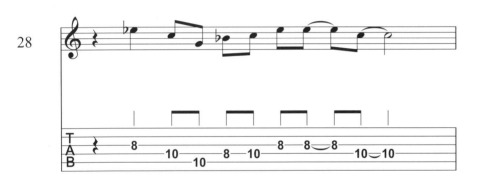

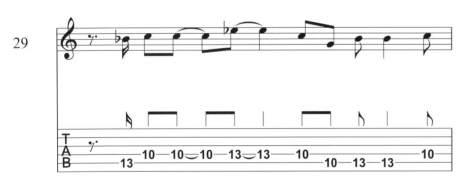

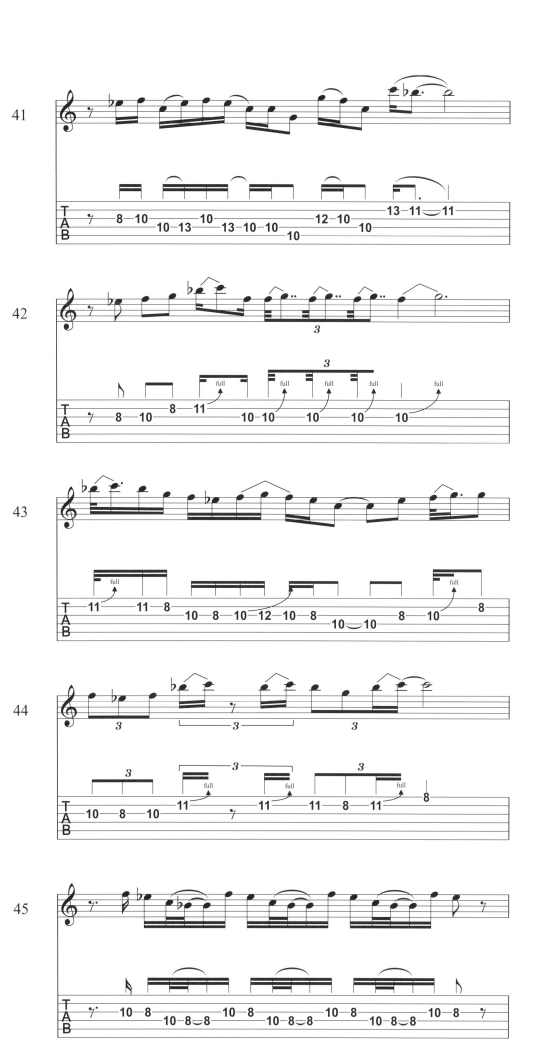

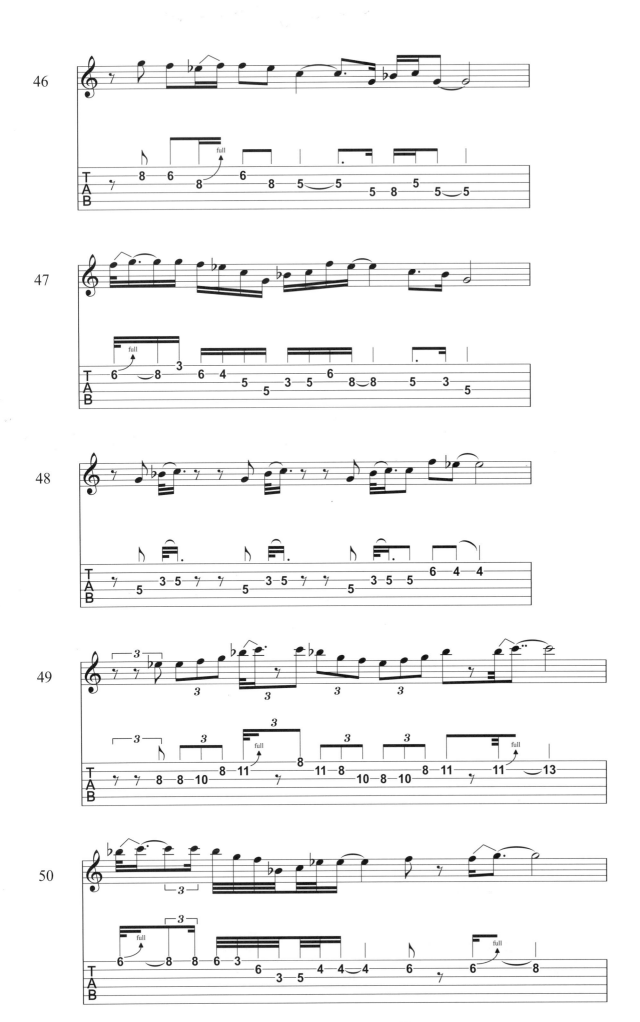

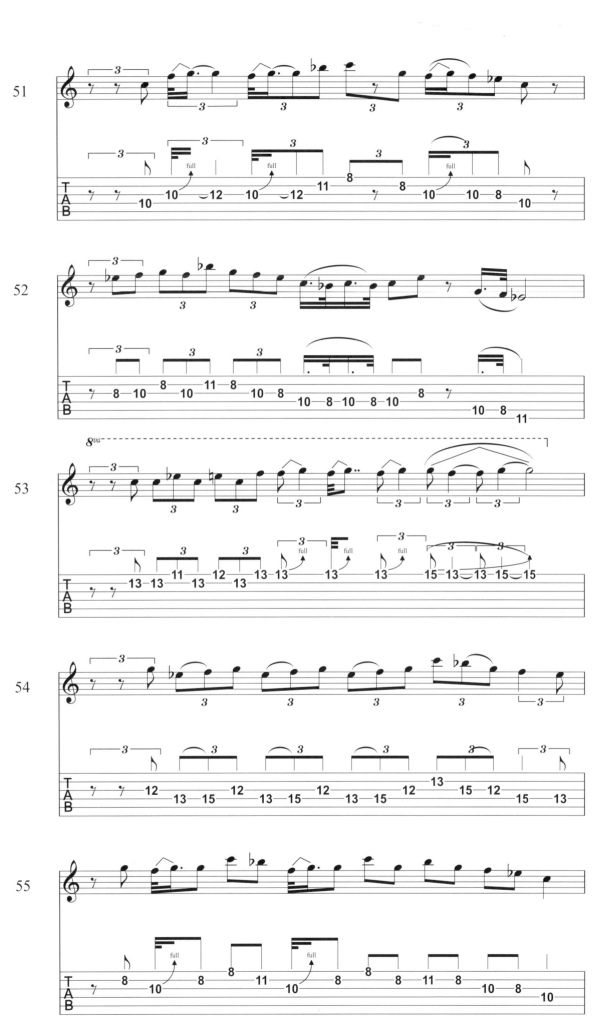

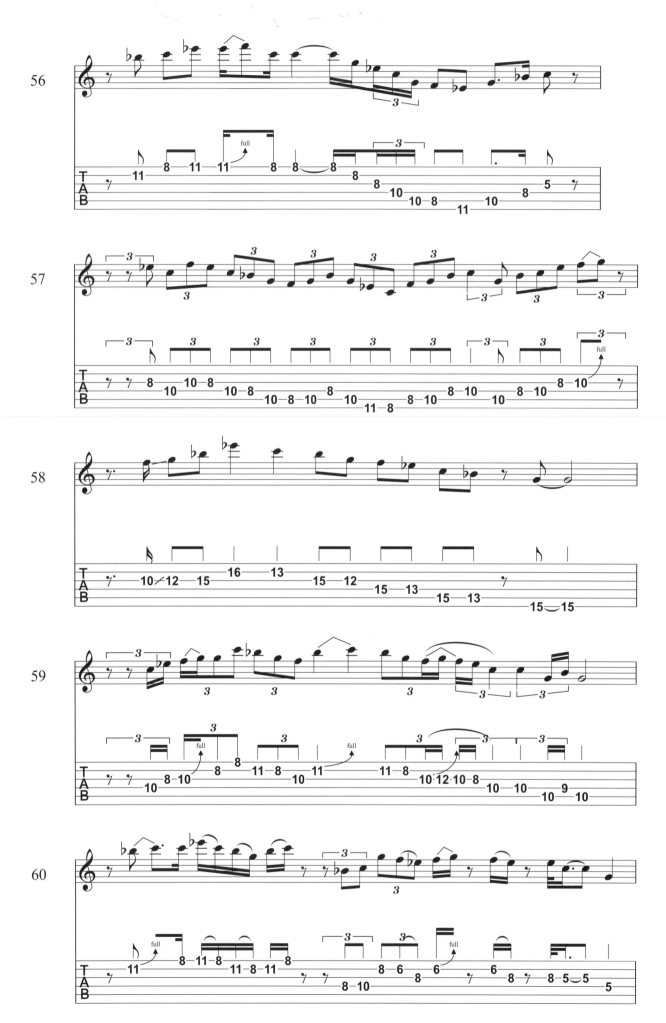

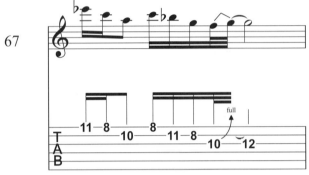

66

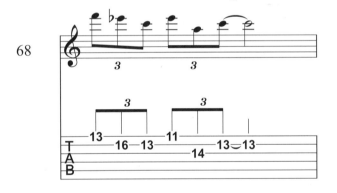

67

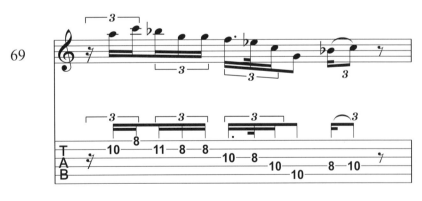

68

Chapter 2:
C Eb F G A Bb

In this chapter, note A is introduced. It is the interval of a sixth above C. Its expressive character is unique in the blues, and has been interpreted as sweet, schmaltzy, uptown, and sophisticated. The sixth is not generally used in music that is predominantly downhome, earthy, gritty, dirty, and funky. One important feature of the note A is that it is rarely used directly before or right after the note Bb. Playing these two notes in succession produces the interval of a semitone. The semitone in blues is usually reserved for the notes Eb E F and F F# G, as will be discussed later. In a 12-bar blues, the note A has a notable decorative, non-essential quality, which allows it to float over the chord progression in a gentle and ambiguous way, as can be heard in much of B.B. King's playing.

69

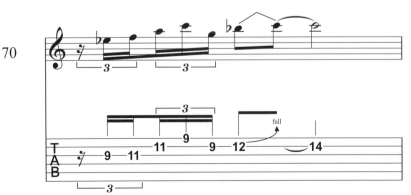

70

B.B. King

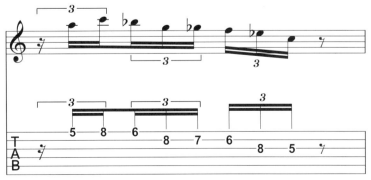

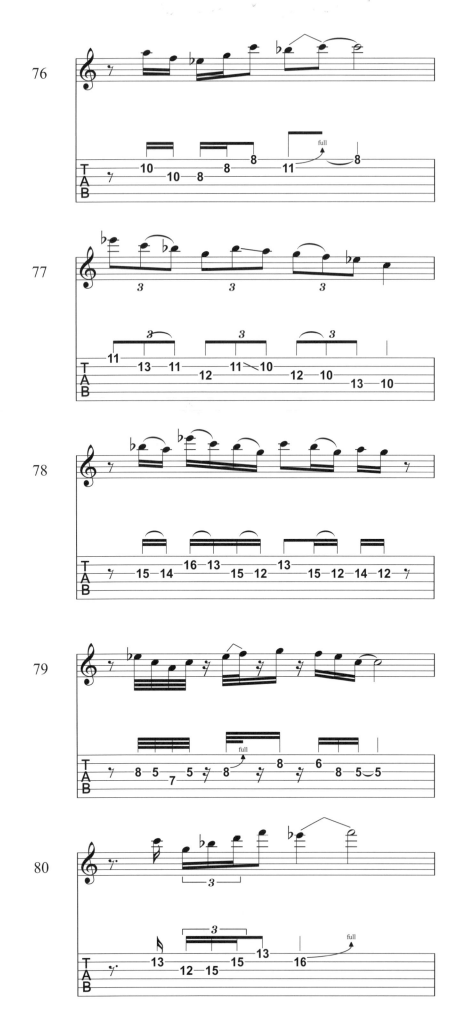

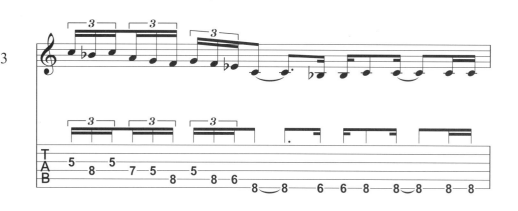

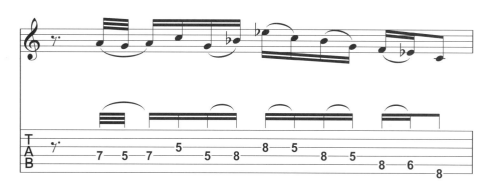

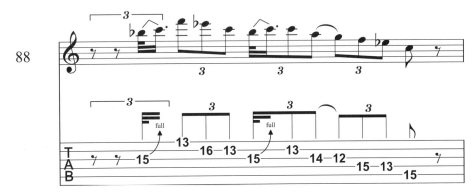

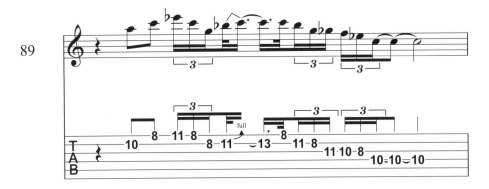

91

92

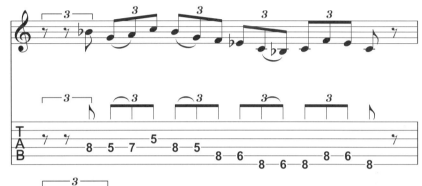

Stan West

93

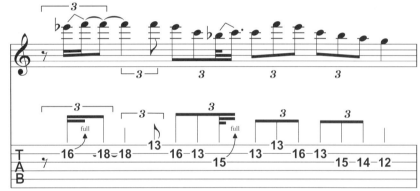

94

95

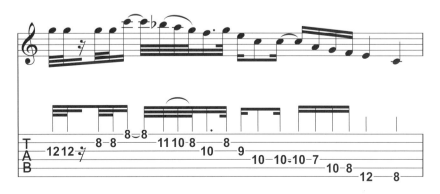

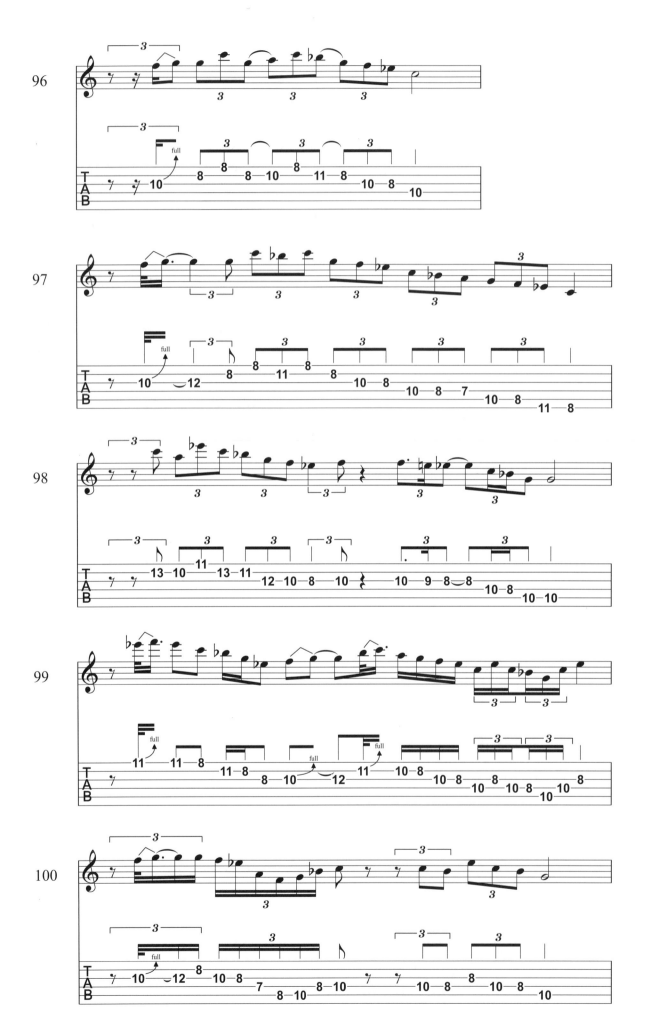

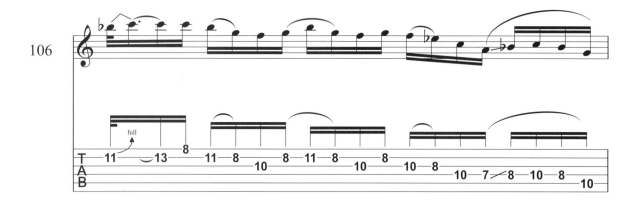

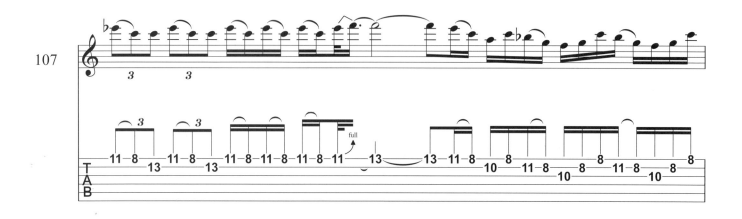

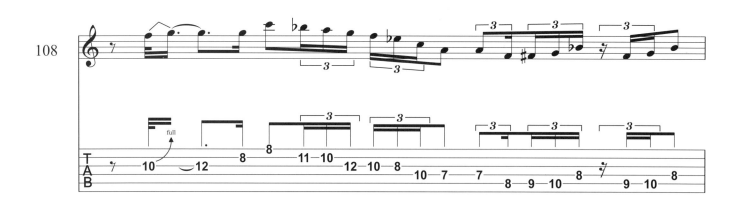

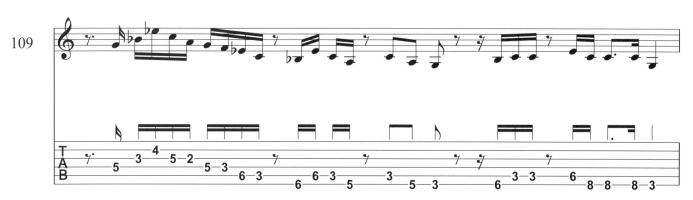

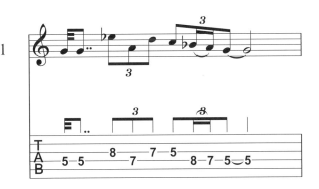

110

111

112

113

114

Chapter 3:
C D Eb F G A Bb

The licks in this chapter introduce the note D. This note forms the interval of a second above C. This note shares some of the qualities of the note A. Like A, the note D has a less gritty feel than the notes of the C minor pentatonic and it can seem to float over the 12-bar blues progression, with no particular need to resolve. It forms the interval of a semitone with the note Eb. The two notes in in succession are rarely heard in the earthier forms of blues. The notes C D Eb F G A Bb can be thought of as either a C dorian mode or a Bb major scale.

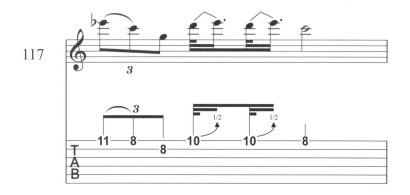

Blind Boy Fuller

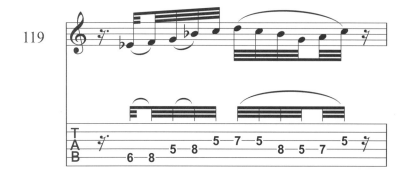

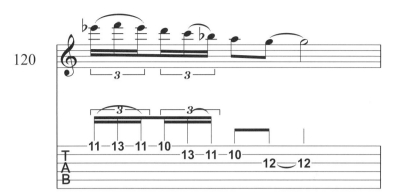

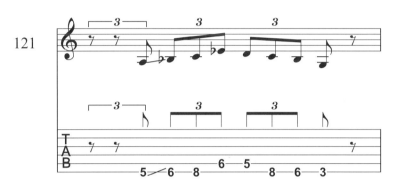

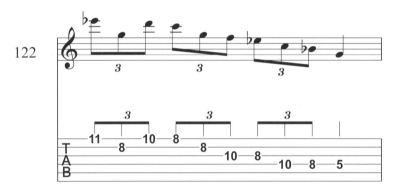

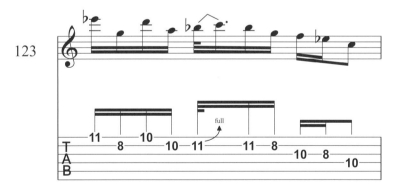

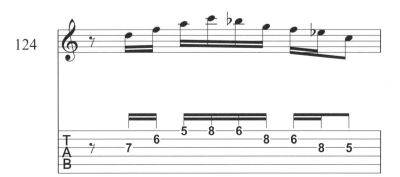

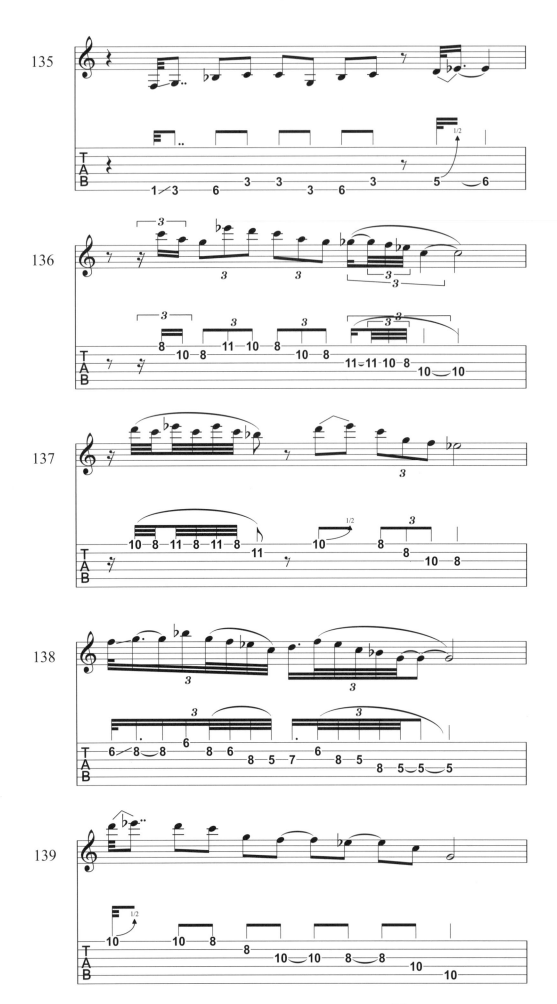

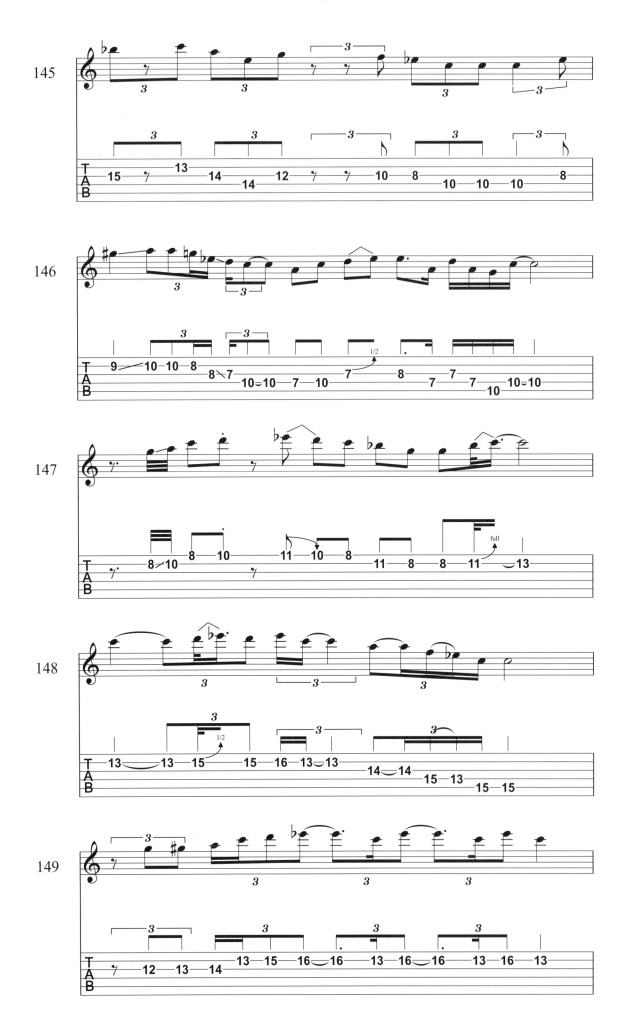

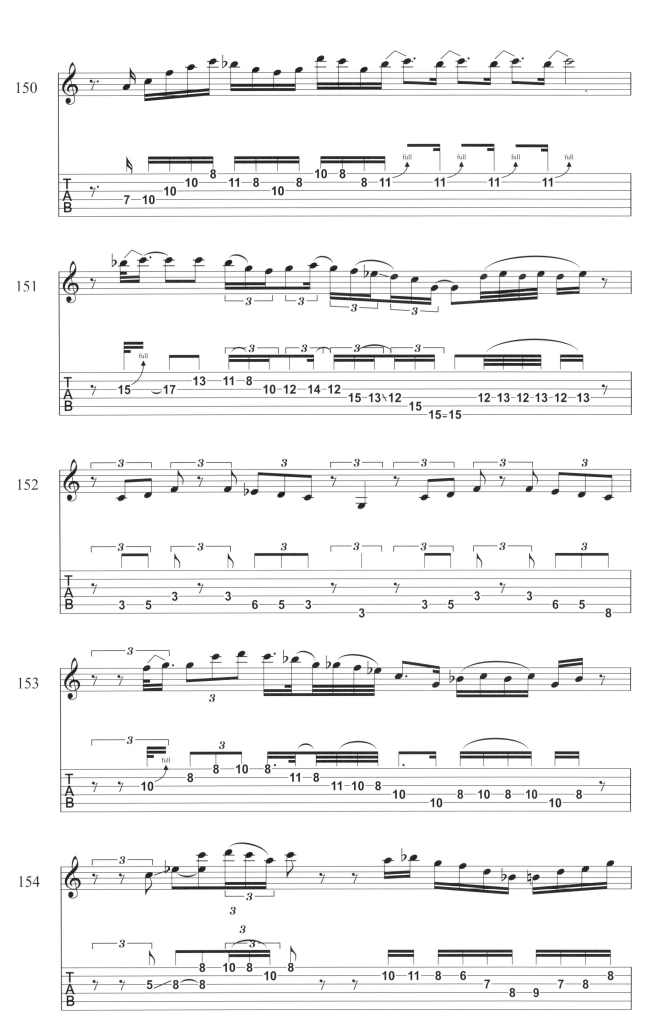

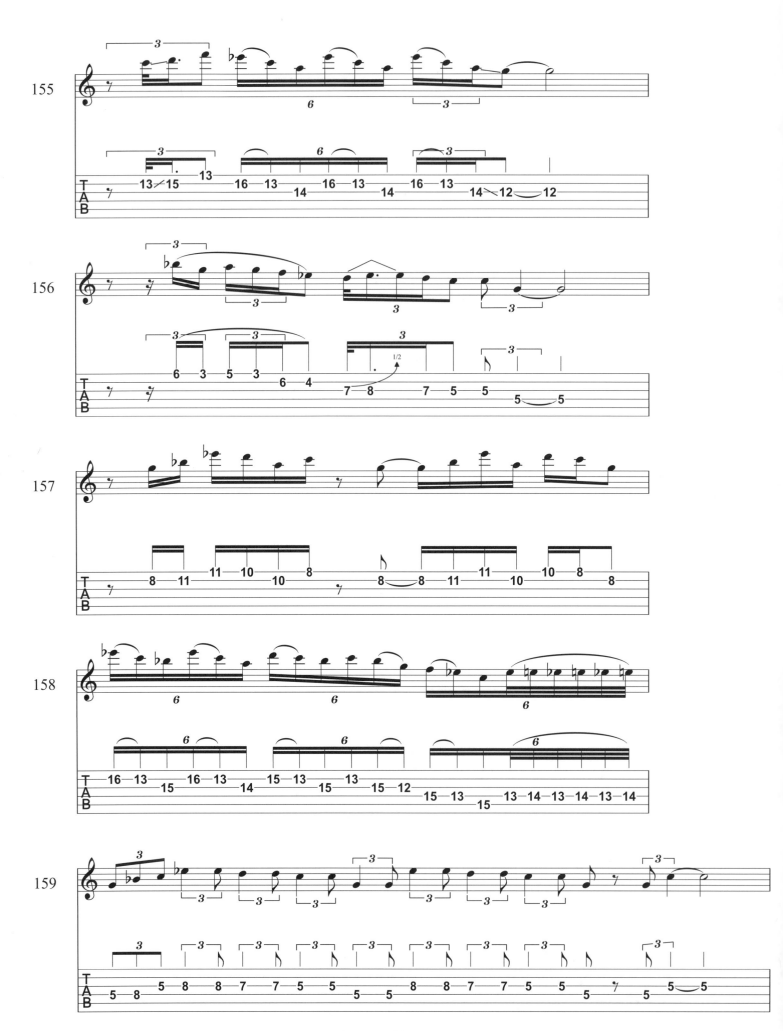

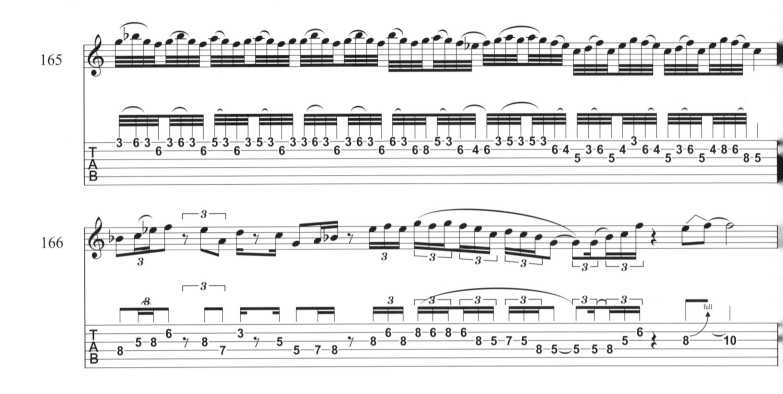

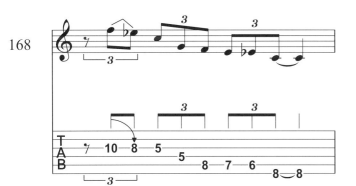

167

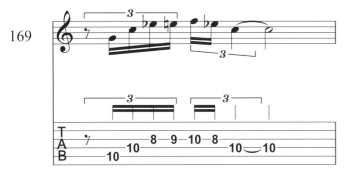

168

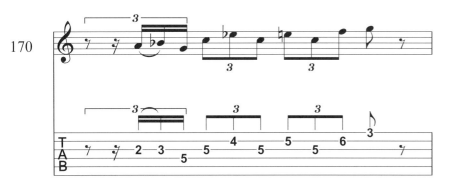

169

Chapter 4:
C Eb E F G Bb

The licks in this chapter incorporate the note E, a major third above C. While the note Eb, a minor third above C, has a sad, dark quality, the note E brightens the mood. The semitone between Eb and E is one of the most striking intervals used in blues guitar solos. Some guitarists, such as Albert King, bend up from C to Eb and C to E, while also exploring the microtones within the semitone. Others, most notably T-Bone Walker, outline a modified triad C Eb E G as a signature lick in a song or solo. Otis Rush often uses Eb throughout a solo, but ends important phrases on an E natural, creating an unexpectedly optimistic, less gloomy atmosphere. This practice of ending a minor phrase on a major third has a long history in music, dating back to Bach and other Baroque-era composers.

170

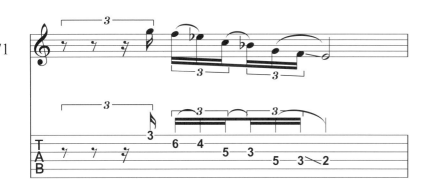

171

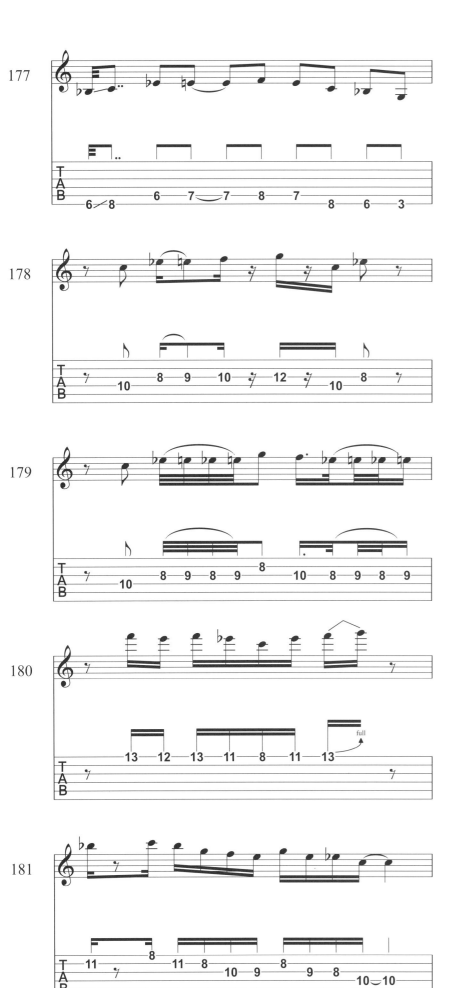

Memphis Willie

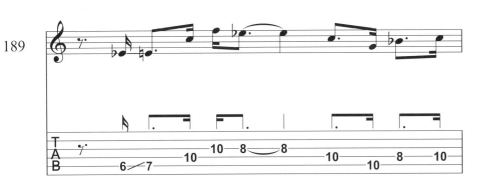

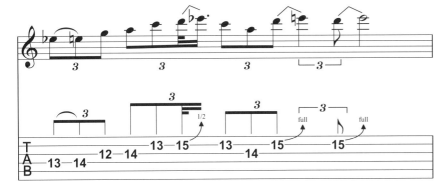

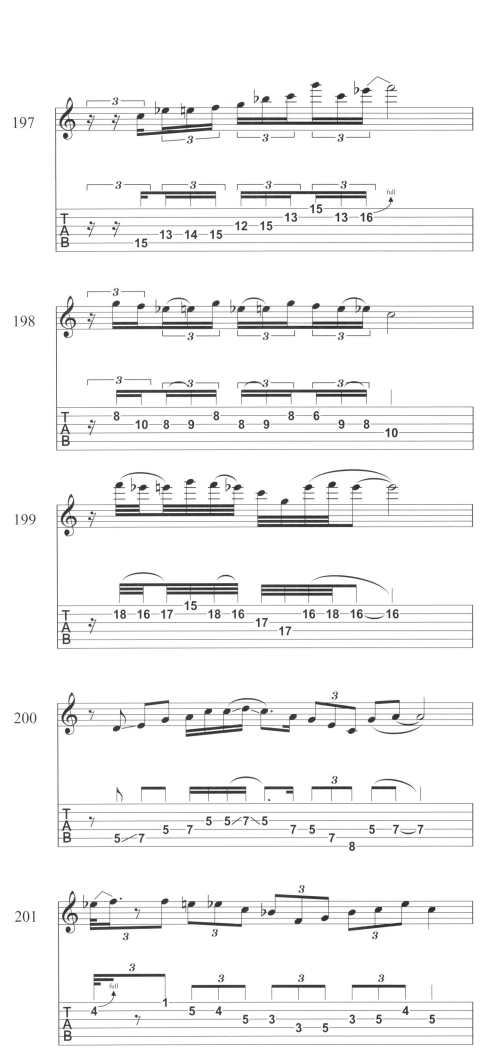

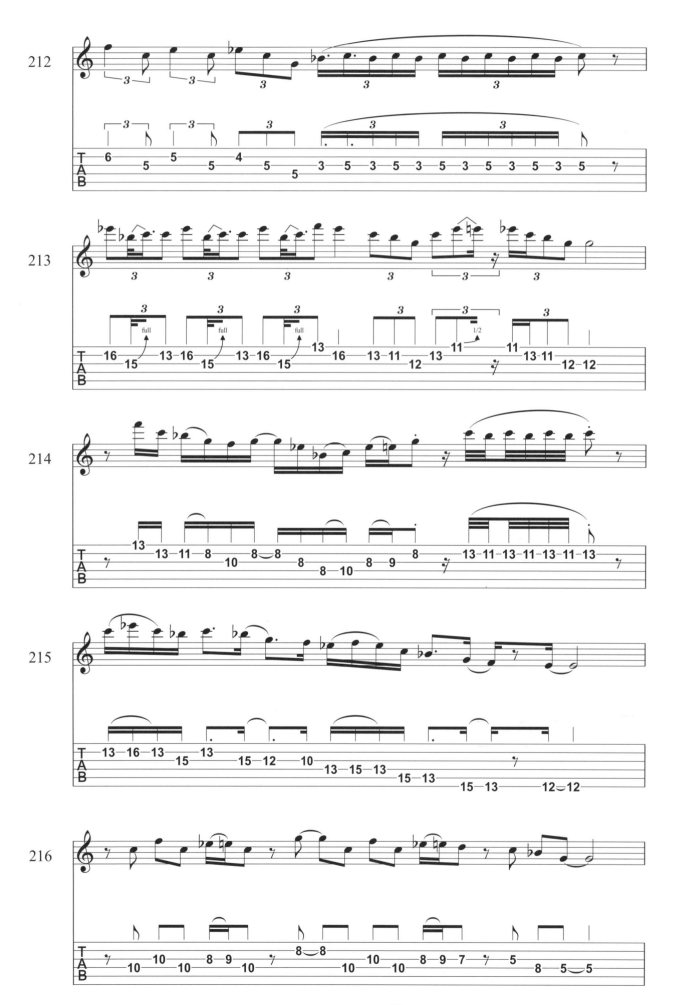

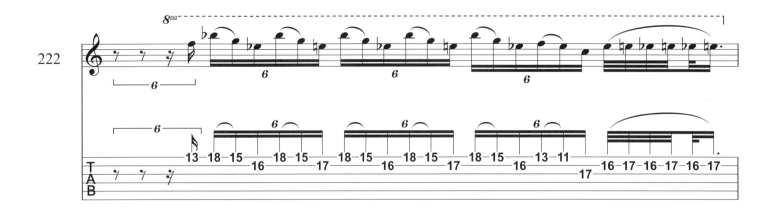

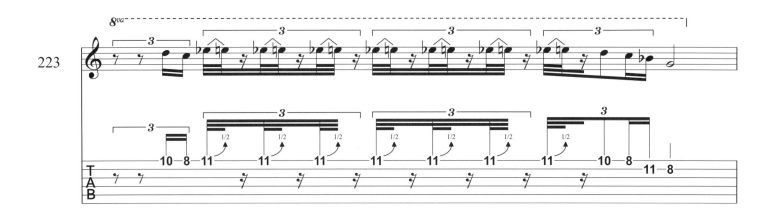

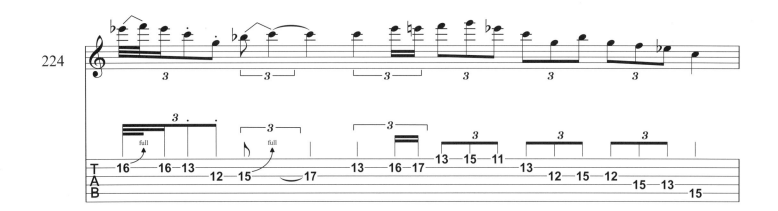

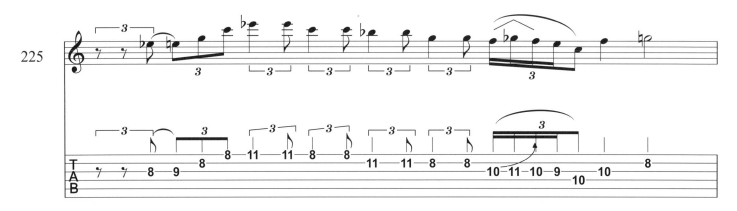

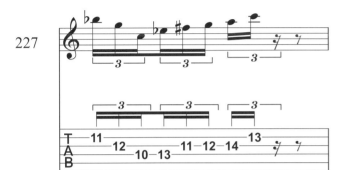

Chapter 5:
C D Eb F Gb G A Bb

This chapter introduces the flat fifth, Gb. Along with Eb and Bb, the note Gb is called a *blue note*. It has a very pungent, tangy quality that easily cuts through thick or complex textures. Because it is not a member of the chords of the 12-bar blues progression, it has a fresh, distinctive quality. This contributes to its instability, and is generally resolved down to F or up to G.

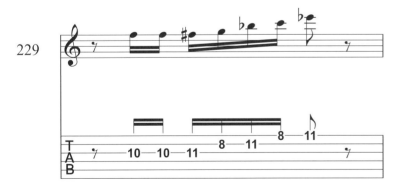

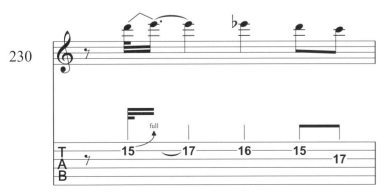

231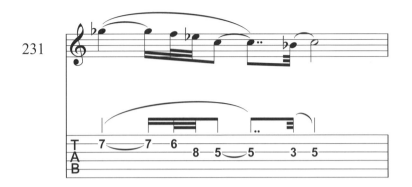

232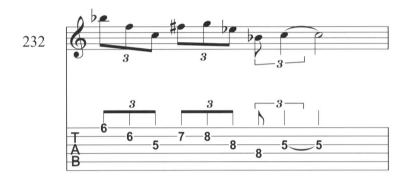

Jeff Beck

233

234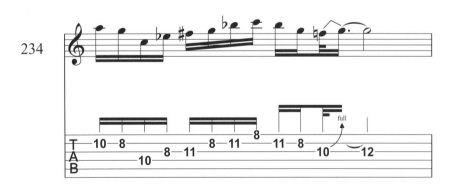

235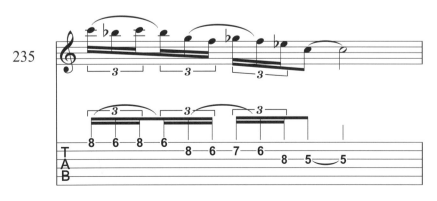

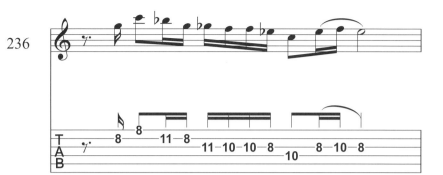

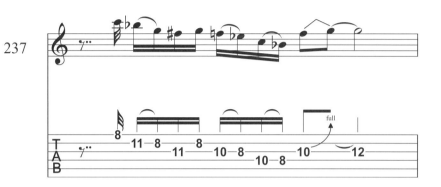

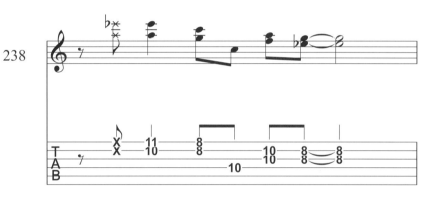

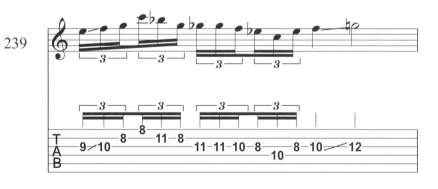

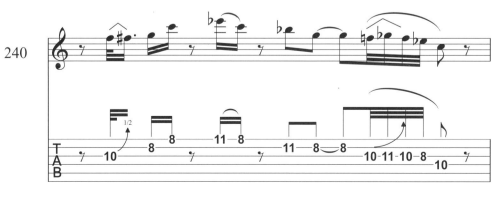

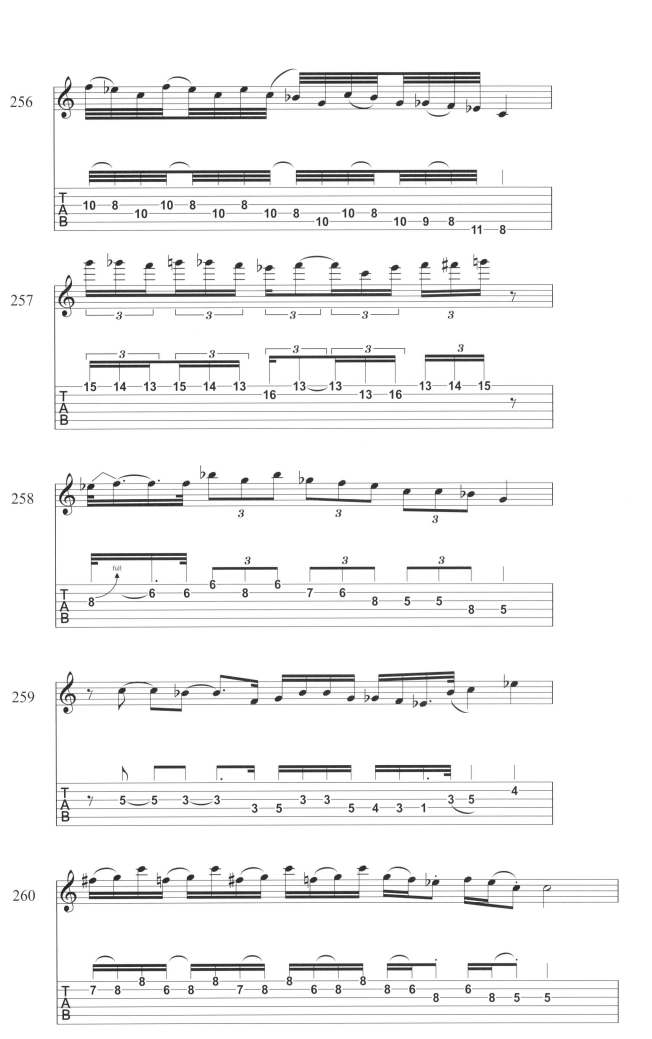

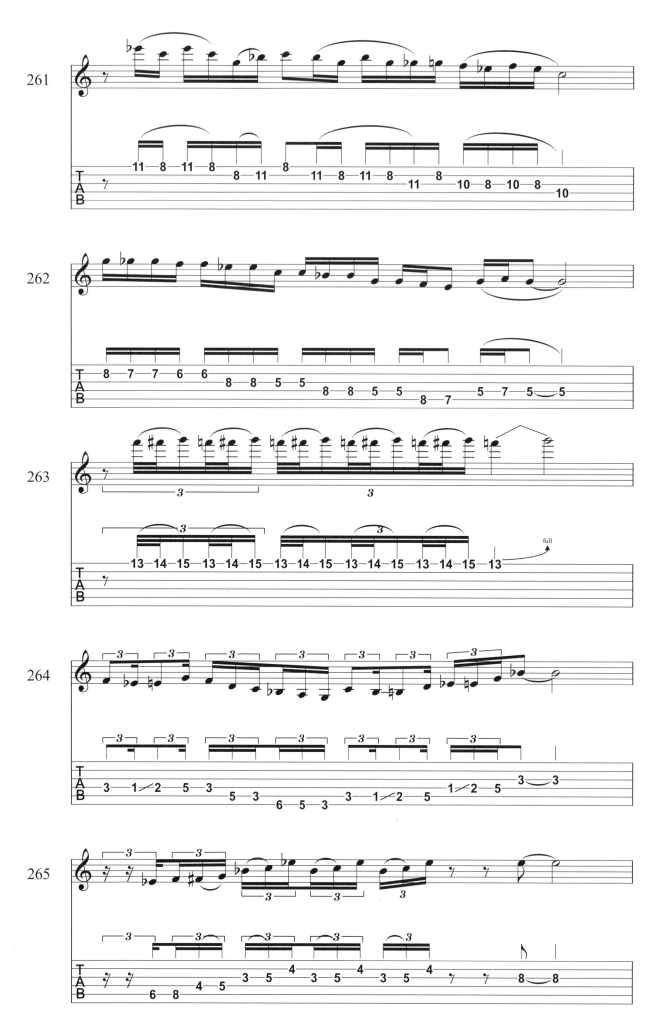

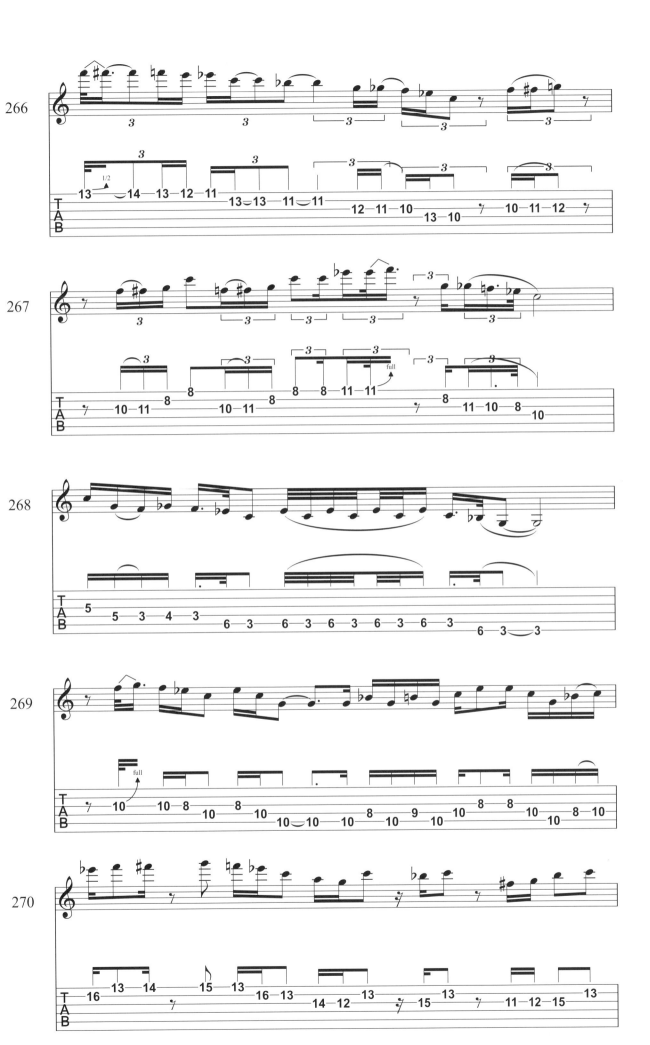

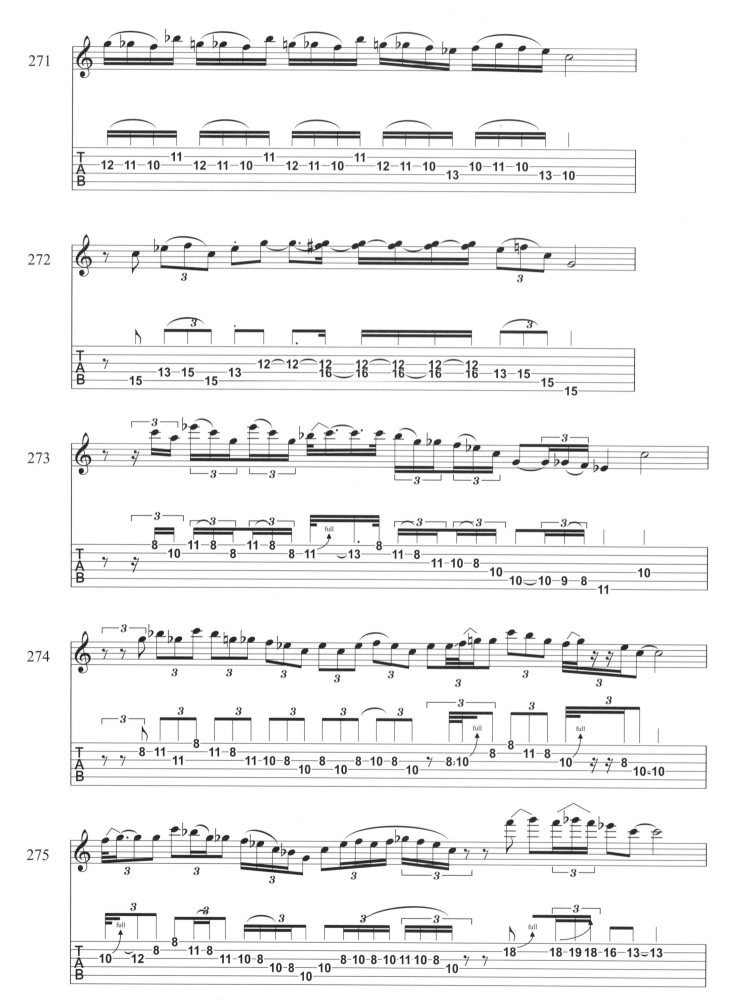

Chapter 6:
C Eb F G Bb B

This chapter introduces the note B. This note is often called the *leading tone* for its very strong tendency to lead up to the tonic note, C. When played over a G7 chord, which contains the notes G B D F, the upward resolution of B to C is very strong. If a player wants to weaken the strength of the leading tone effect, the note B can be followed by a descending semitone down to Bb. The note B, in either utilization, creates a flowing, jazz-like melodic motion found more in west coast, jump, and swing forms of the blues than in the music of the midwest guitarists centered in Chicago and Memphis.

281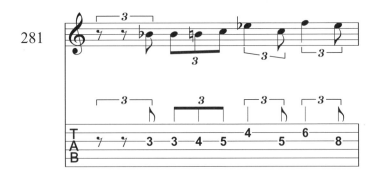

282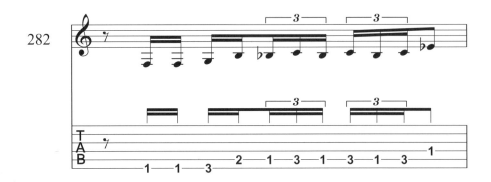

283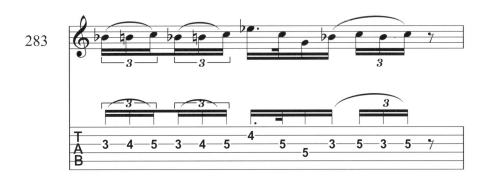

284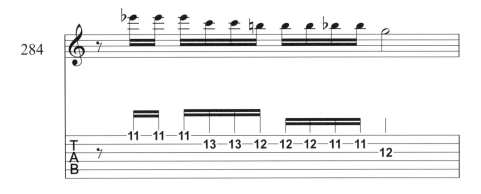

285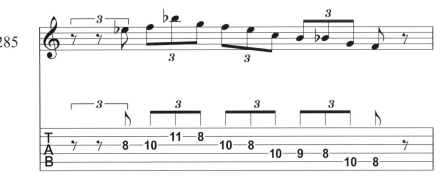

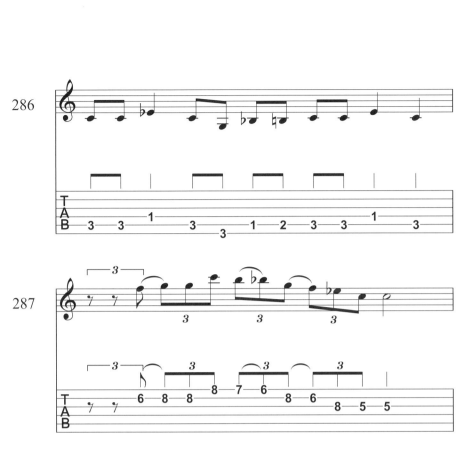

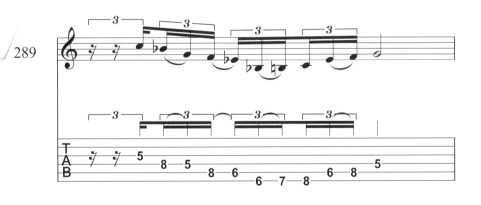

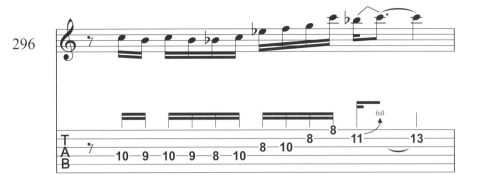

Bukka White

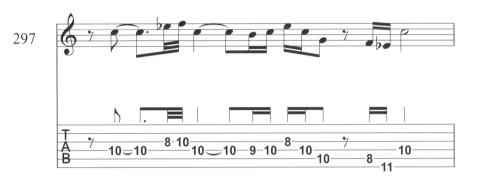

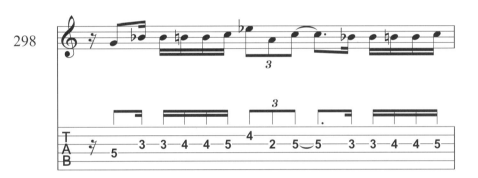

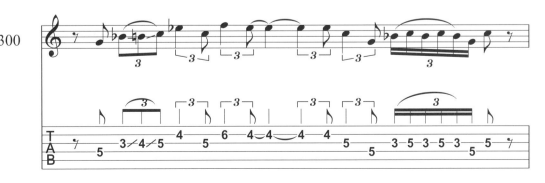

Chapter 7:
C Eb E F Gb G Bb B

The notes E, Gb, and B can be used to embellish the minor pentatonic scale. These notes help form the chromatic figures Eb E F, F Gb G, and Bb B C. These figures can be played either ascending or descending. Played with a full, clean sound, these figures create a distinctly jazz-like texture.

306

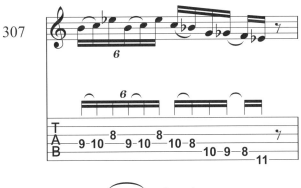

307

308

309

310

64

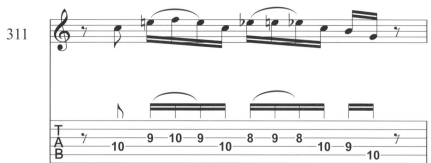

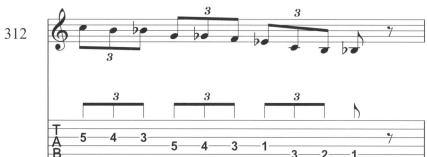

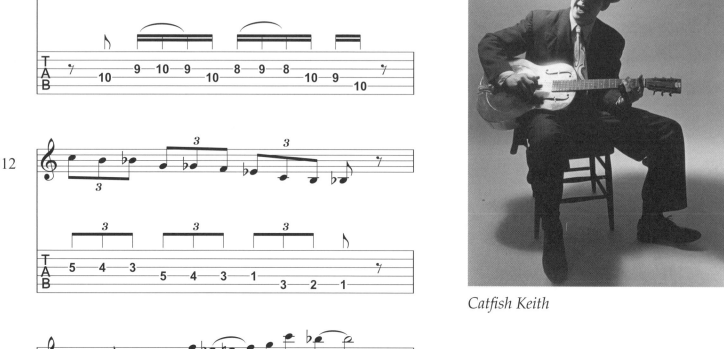

Catfish Keith

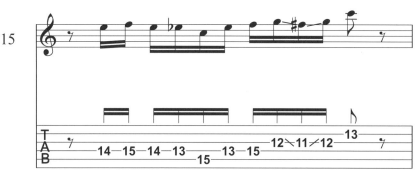

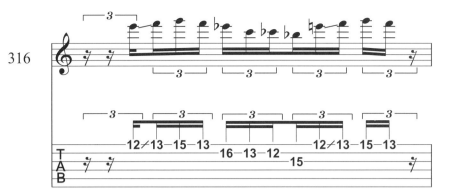

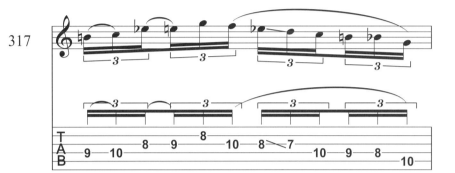

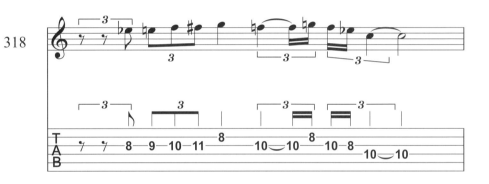

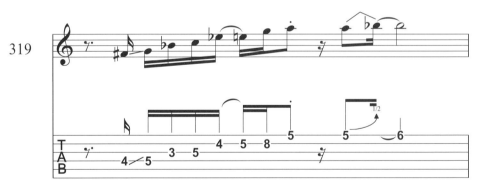

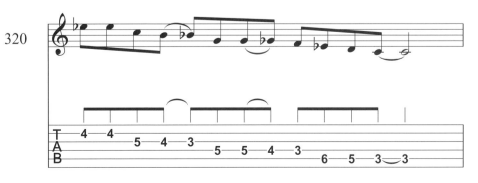

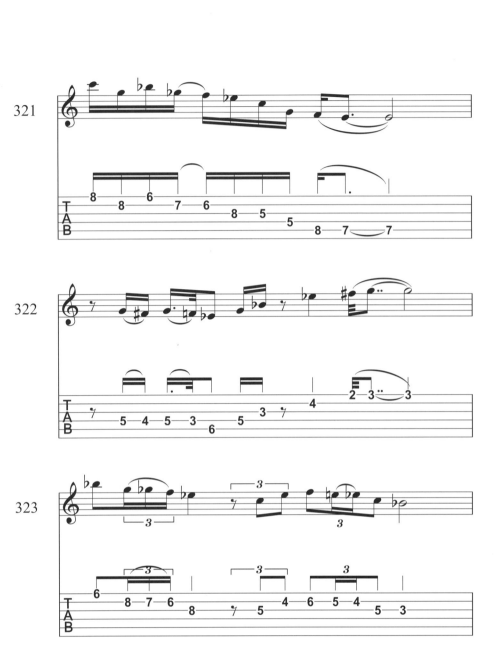

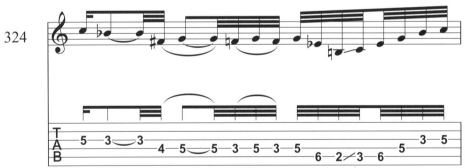

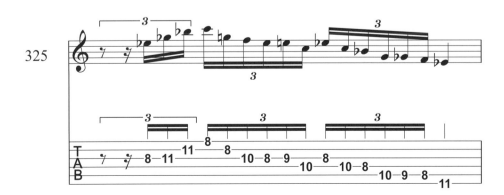

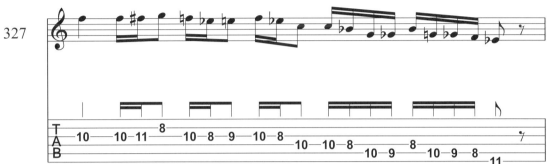

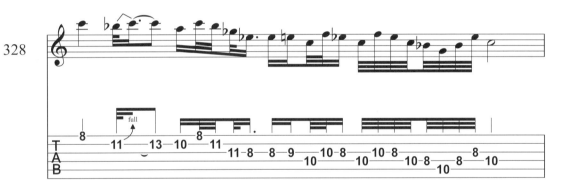

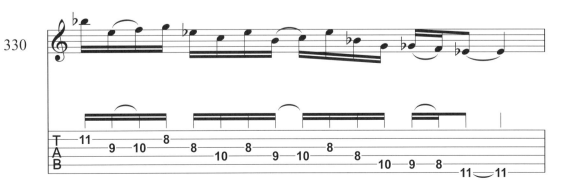

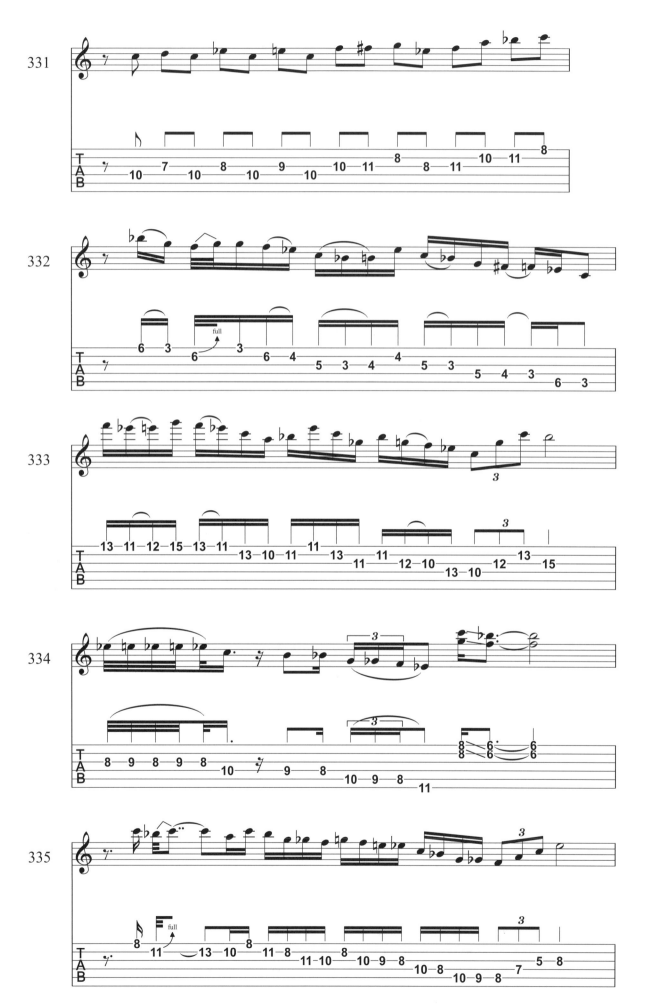

Chapter 8:
Slurs

The slur is a *legato* technique used to create a smooth, vocal-like character in phrase. Also called *hammer-on* and *hammer-off*, slurs combine clear, articulated attacks with smooth, soft attacks to create dynamic patterns that give equal-duration note values a unique type of rhythmic vitality and energy. Slurs are highly effective as expressive tools when the guitarist employs a warm, rich, overdriven sound that sustains easily.

356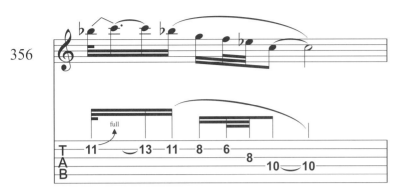

357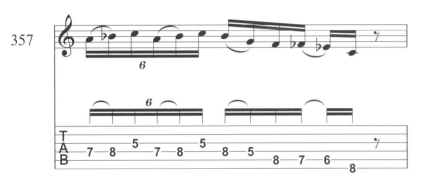

358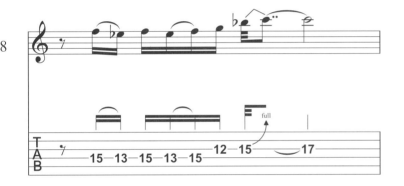

359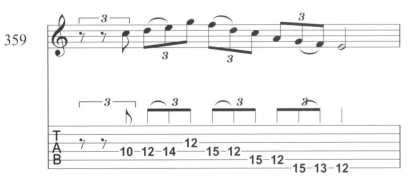

360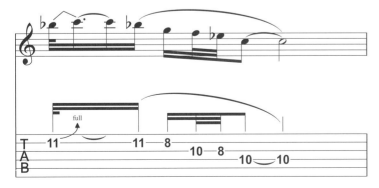

Kenny Sultan

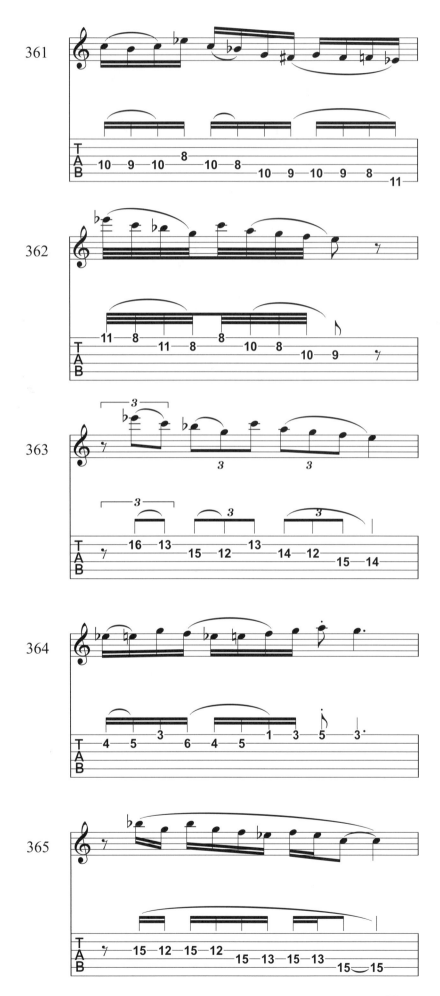

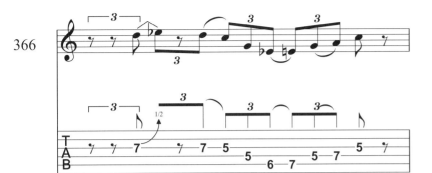

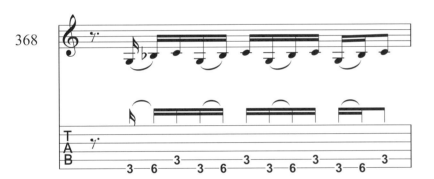

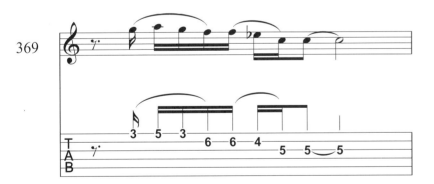

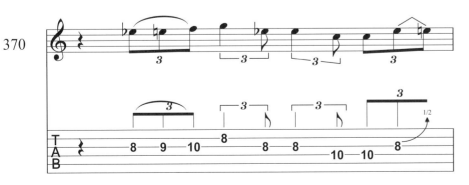

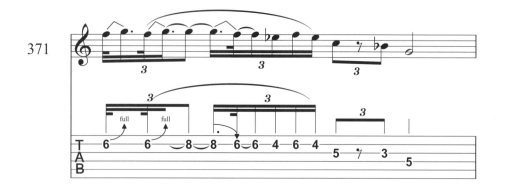

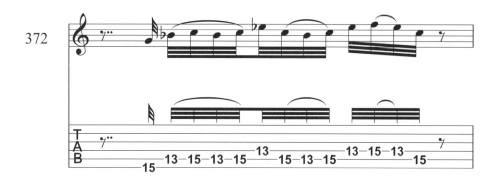

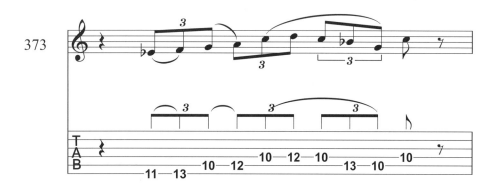

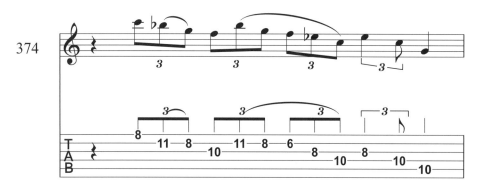

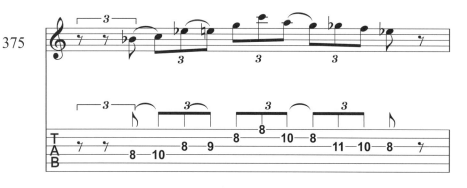

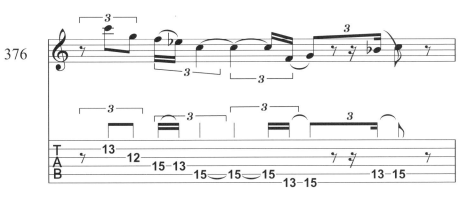

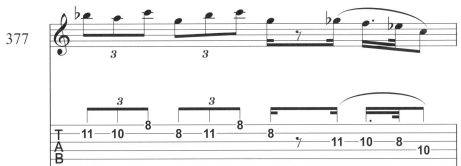

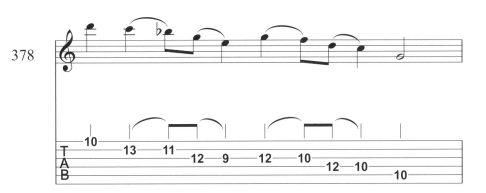

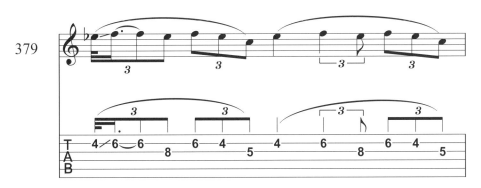

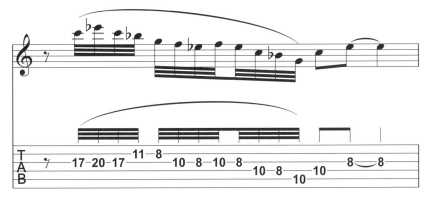

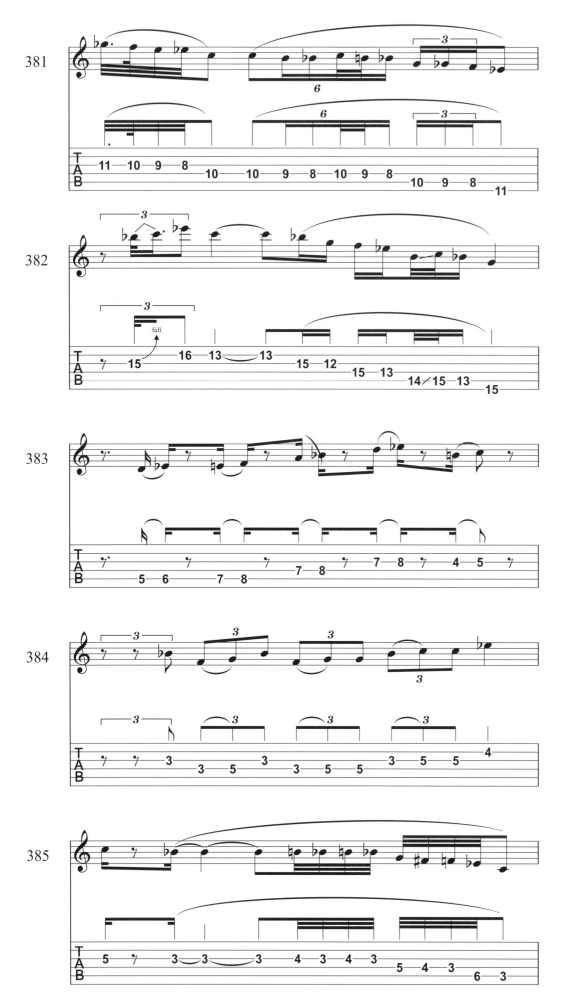

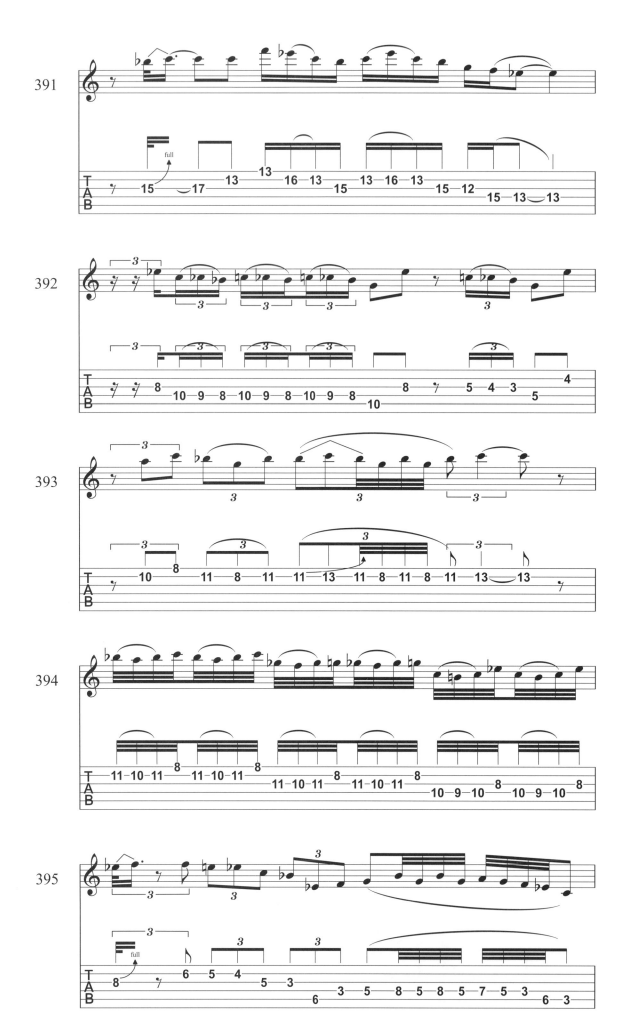

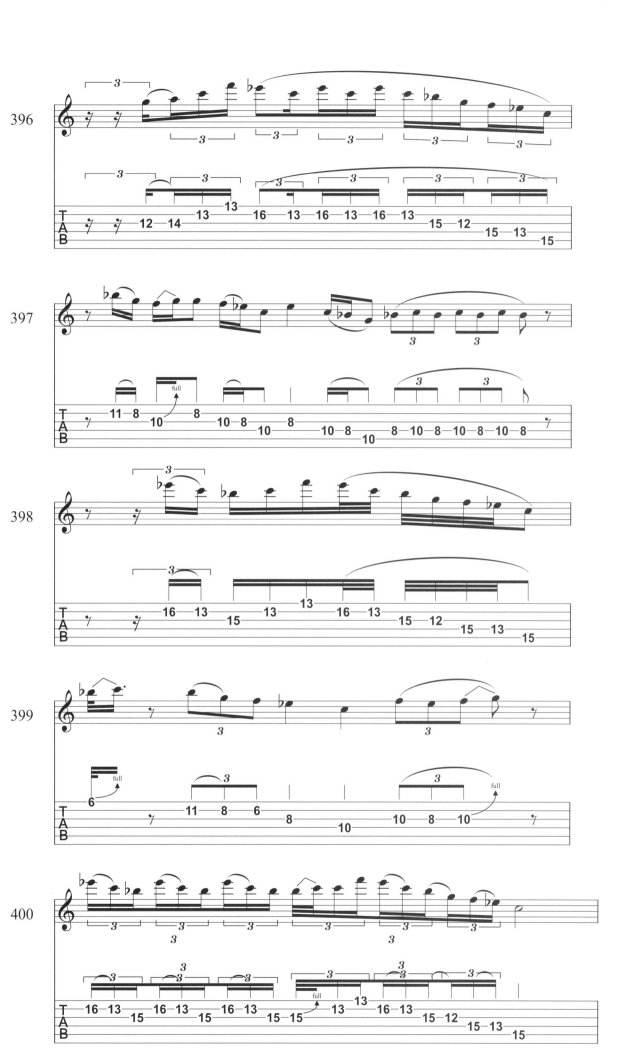

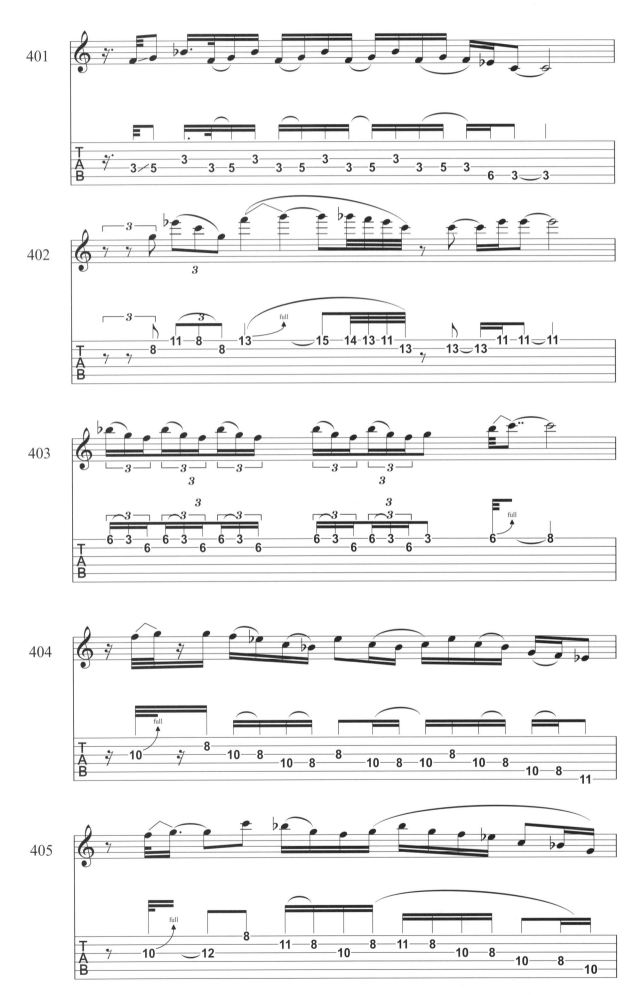

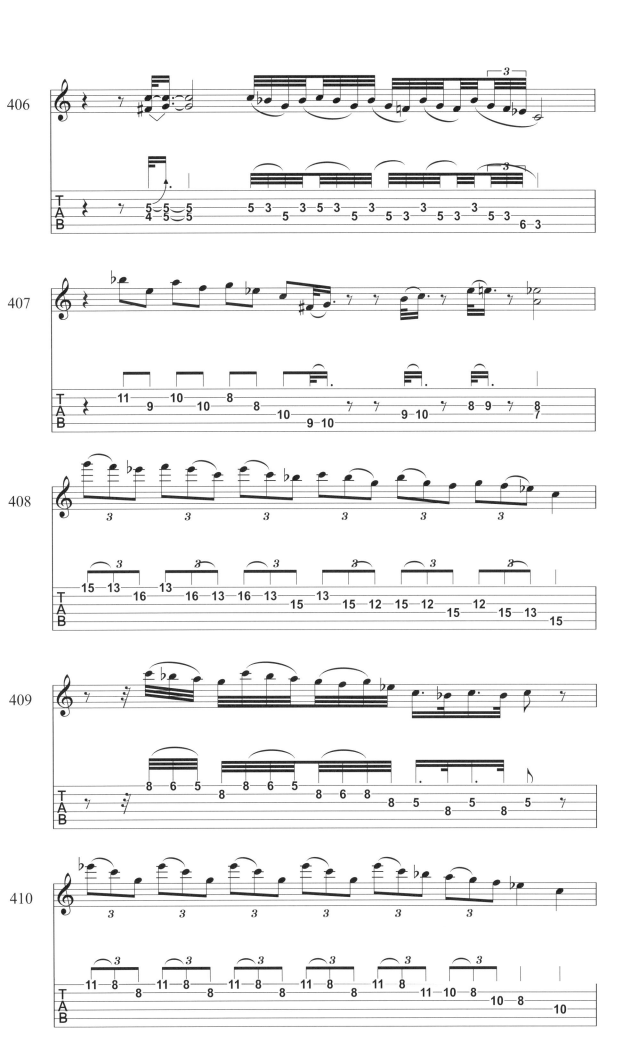

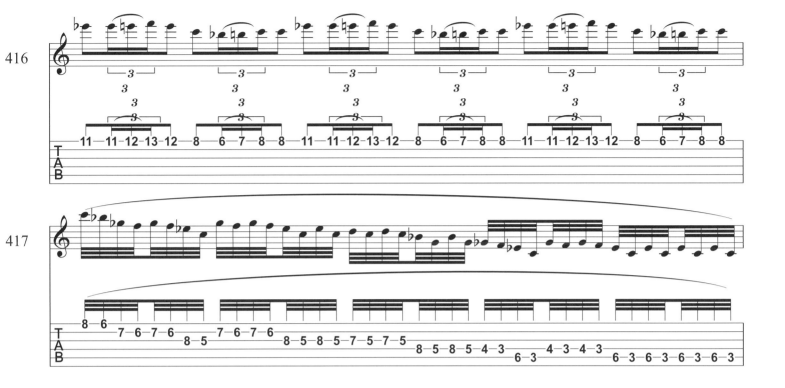

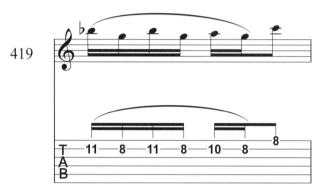

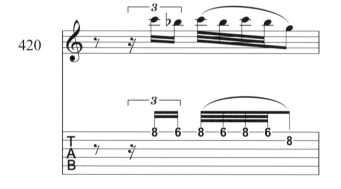

Chapter 9: Trills and Turns

Trills and turns are slurs between two notes, usually 1-2 semitones apart. A turn begins on a note, slurs up or down by step, then returns to the original note. A trill is similar, except that the two notes are sounded 4 or more times. Trills and turns are highly idiomatic in the blues. They can sound dark and foreboding in the low register and sweet and ornamented in the higher registers. Trills can be played as sixteenth-notes or eighth-note triplets, and can begin on strong and weak subdivisions of the beat for rhythmic variety.

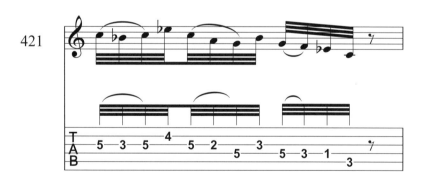

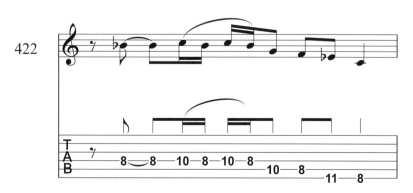

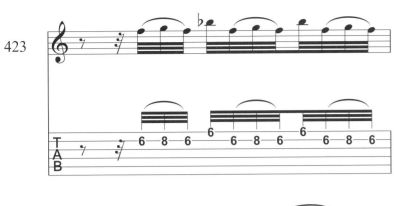

423

424

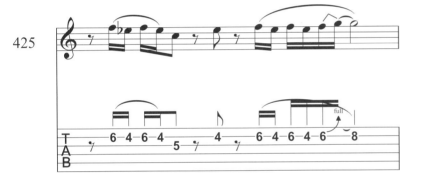

425

Dave Celentano

426

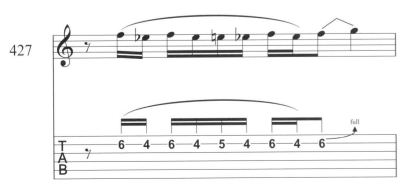

427

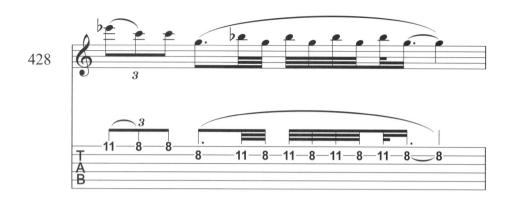

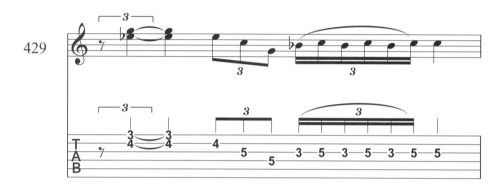

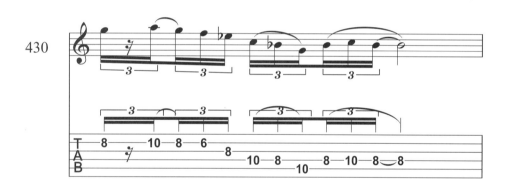

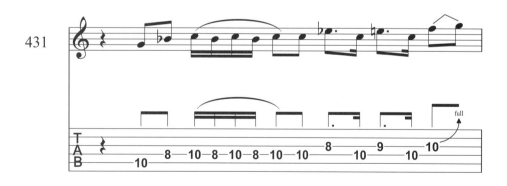

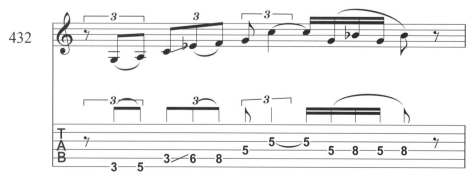

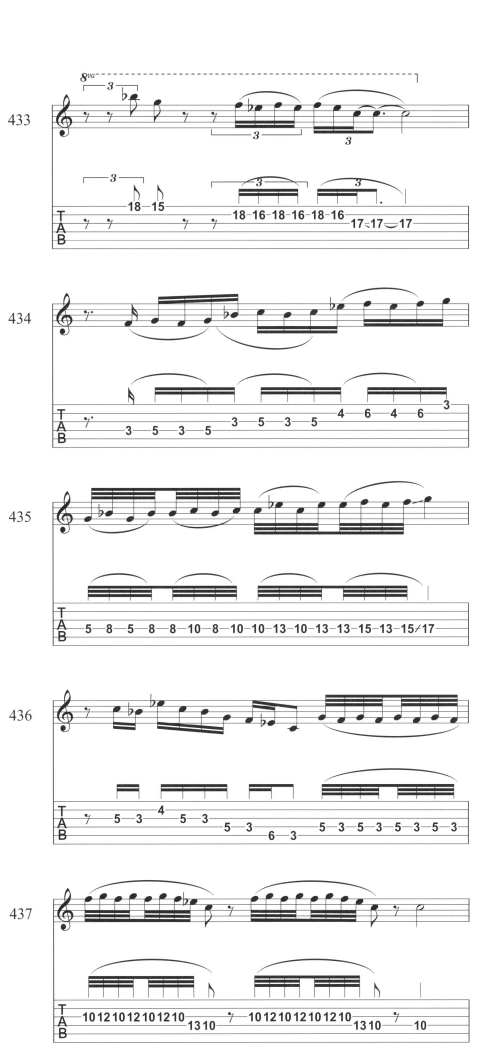

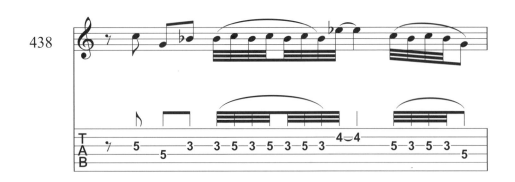

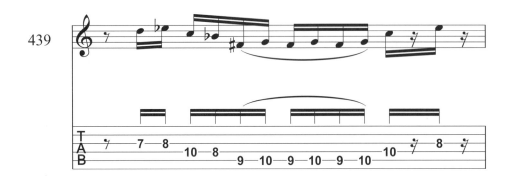

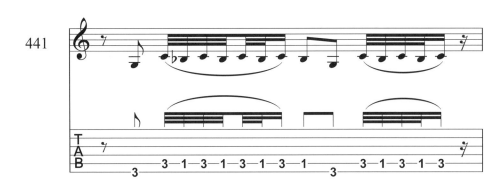

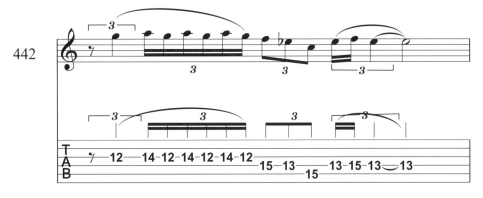

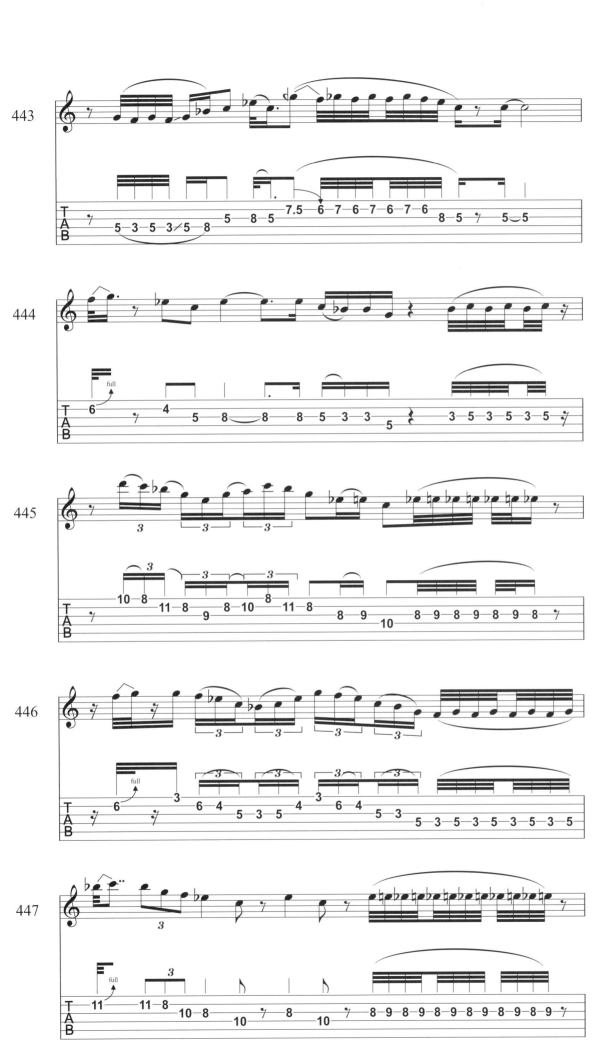

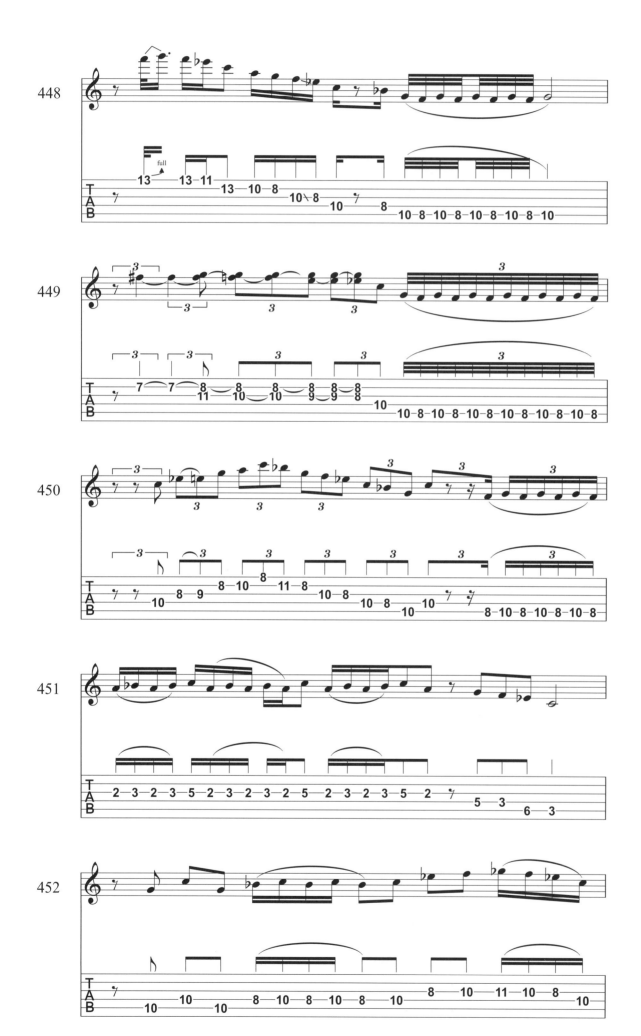

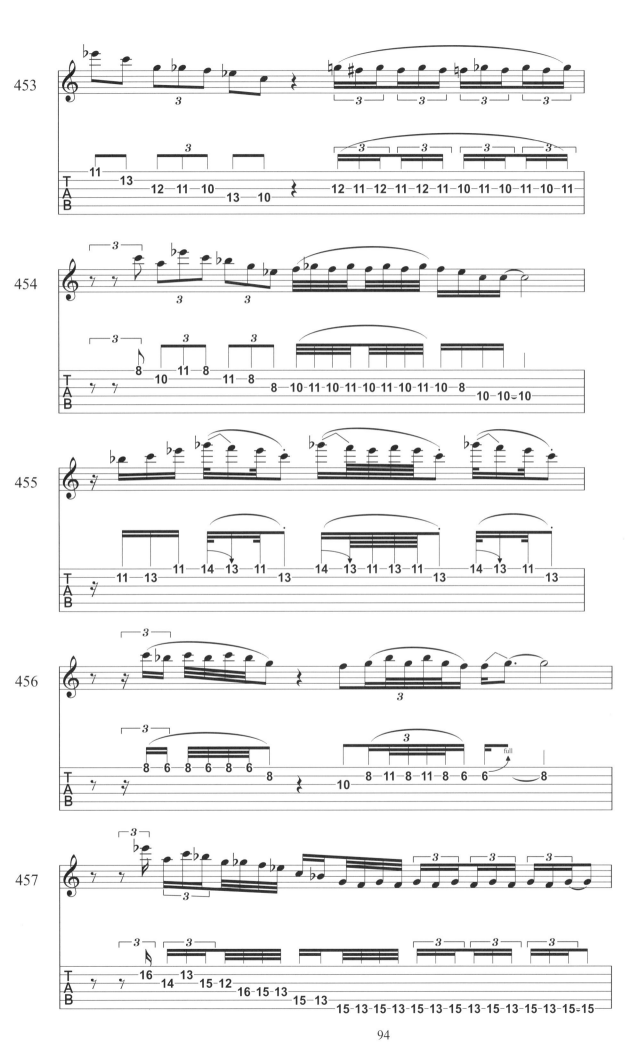

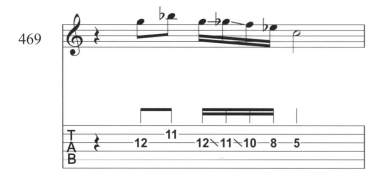

468

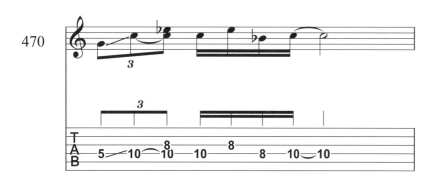

469

Chapter 10:
String Slides

The string slides in this chapter are not played with a metal or glass slide, but rather by sliding up or down the frets with the string depressed by a finger. Short slides of a step are usually very quick and act as an inflection to color a melody or phrase. Longer slides are often used as a lead-in to an important musical idea, in much the same way that a singer dramatically inhales in preparation for a new phrase.

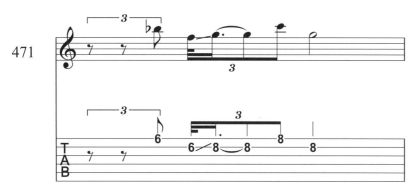

470

471

472

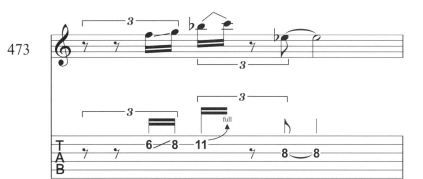

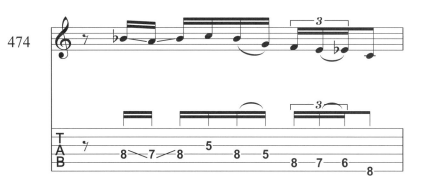

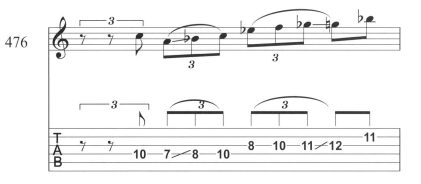

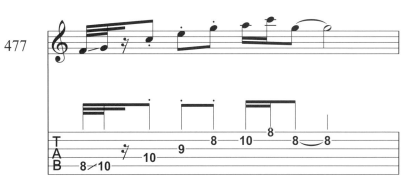

478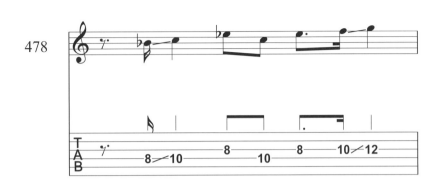

479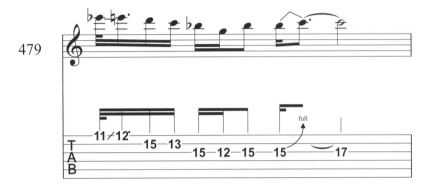

Johnny Hiland

480

481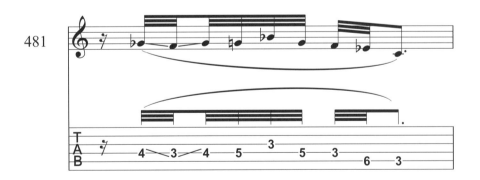

482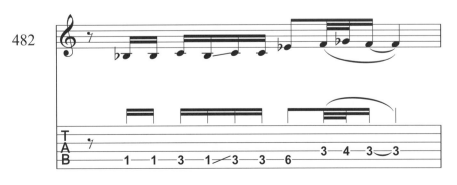

99

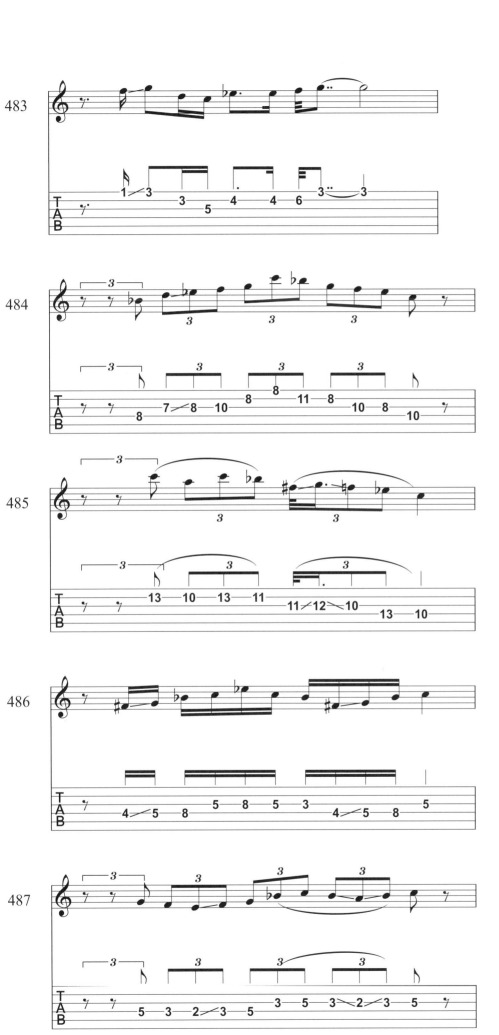

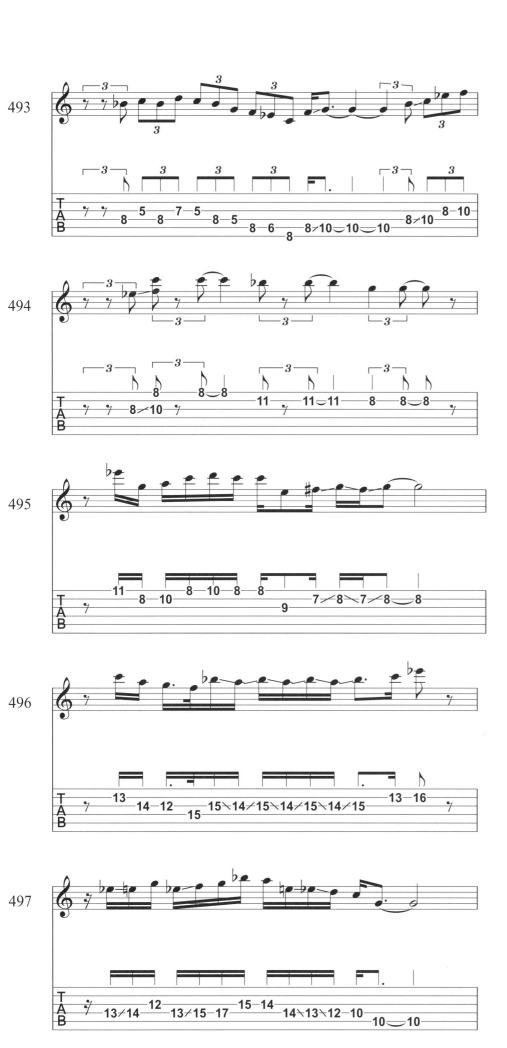

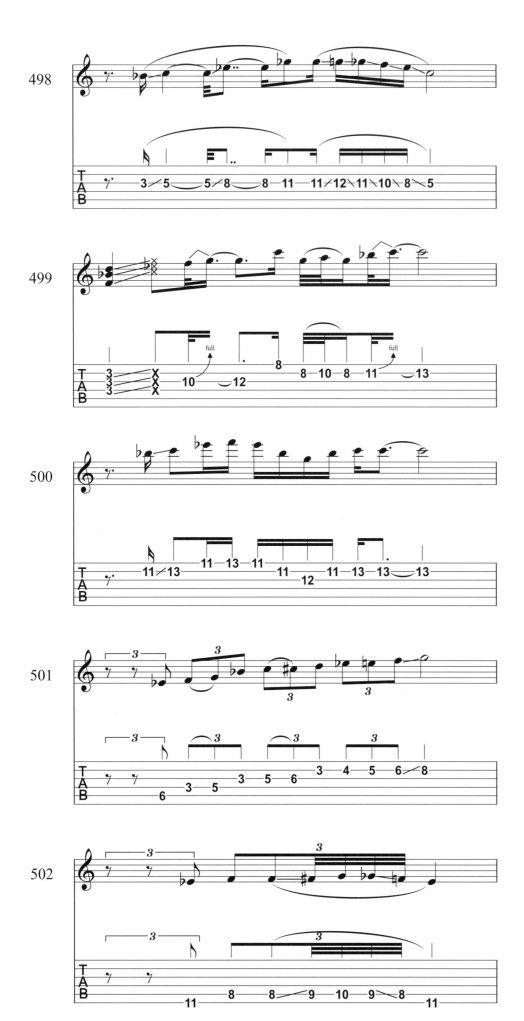

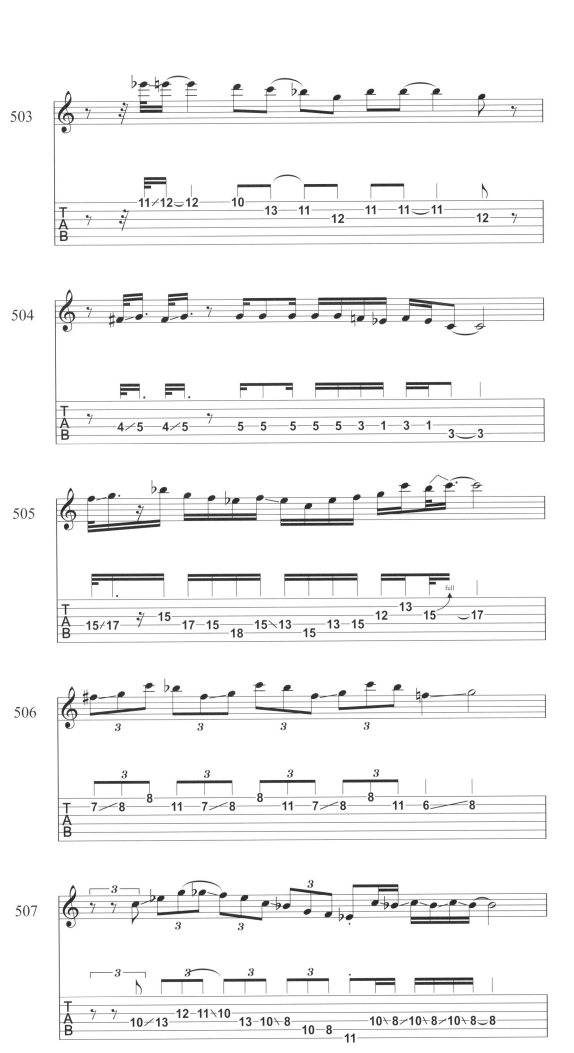

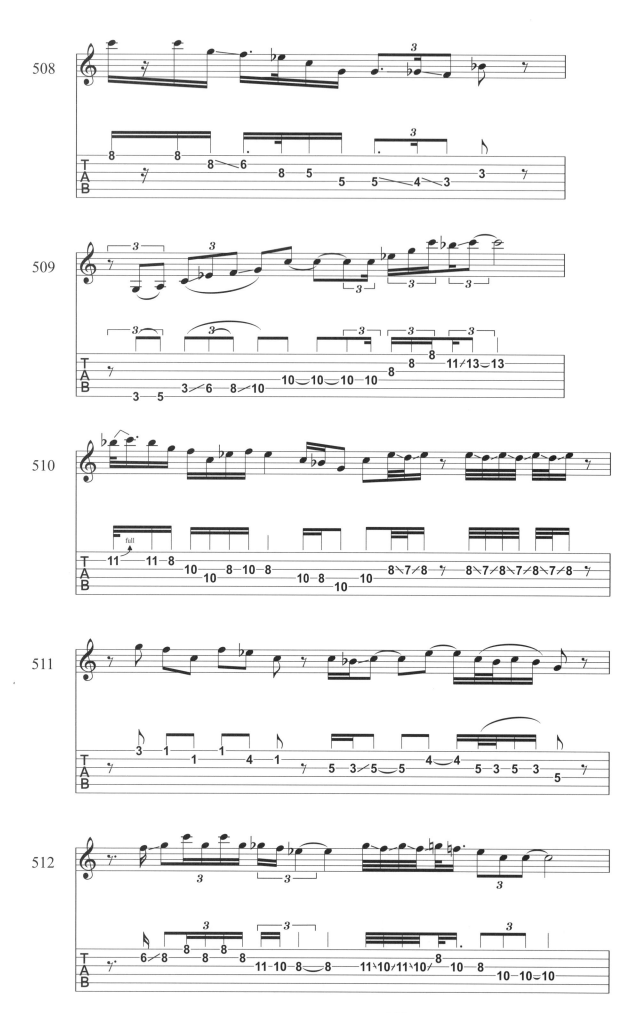

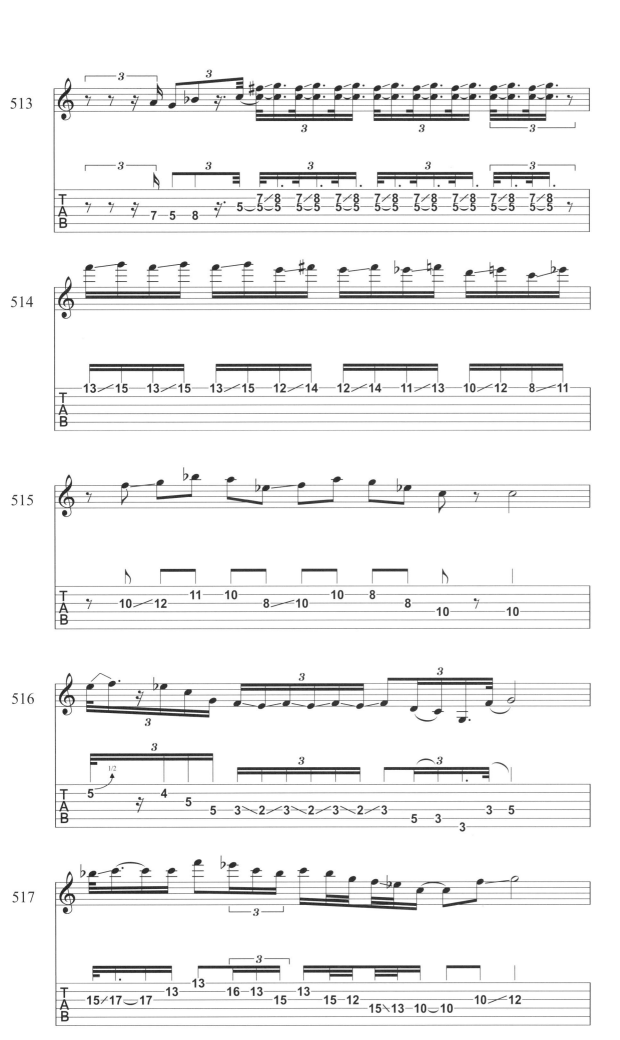

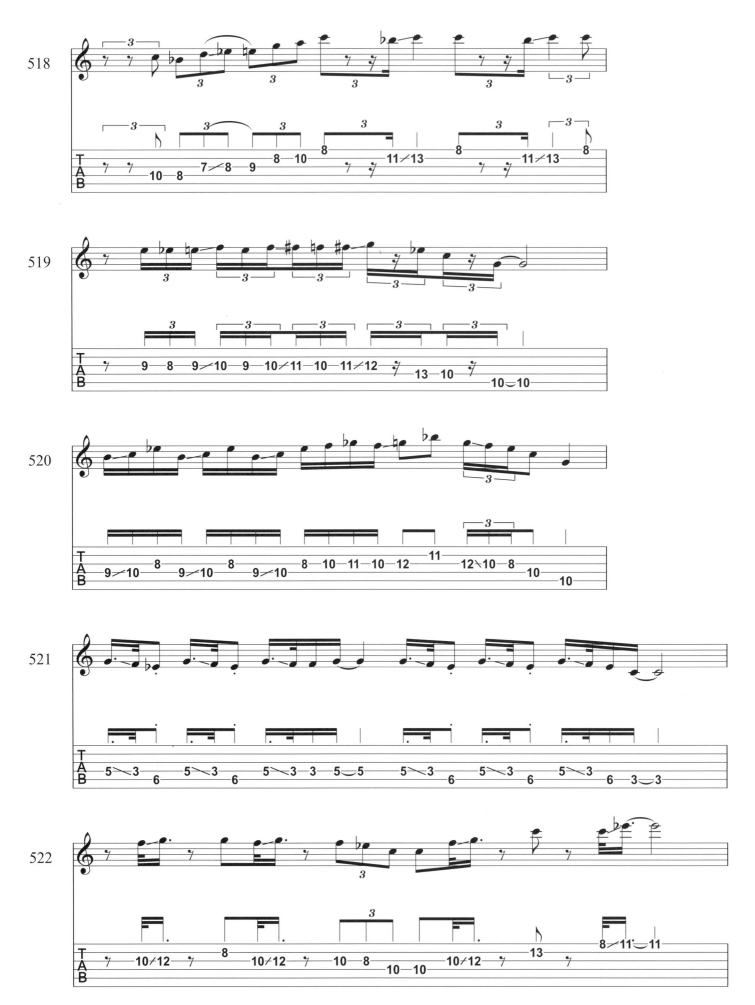

Chapter 11:
Muted Notes

Single muted notes, played with the edge of the right hand on the string near the bridge, add a percussive quality to a phrase. By preventing strings from ringing loudly, they can draw the listener into a solo, almost as if sharing a secret with the musician. Two or more notes can be muted with one or more fingers of the left hand lightly touching the strings. With a quick strum, this can produce a percussive or snare drum-like effect. Playing the muted strings in sequence produces a roll that is highly idiomatic in blues guitar playing.

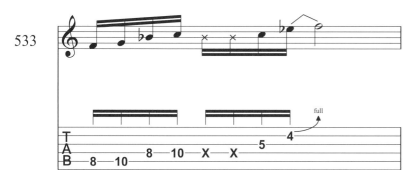

533

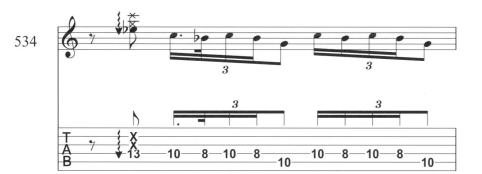

534

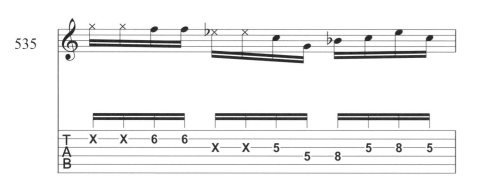

535

536

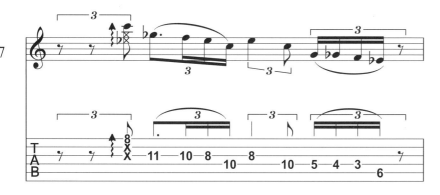

537

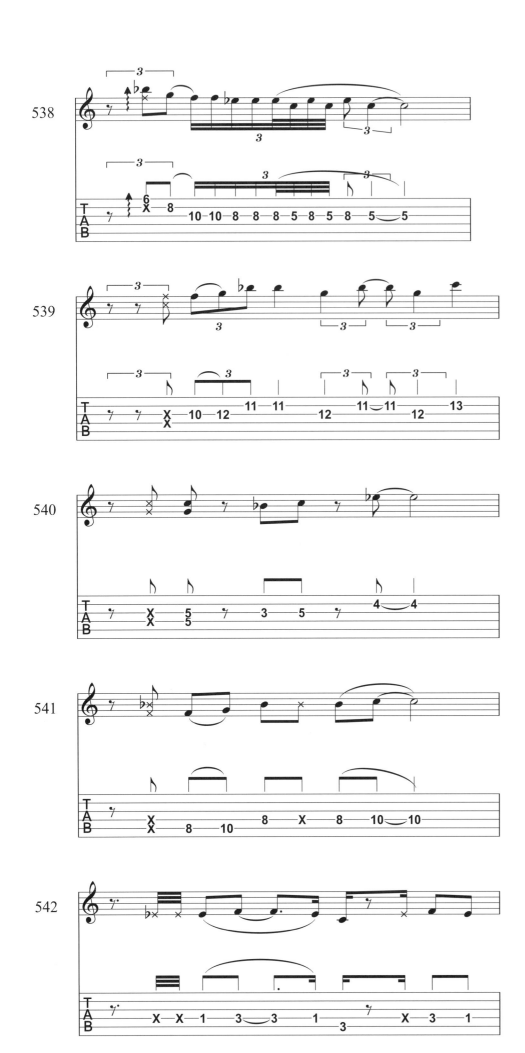

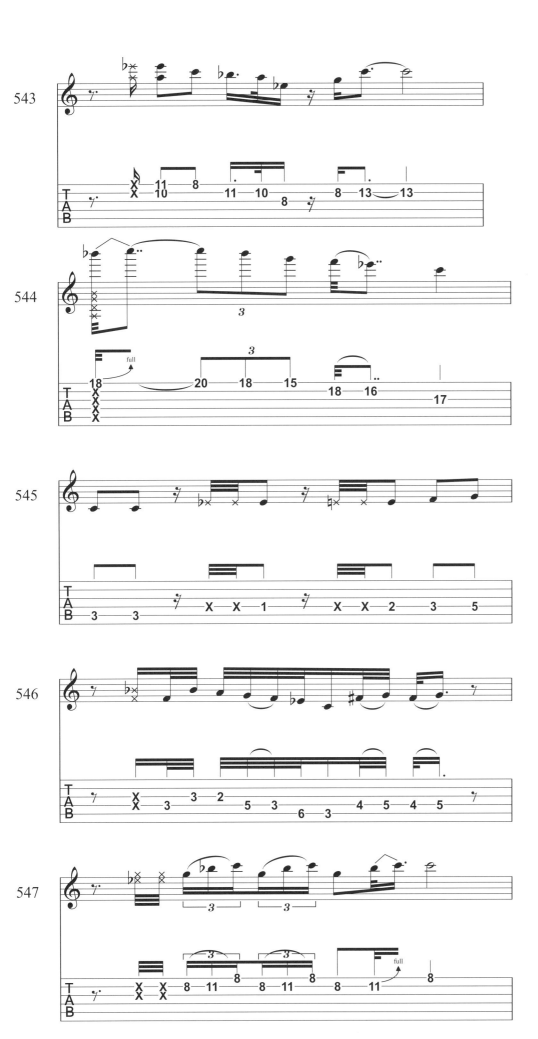

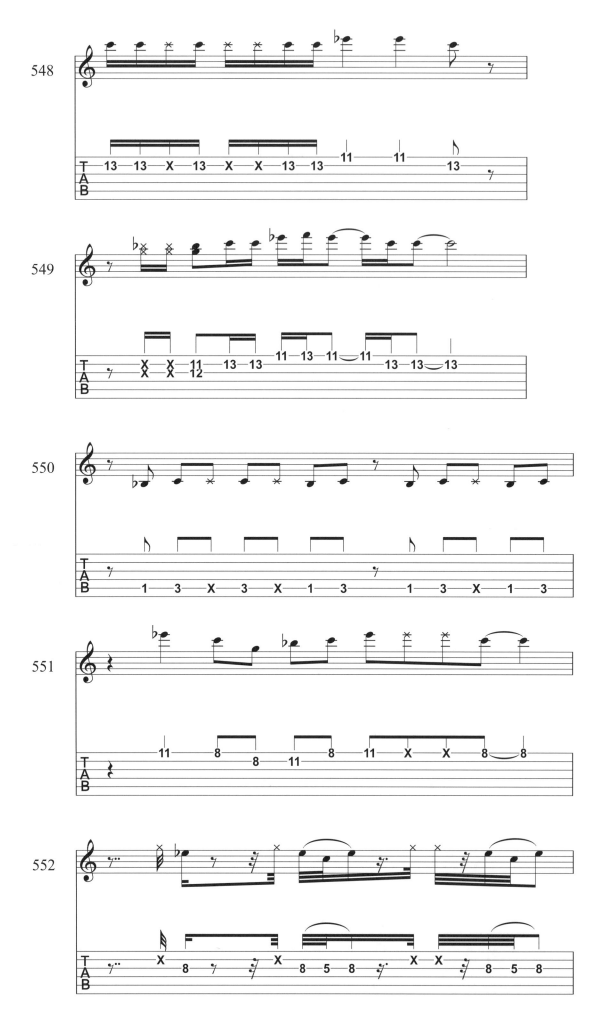

563

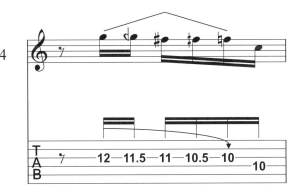

Chapter 12:
String Bends

There is no idiomatic technique in blues guitar playing more widely used than the string bend. As shown in this chapter, bends can be as small as a semitone and at least as large as a minor third. They can be played from a normal position and bent up, or they may start from a pre-bend and bent down. A bend can also be used in creating a vibrato, as the note oscillates between the peak of the bend and a microtone below. Played with adequate sustain, bends can lend a vocal quality to a guitar solo. Bends can be played very quickly, to create a forceful, stinging sound like B.B. King, or very slowly to create a more mournful, woozy sound like Mike Bloomfield.

564

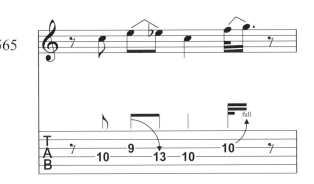

565

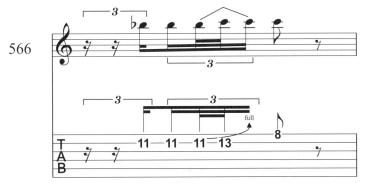

566

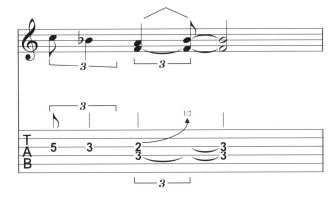

567

568

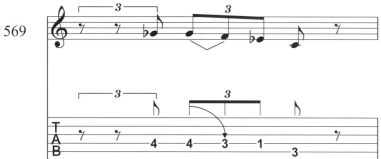

569

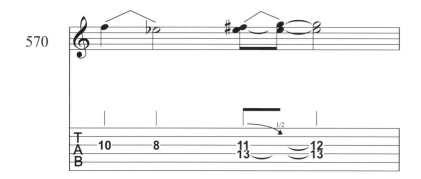

570

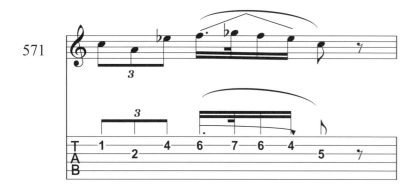

571

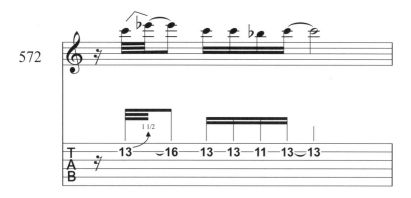

572

Tommy Emmanuel

117

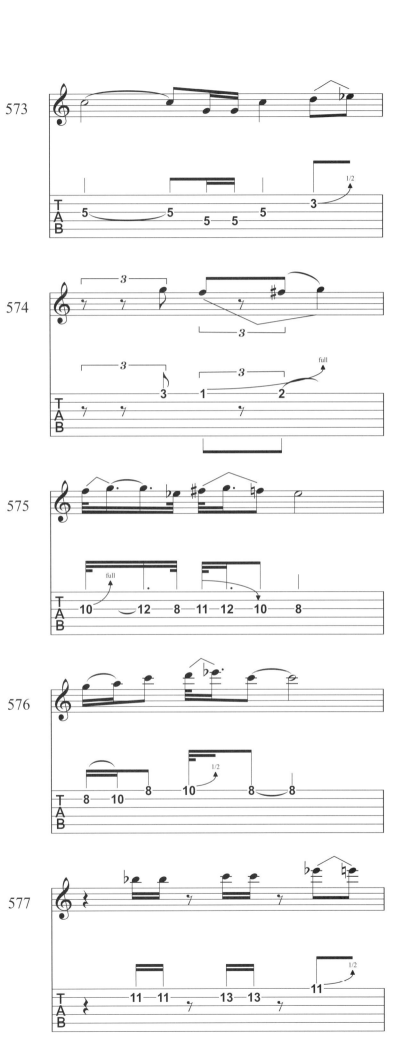

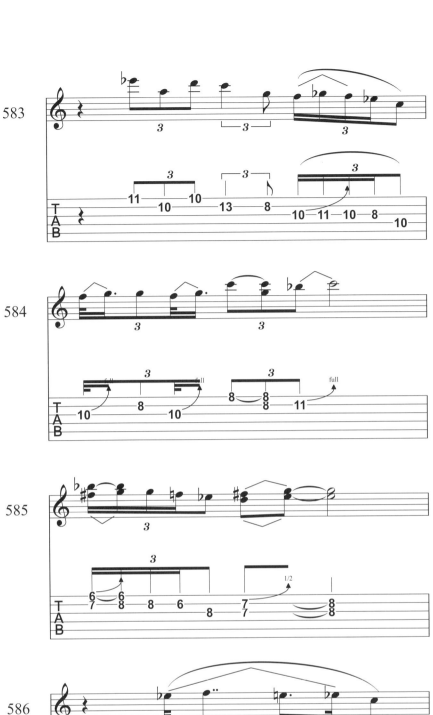

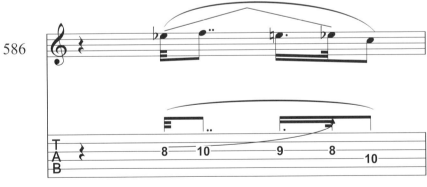

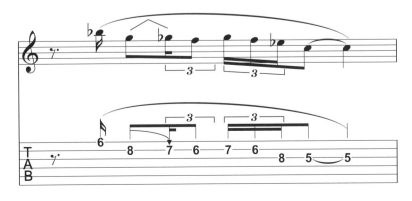

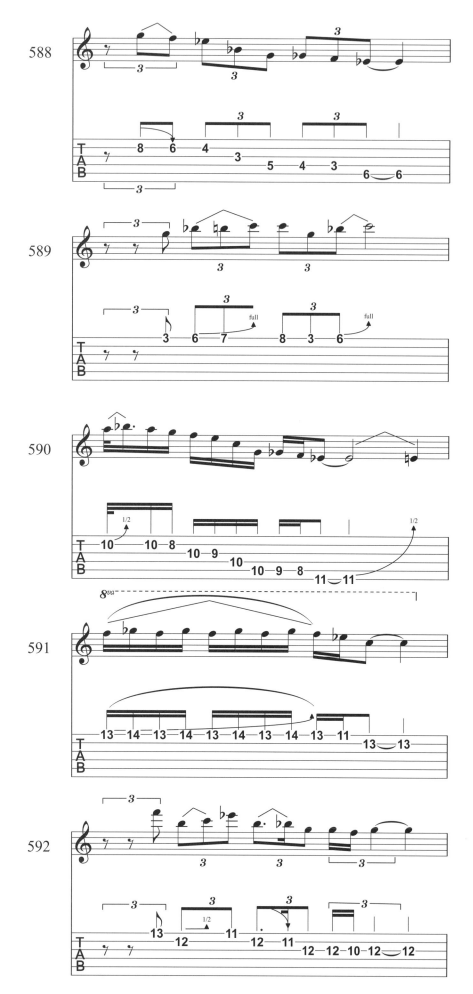

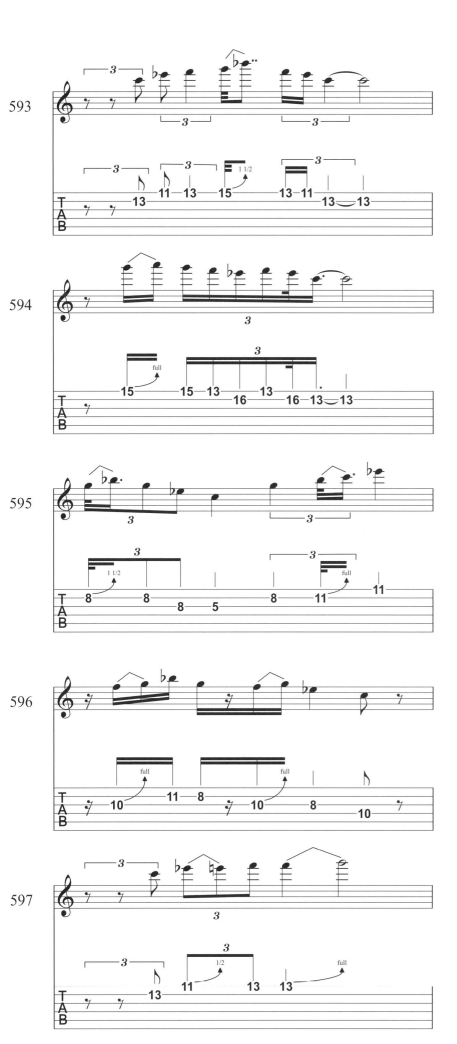

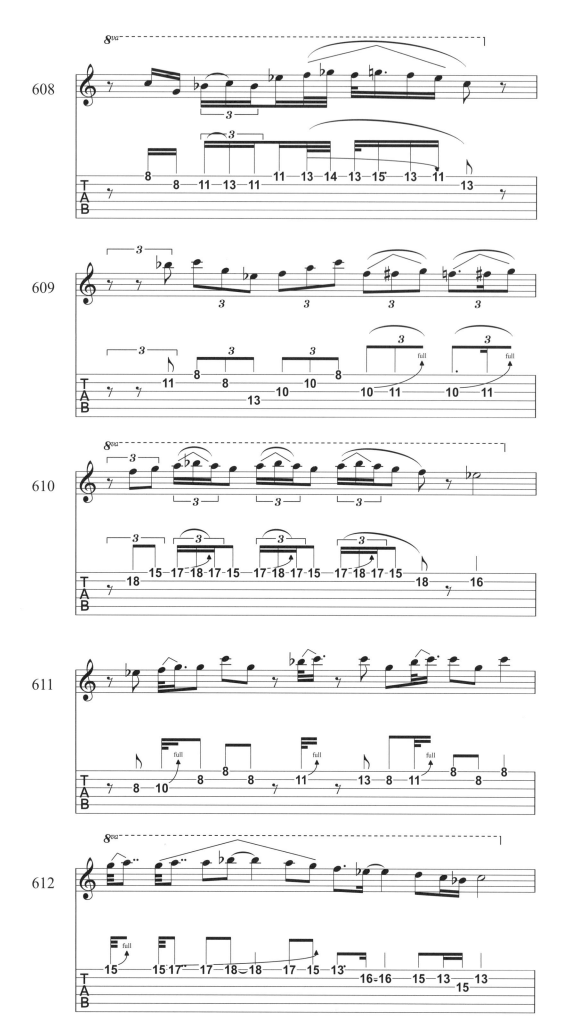

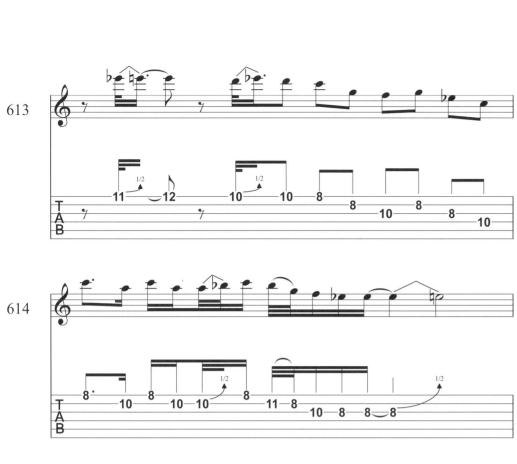

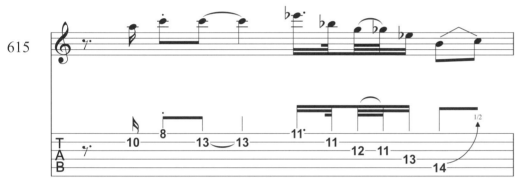

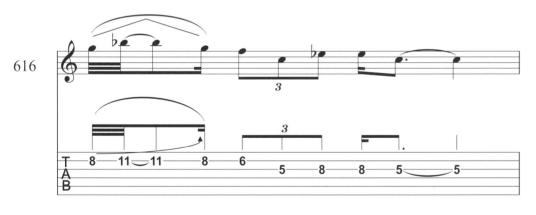

127

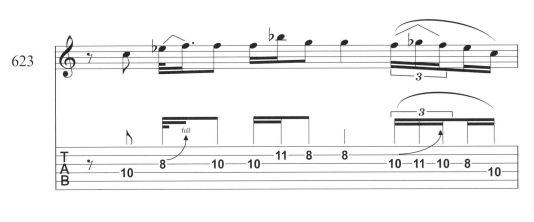

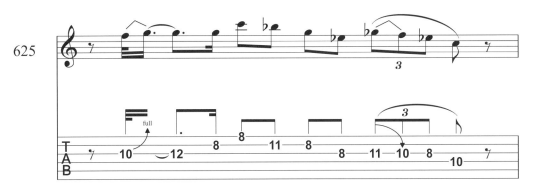

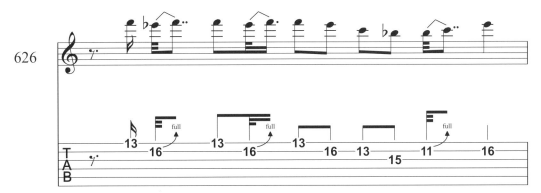

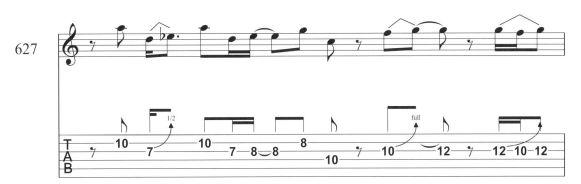

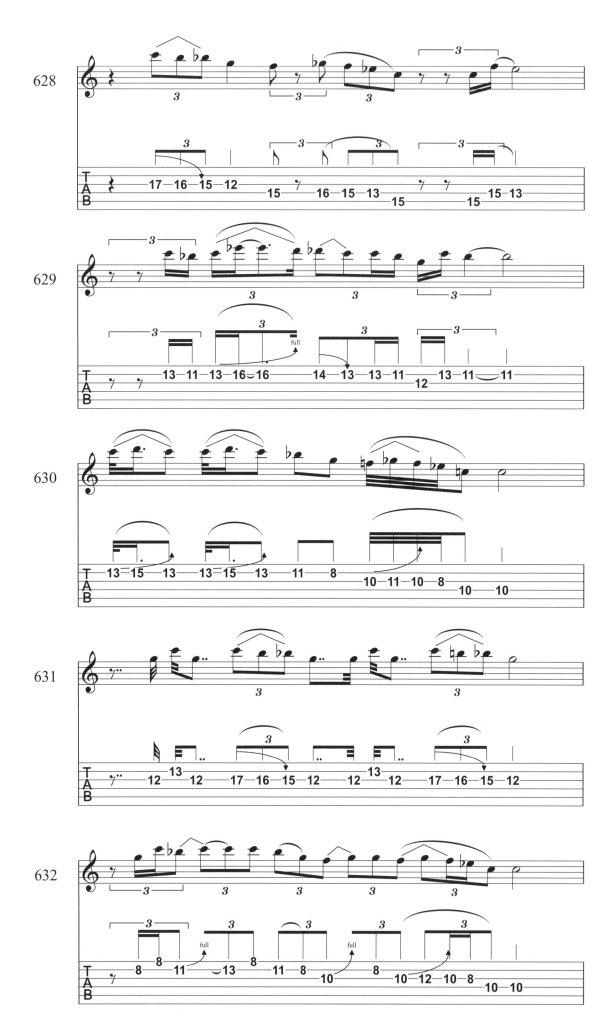

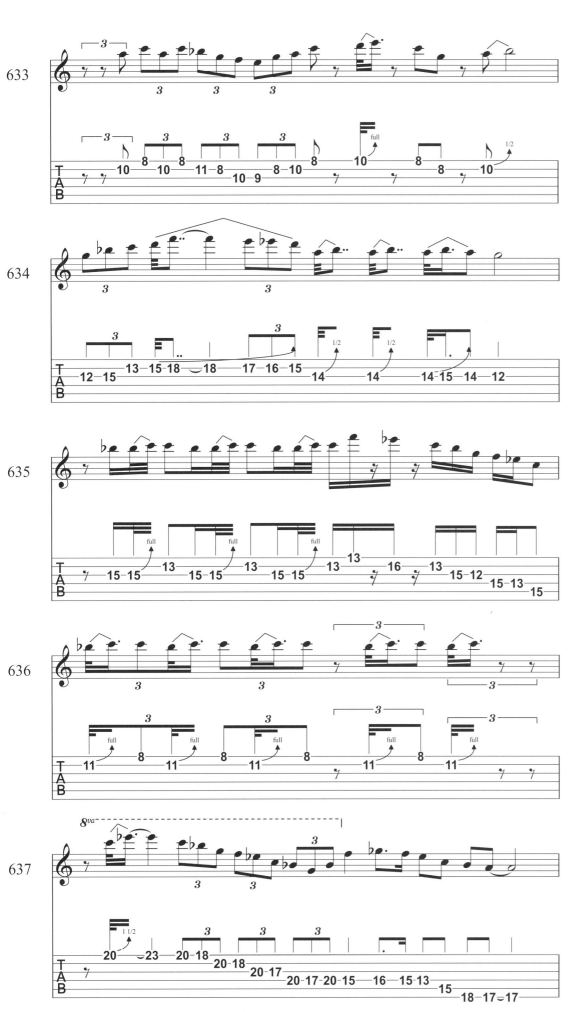

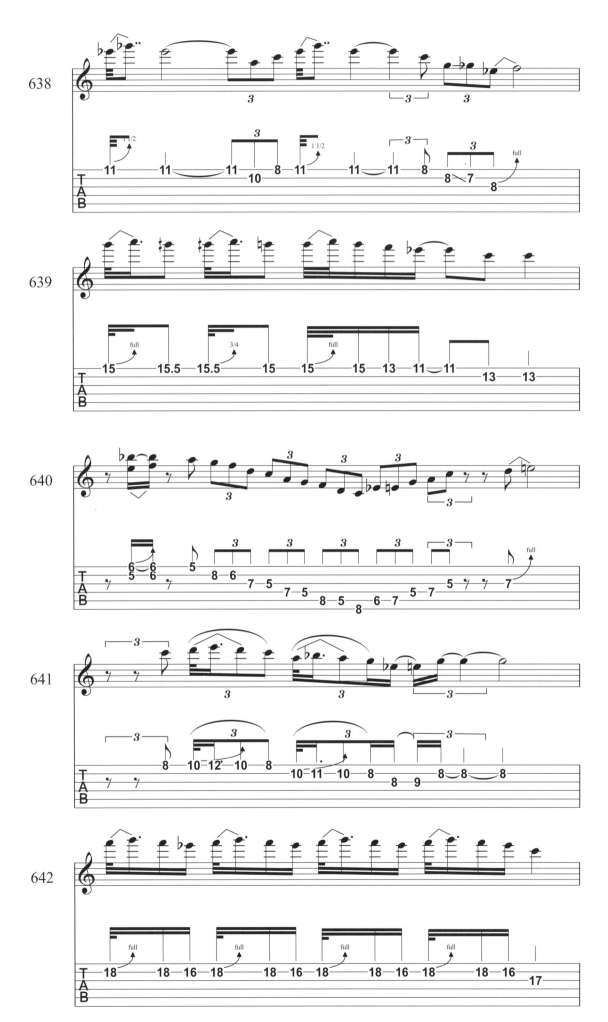

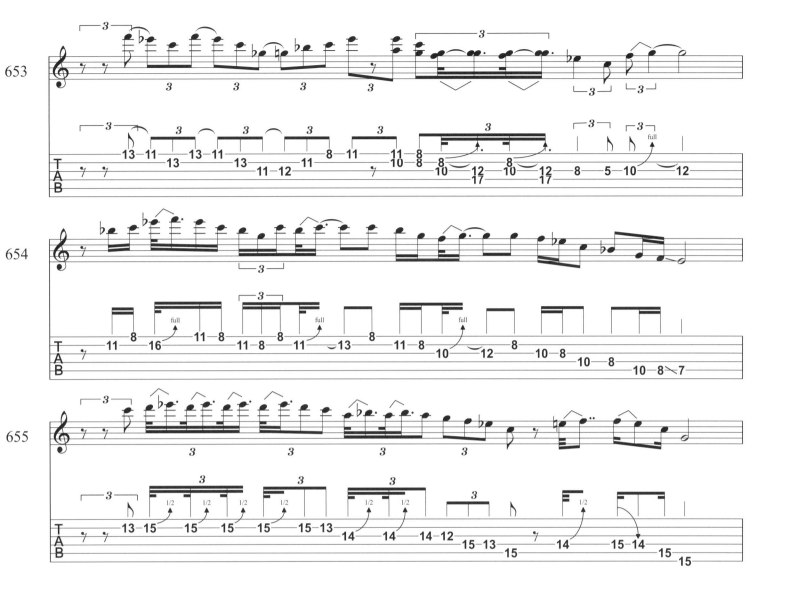

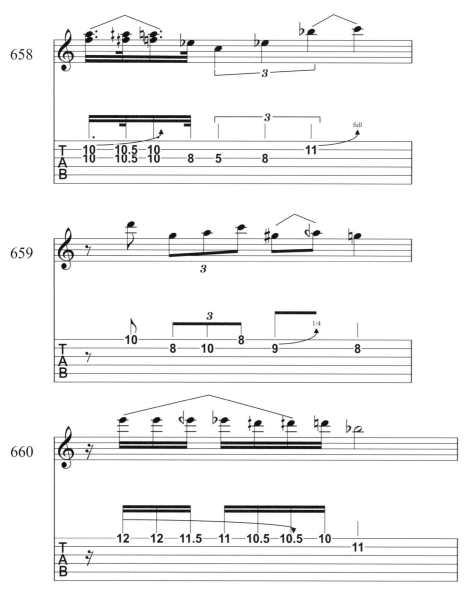

Chapter 13:
Microtones

A microtone is an interval smaller than a semitone played on the guitar by bending a string to produce the desired pitch. The microtones in this chapter are denoted as a quarter-tones sharp or flat, although fifth- and sixth-tones may be played if they suit the ear. Some guitarists, such as Albert King, often explore the microtones found within a minor third. The most common microtones used in the blues are found between the notes Eb-E, F-Gb, and Gb-G.

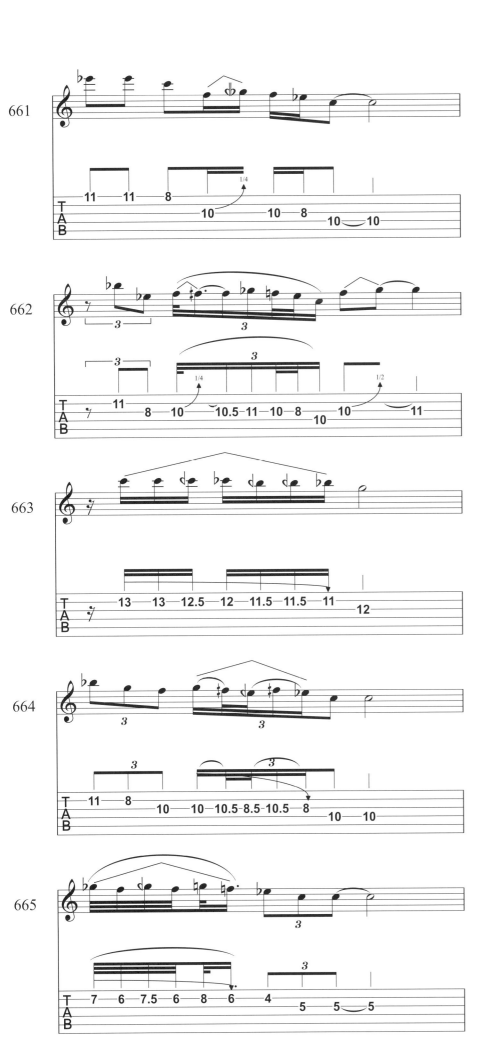

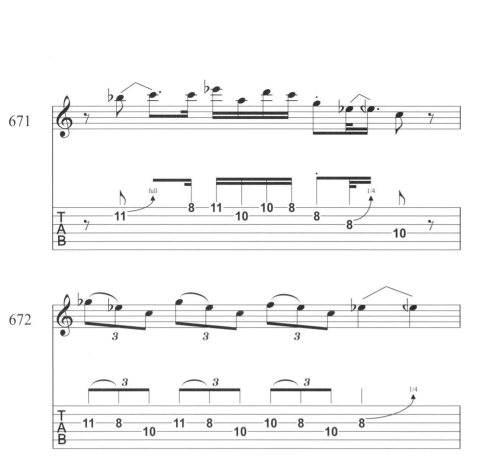

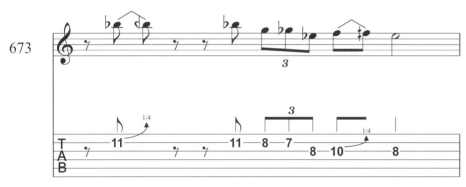

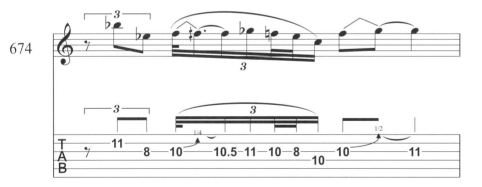

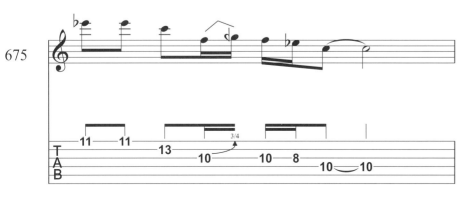

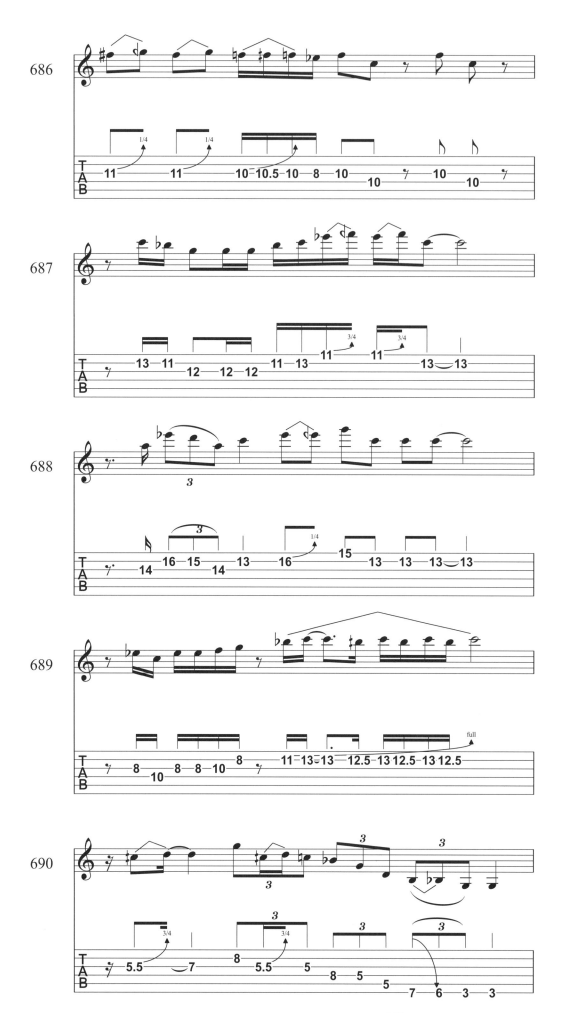

Chapter **14**:
Combined Techniques

The licks in this chapter combine slurs, turns, trills, slides, muting, bends, and microtones. Jimi Hendrix, Johnny "Guitar" Watson, and Stevie Ray Vaughan created phrases of great expressive color by compressing several techniques into a single lick.

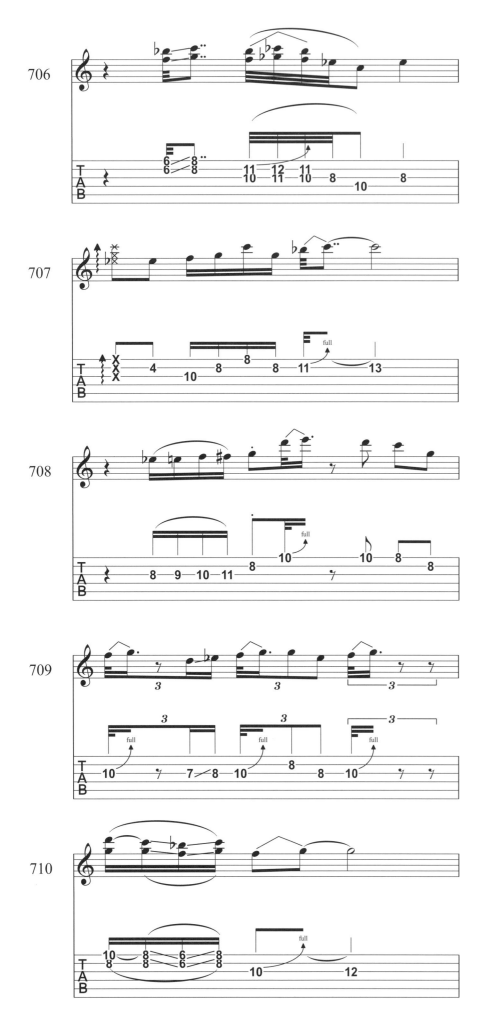

Paul Geremia

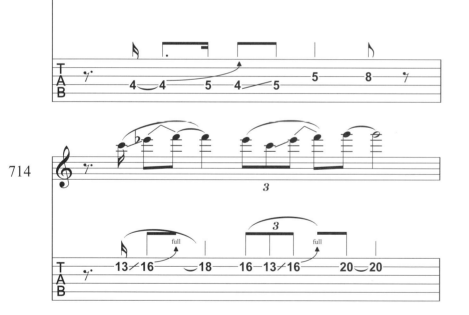

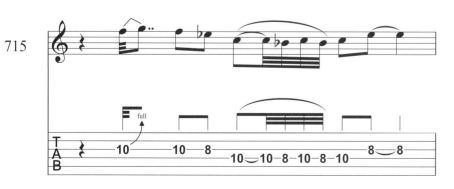

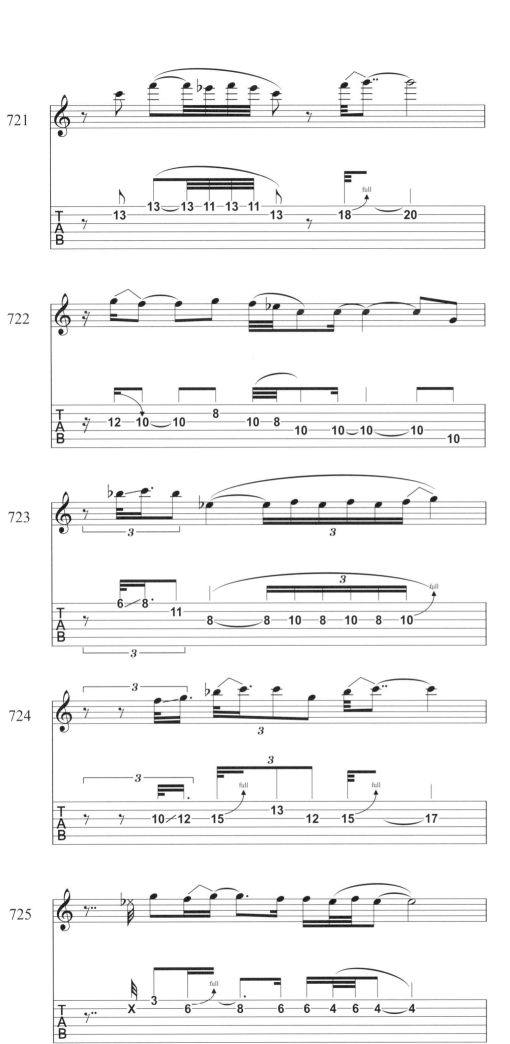

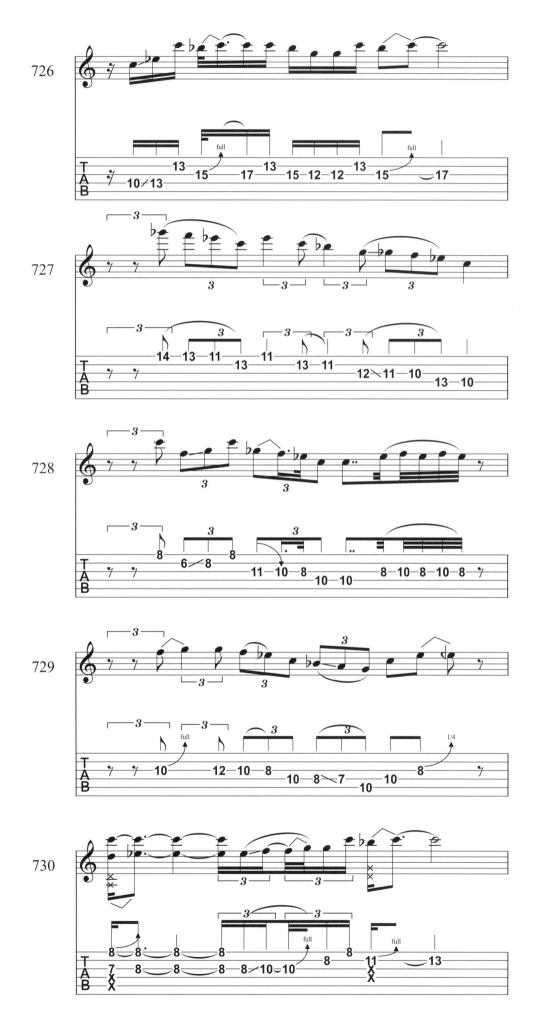

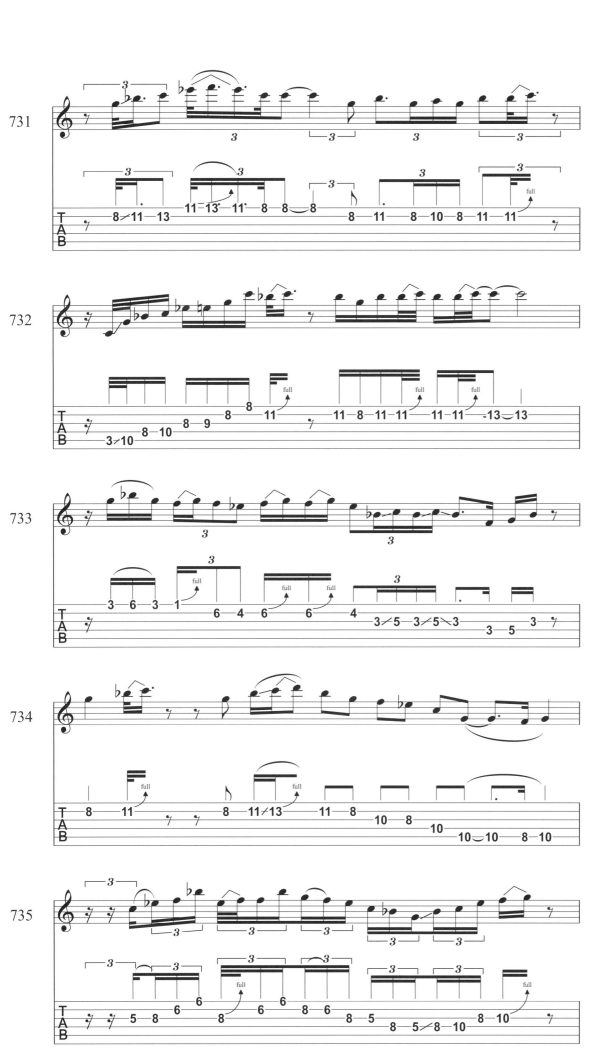

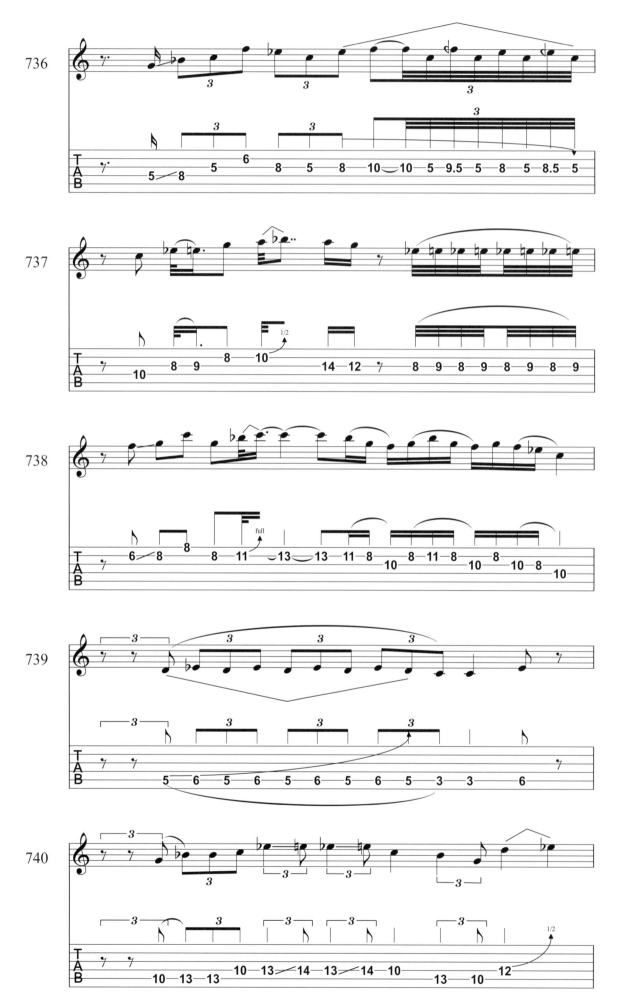

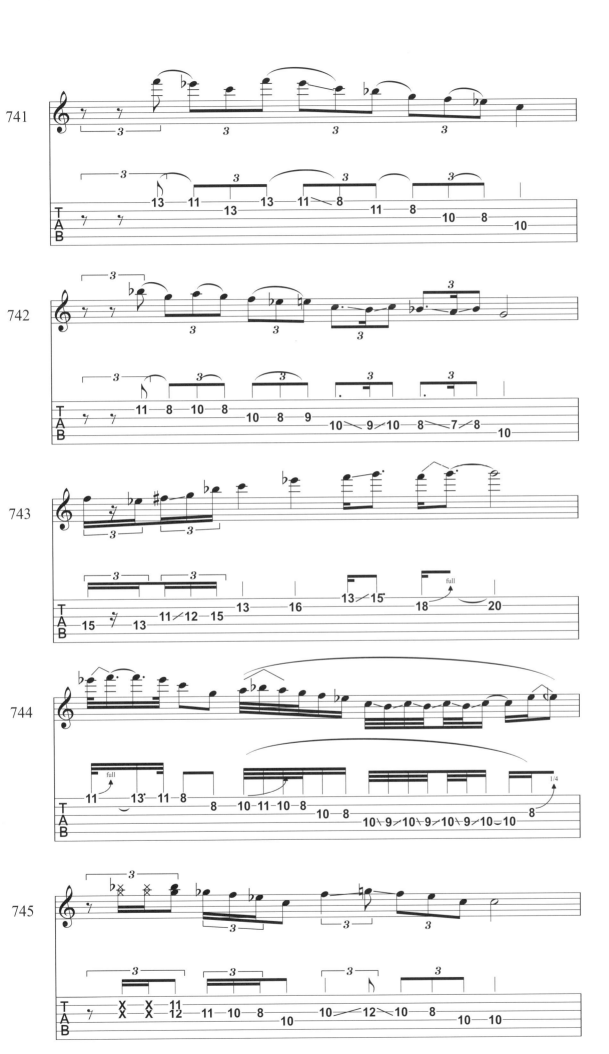

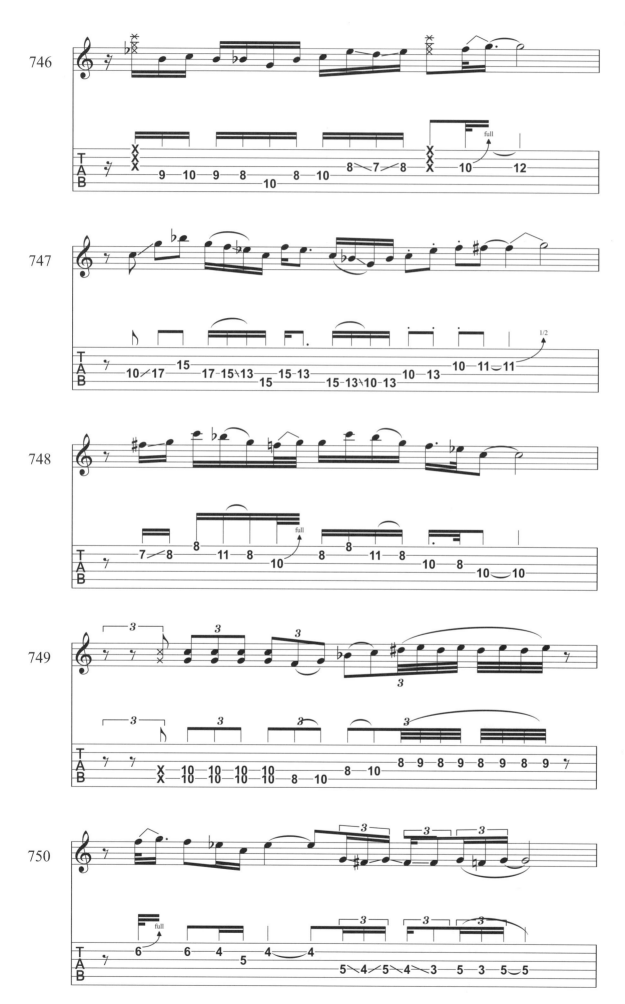

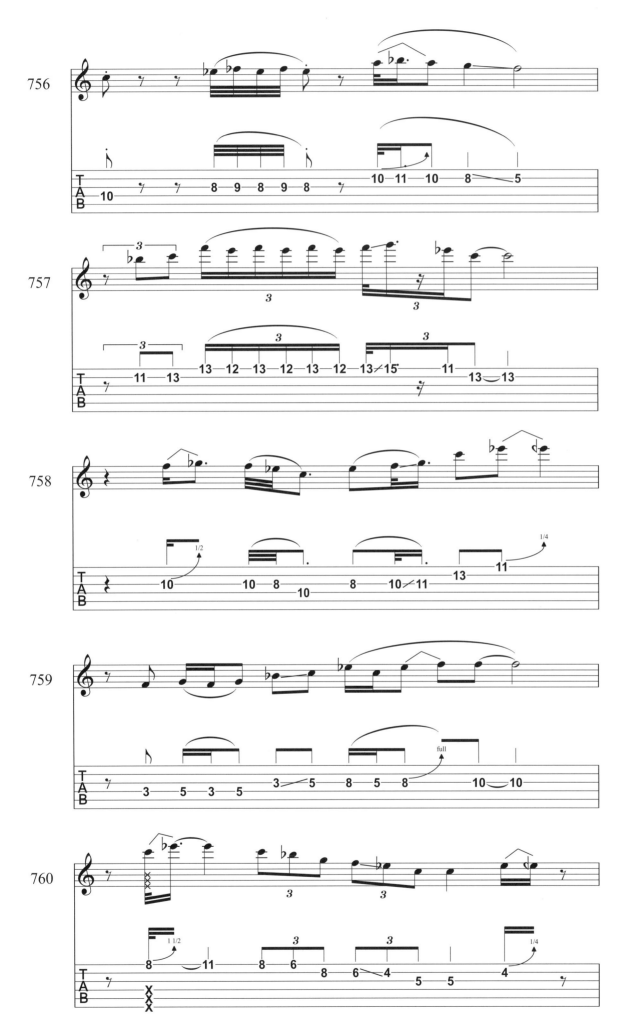

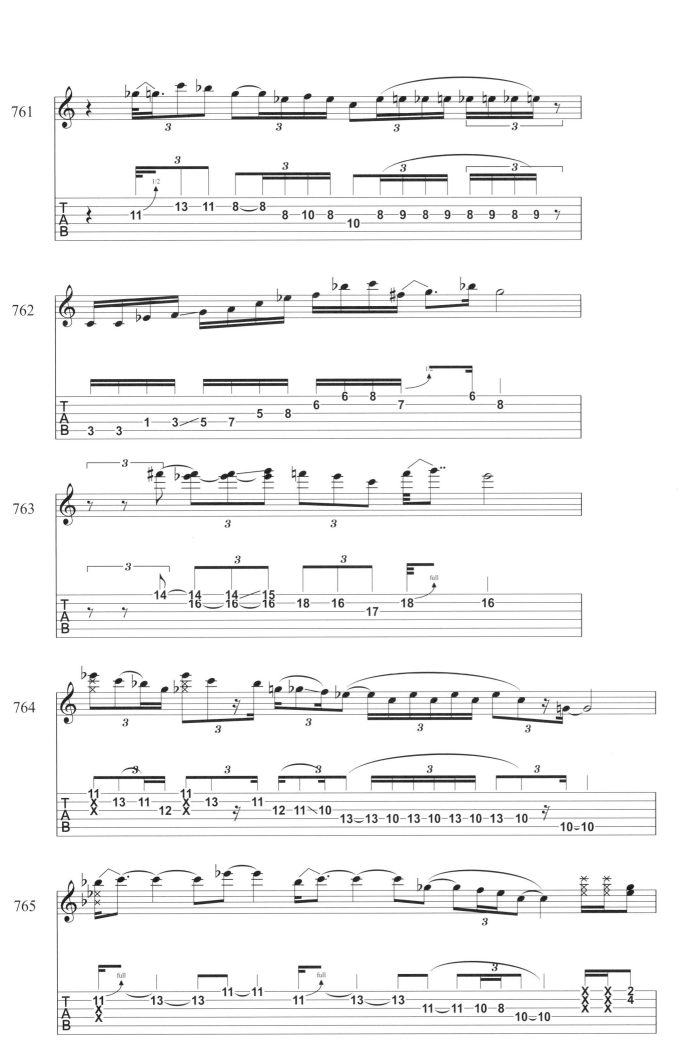

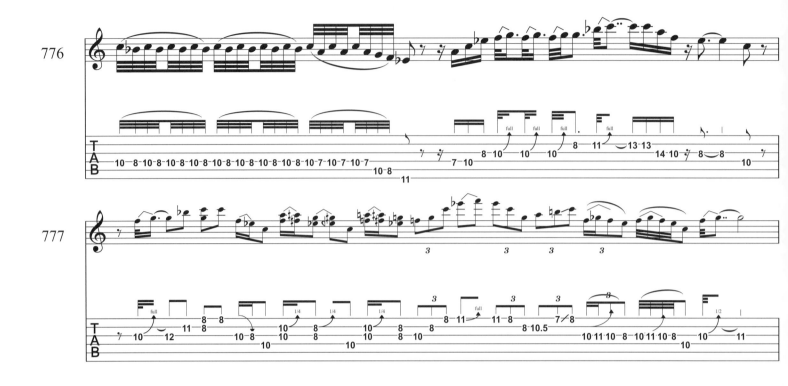

Chapter 15:
Dyads in Thirds and Sixths

Two notes played together on the guitar are called double-stops or dyads. The most harmonious of these are thirds and sixths. These intervals are closely related. For example, in the C minor pentatonic scale, a third higher than the note C is the note Eb. If, on the other hand, the note Eb is played below the note C, the interval of the dyad is a sixth. Dyads in both thirds and sixths are often played ascending or descending motion, usually staying on the same pair of strings.

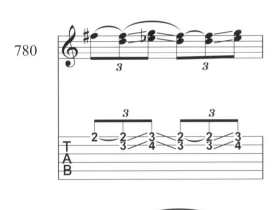

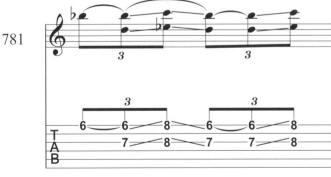

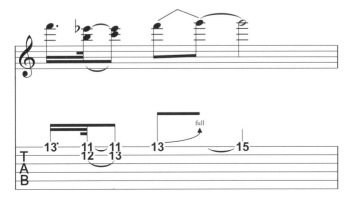

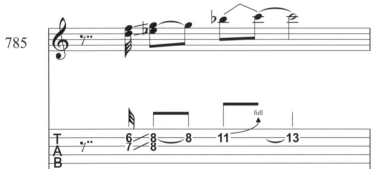

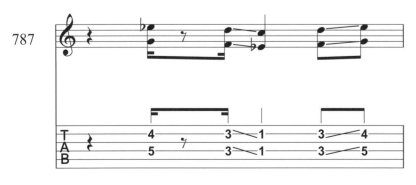

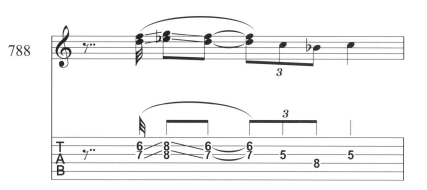

Little Charlie Baty

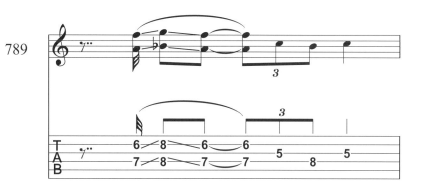

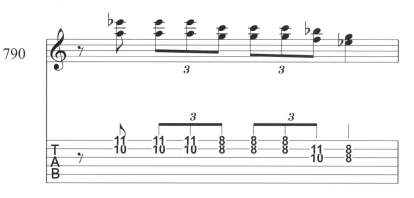

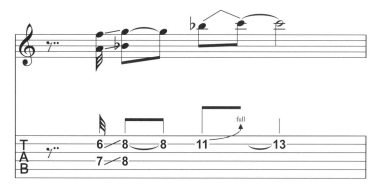

162

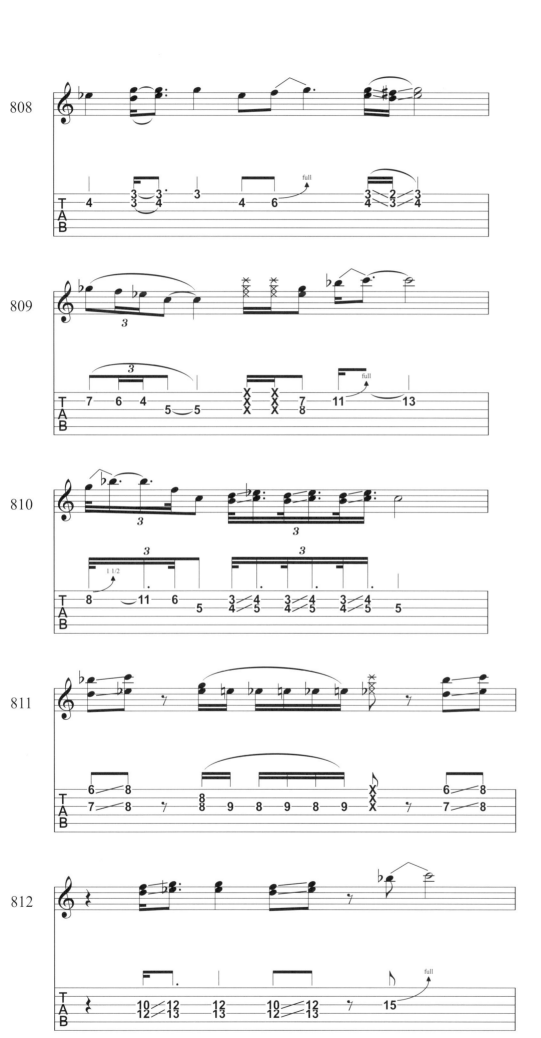

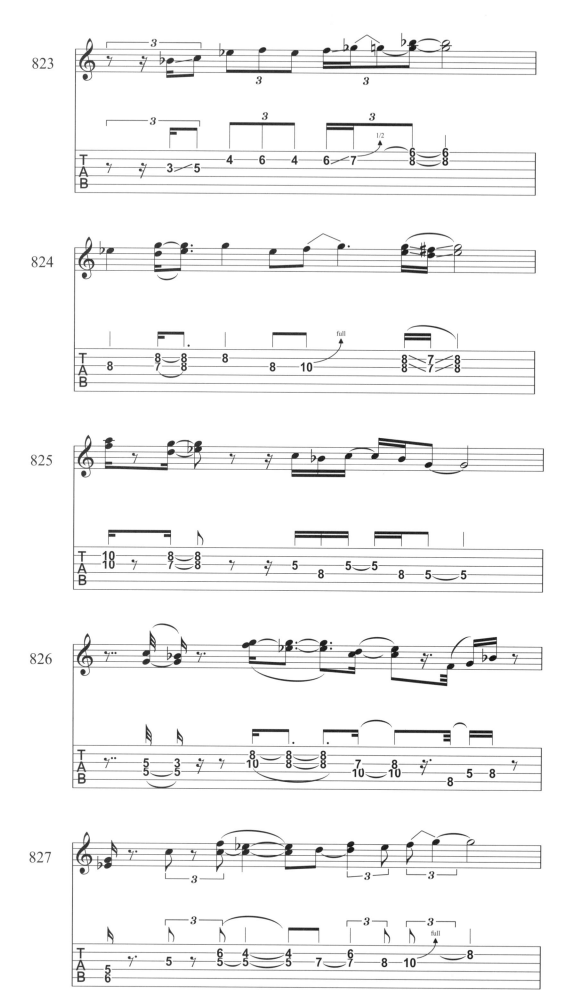

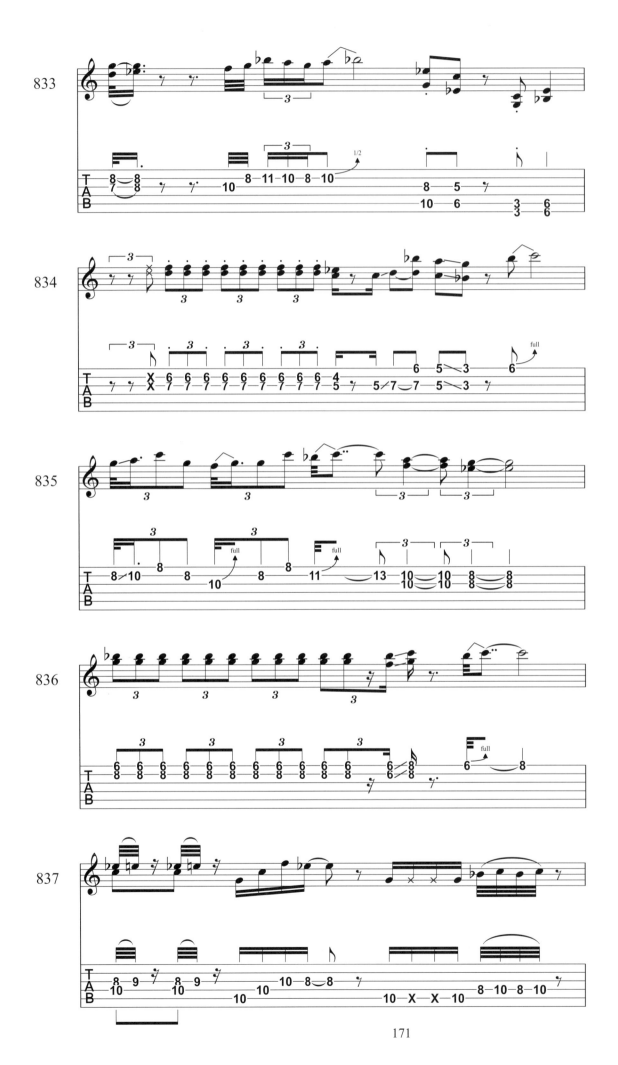

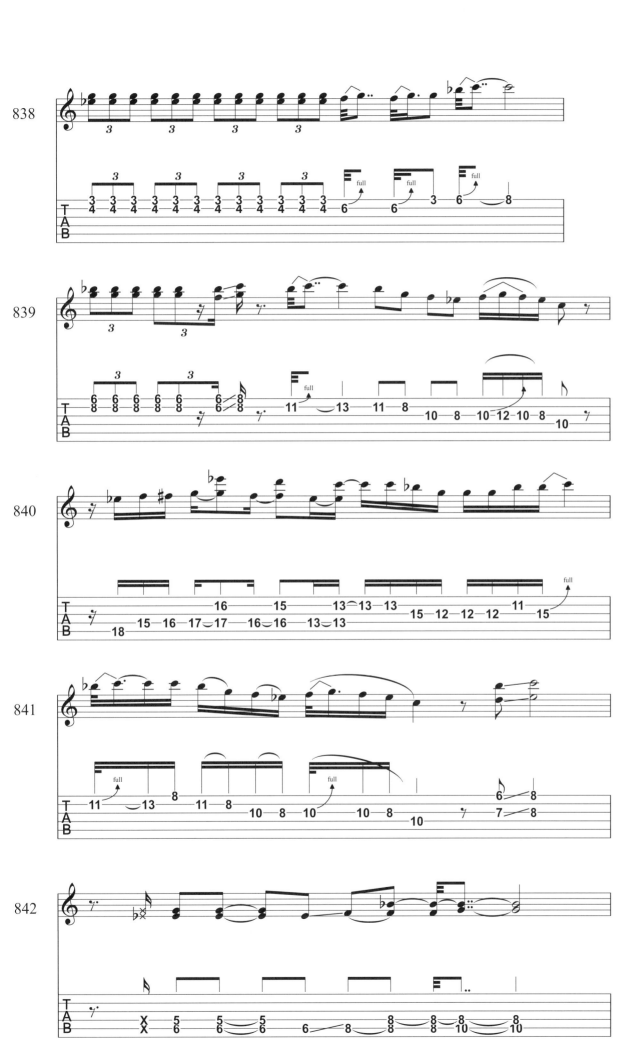

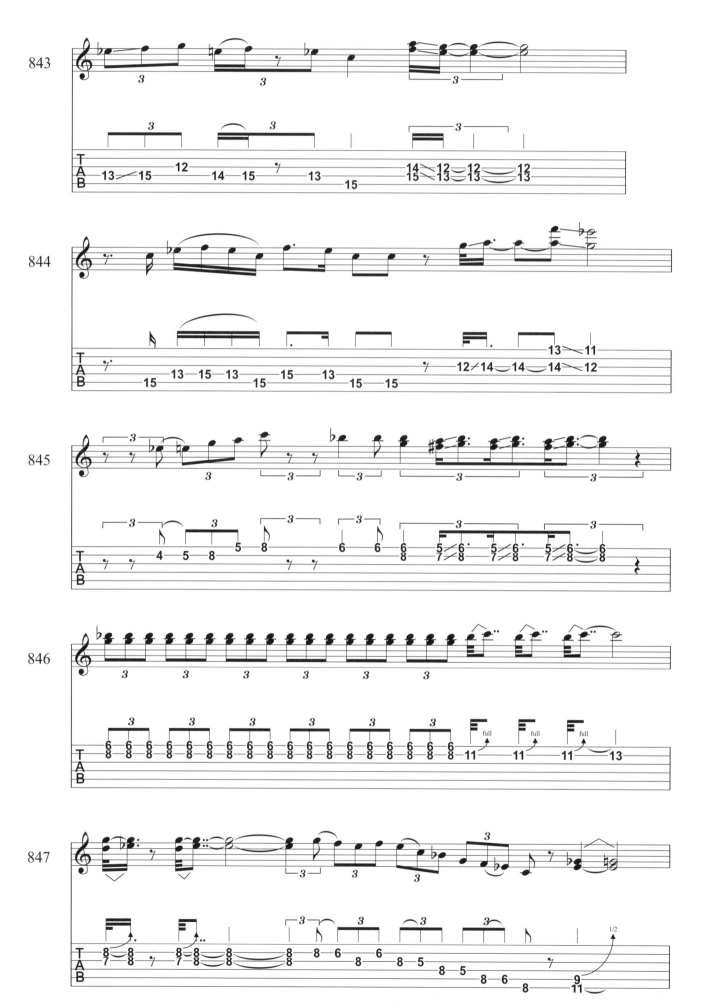

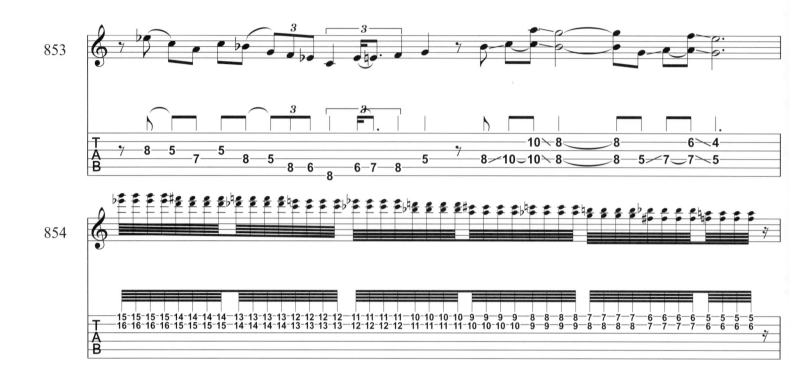

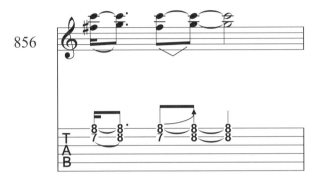

Chapter 16:
Other Dyads

This chapter explores other dyads used in blues guitar playing, the most important of which are fourths and octaves. The fourth easily conjures up the sound of bottleneck slide guitar. Because when the slide plays dyads on any adjacent strings except 2 and 3, the interval of the fourth is produced. Since the bottleneck tradition is so identified with blues guitar, dyads in fourths sound highly authentic. Dyads in octaves, on the other hand, tend to be associated with the mainstream jazz guitar sounds popularized by Wes Montgomery.

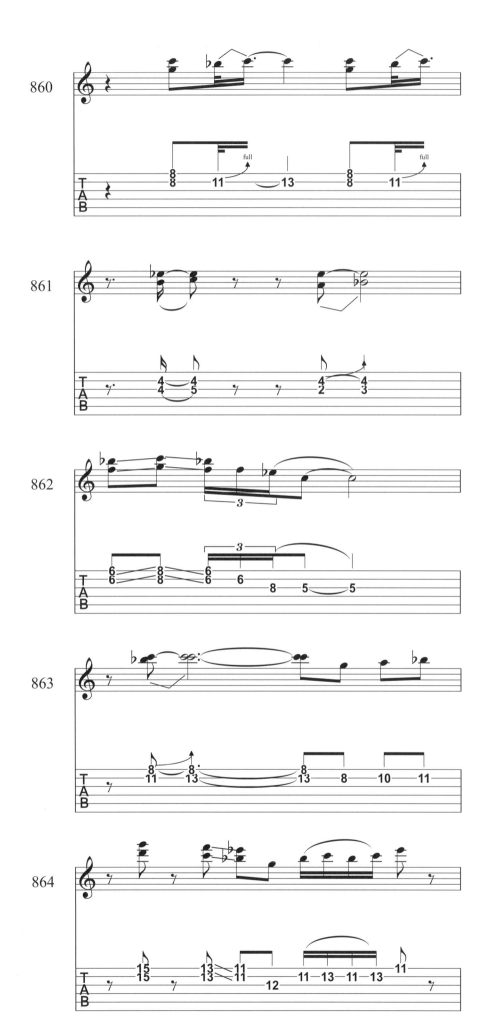

Ed King

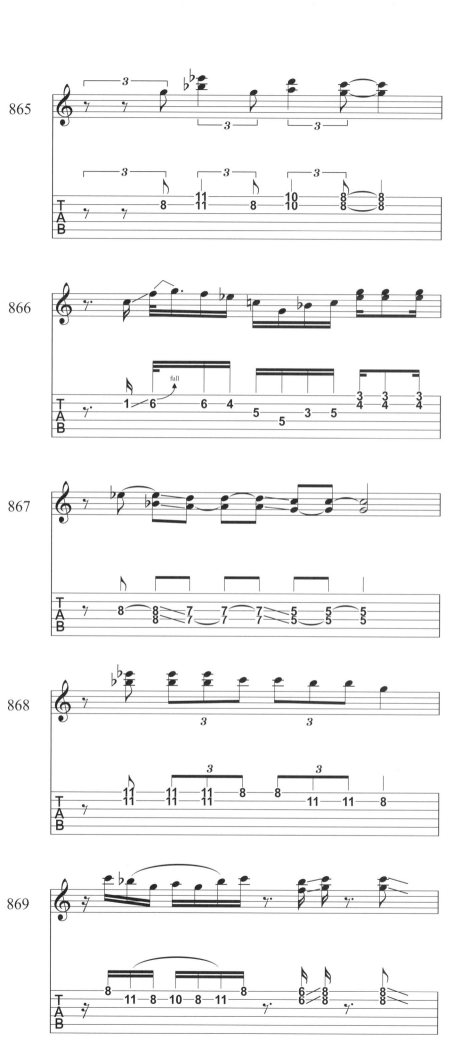

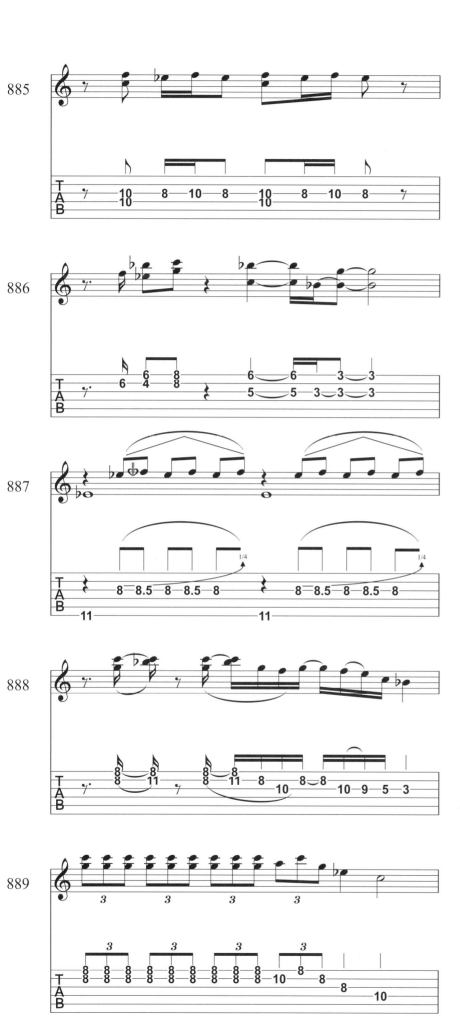

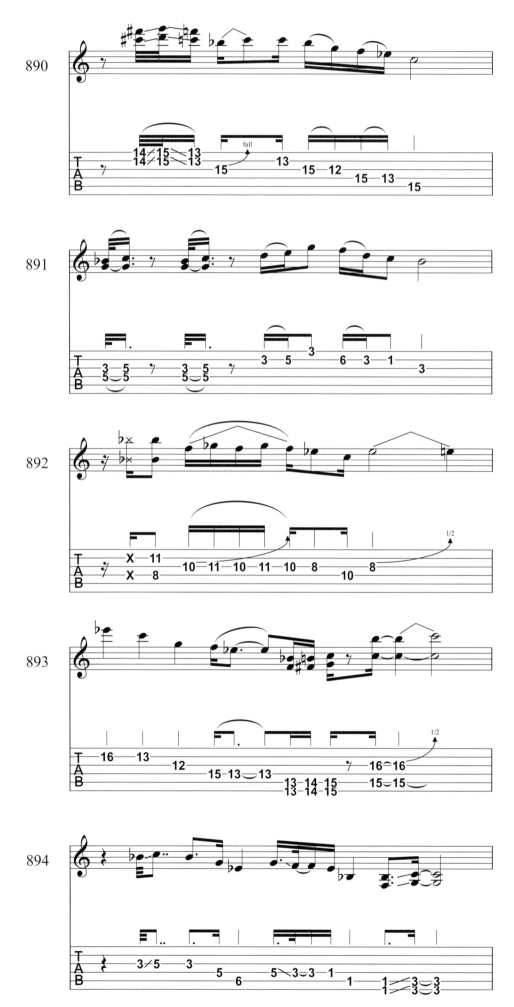

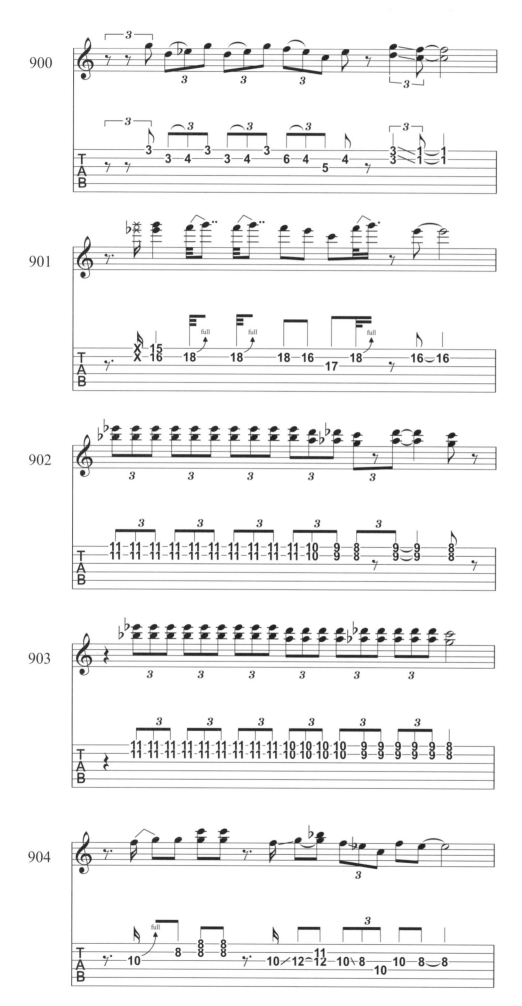

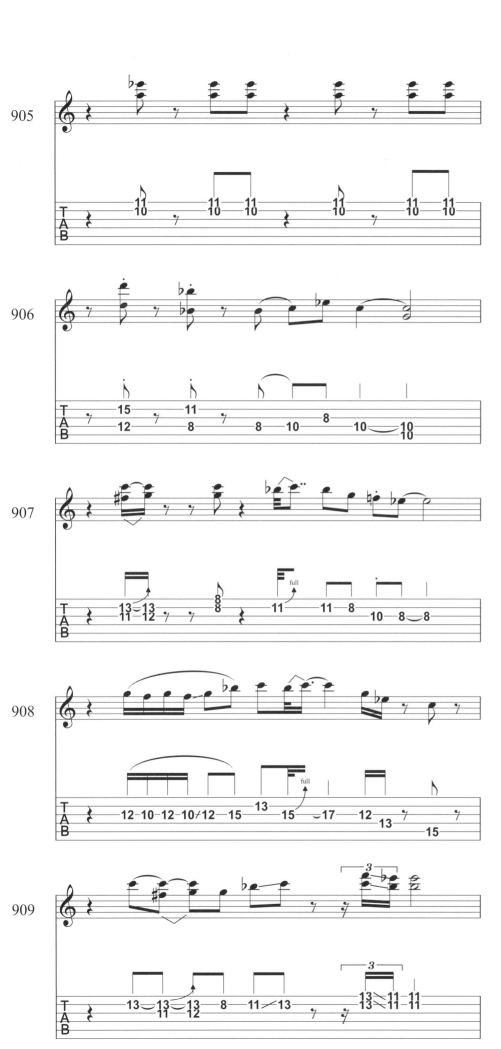

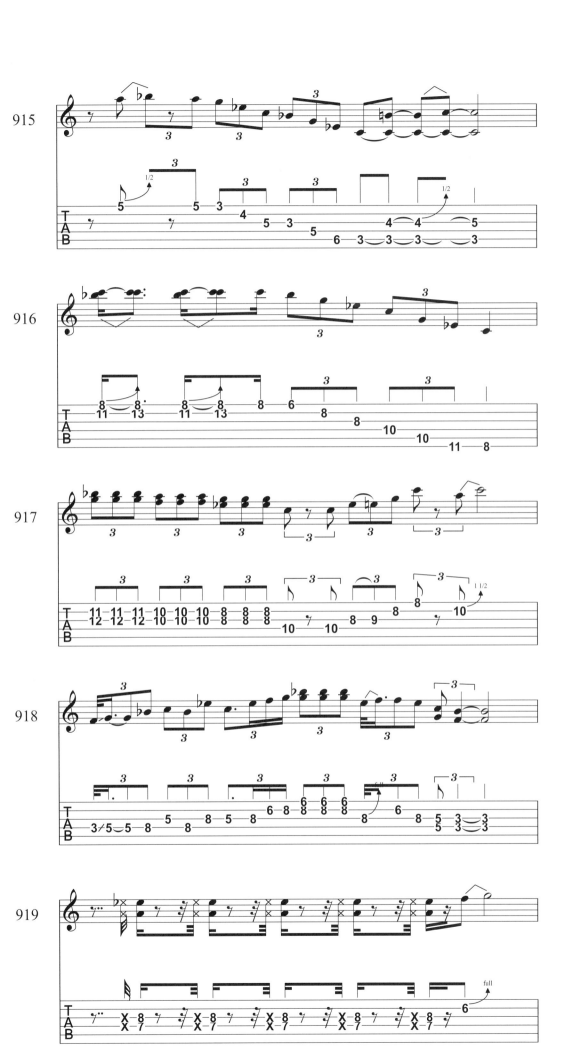

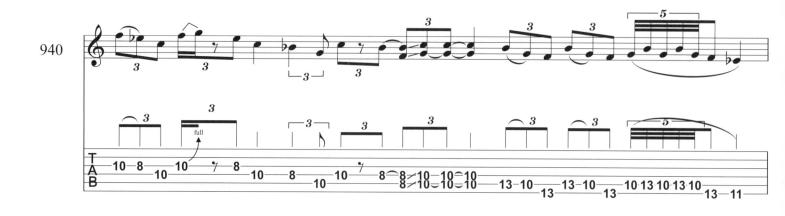

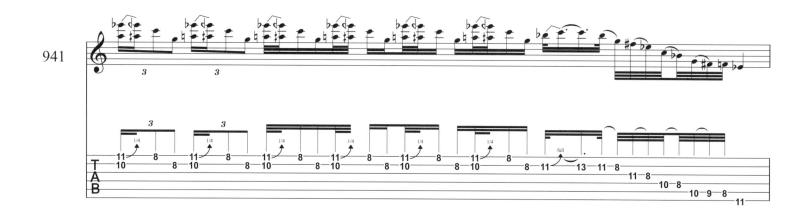

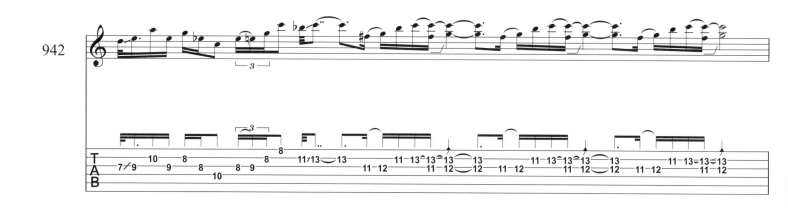

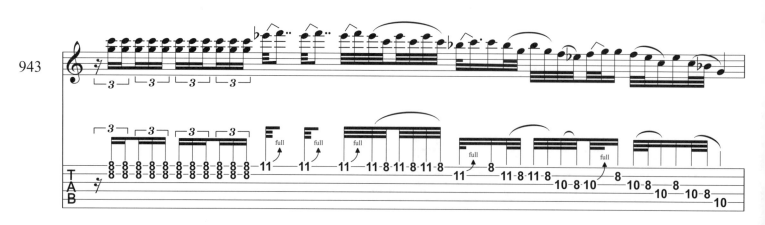

Chapter 17: Triads

A triad can be regarded as any combination of three notes, not limited to the familiar major, minor, augmented, and diminished chords. This allows the musician a great deal of creative latitude in incorporating chords in a melodic setting. Triads can be strummed like other chords, arpeggiated by picking notes individually, and raked, by sweeping the pick over the strings in quick succession. Triads can also be played up and down the fingerboard in parallel motion. All of these actions bring new expressive textures, energy, and freshness to a guitar solo.

949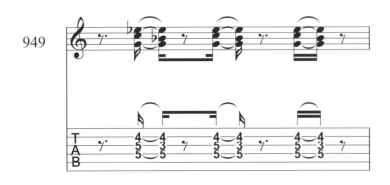

950

Depression Blues

951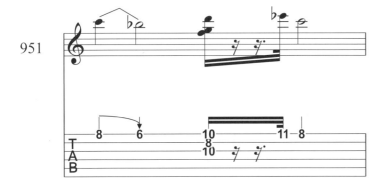

952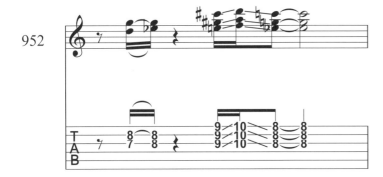

953

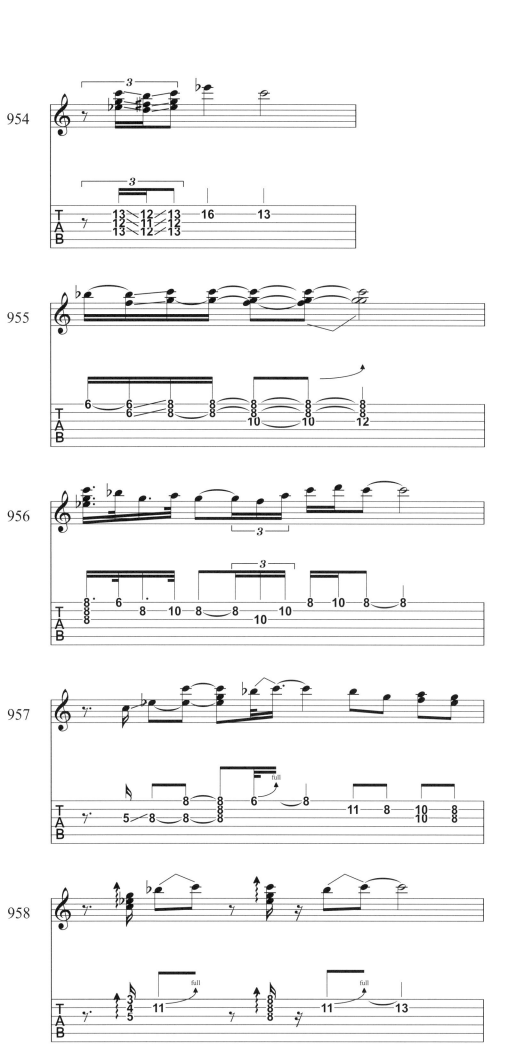

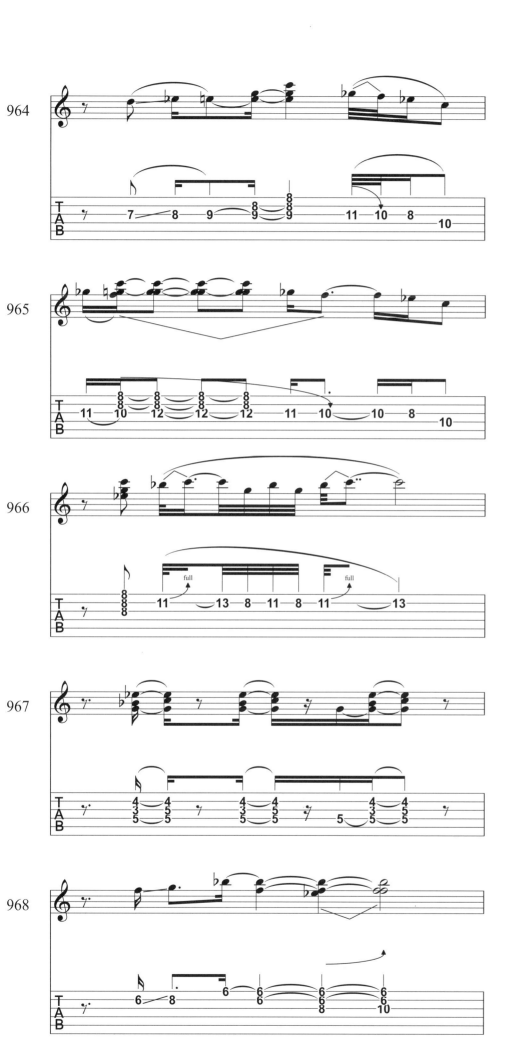

Chapter 18:
Repeated Notes

This chapter focuses on one of the most fundamental building blocks of phrasing, the repeated note. Using the singing voice as a model, as many guitarists do, consider how certain words in a song would be incomprehensible if every syllable was sung on a different pitch. In practice, vocal melodies often use two or more notes on the same pitch for the simple reason that this is more speechlike and makes individual words more comprehensible. Another consideration is that repeating notes of the same pitch imparts to the phrase a rhythmic energy and focus. This technique can serve as an effective antidote to the possible overuse of scale-like patterns that some musicians might find antithetical to blues soloing.

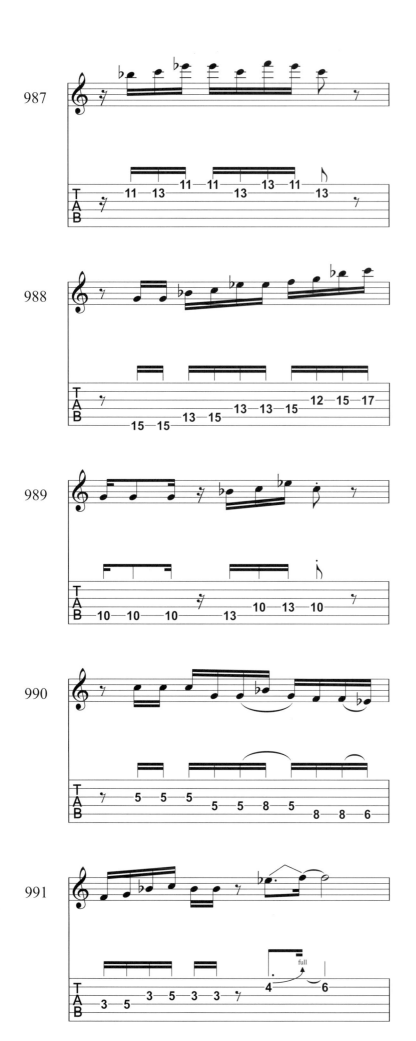

Tony Rombola

203

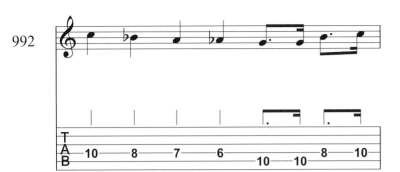

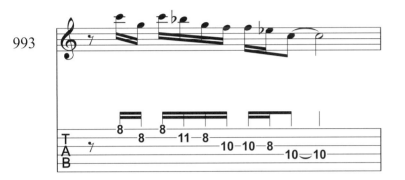

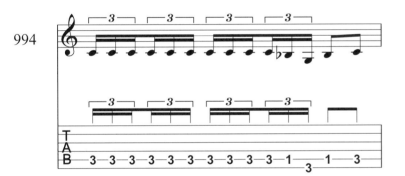

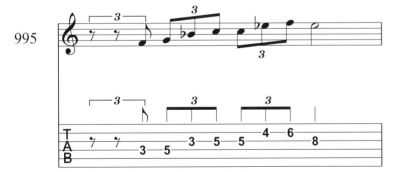

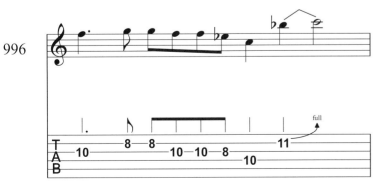

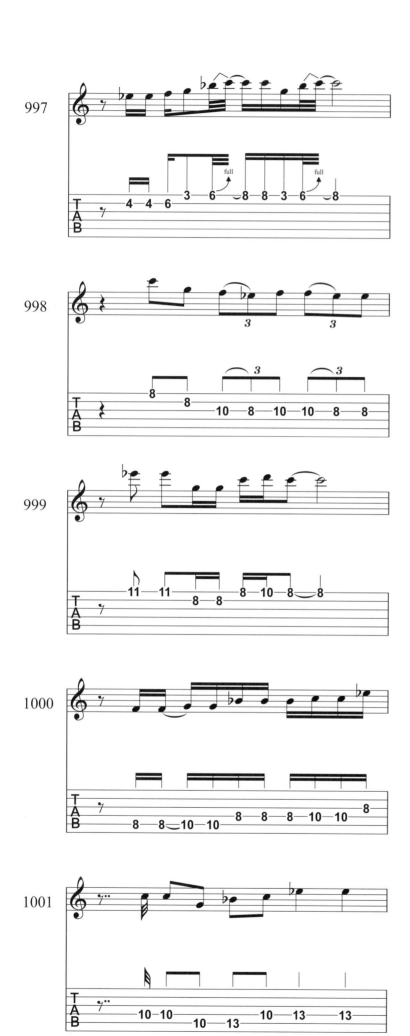

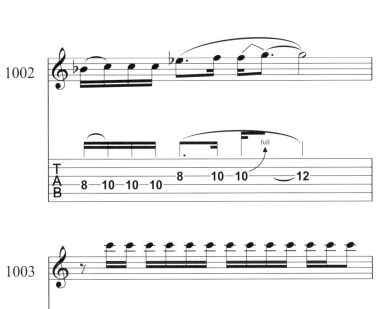

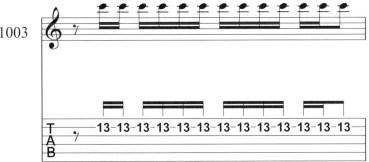

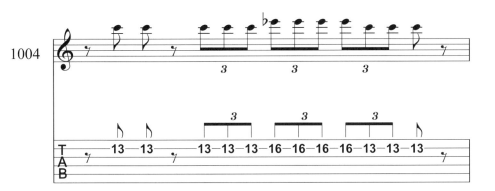

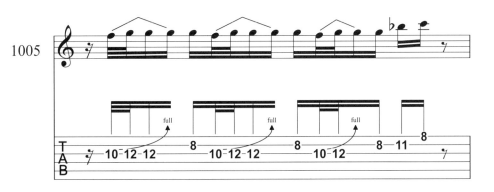

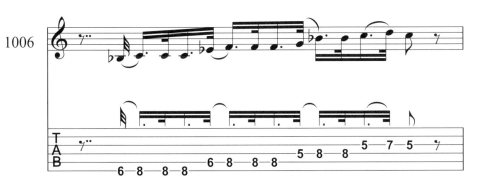

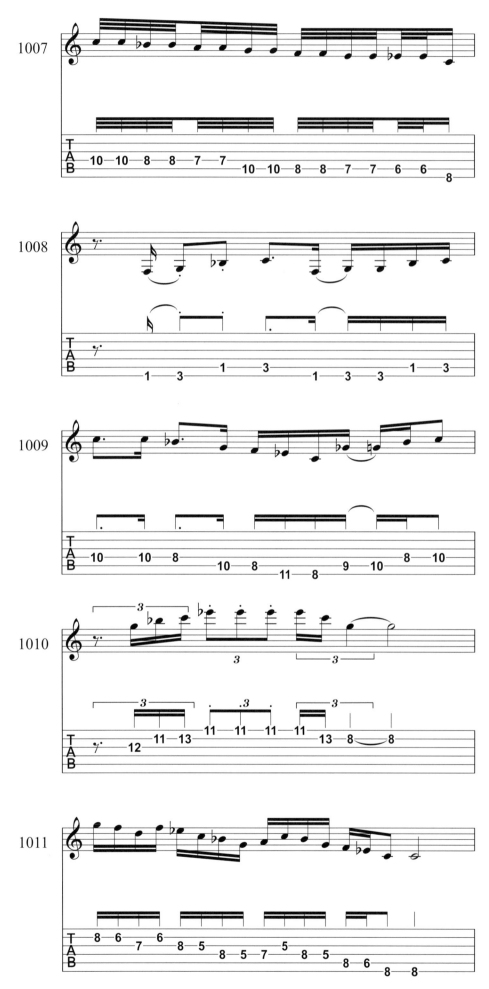

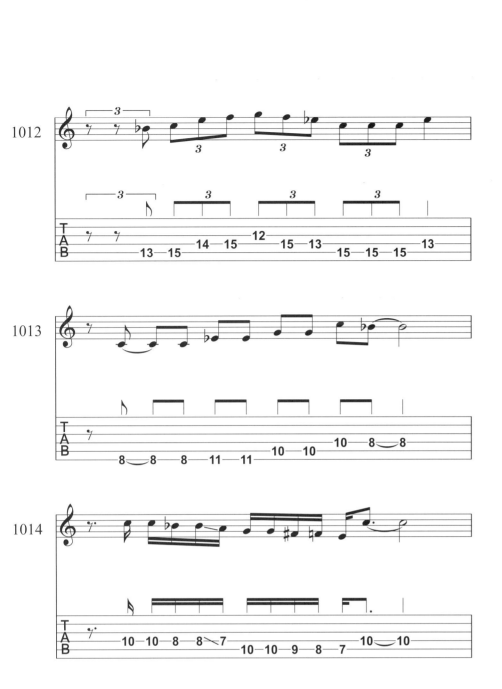
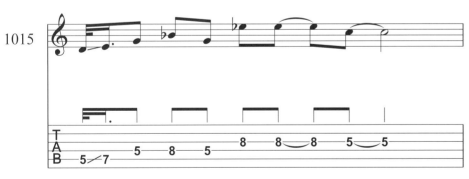
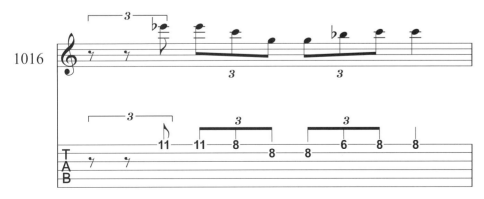

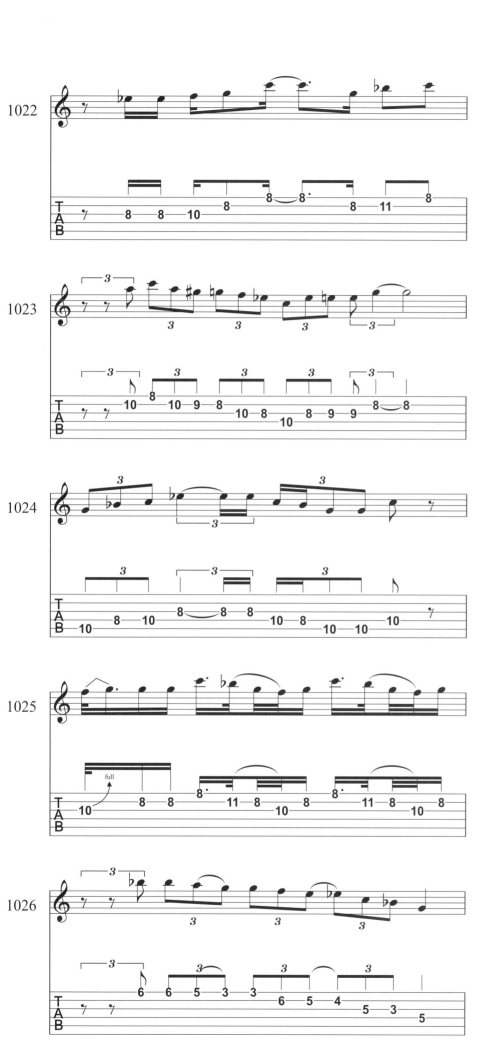

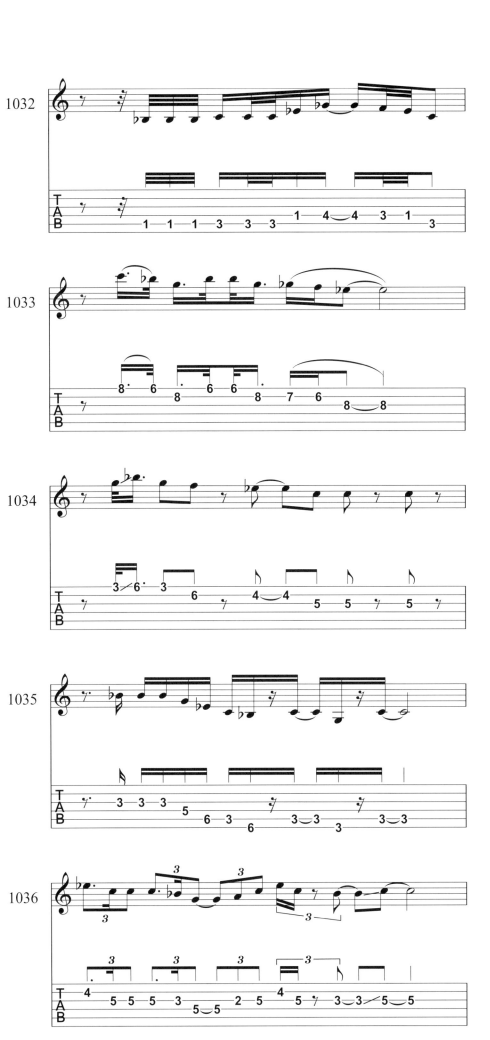

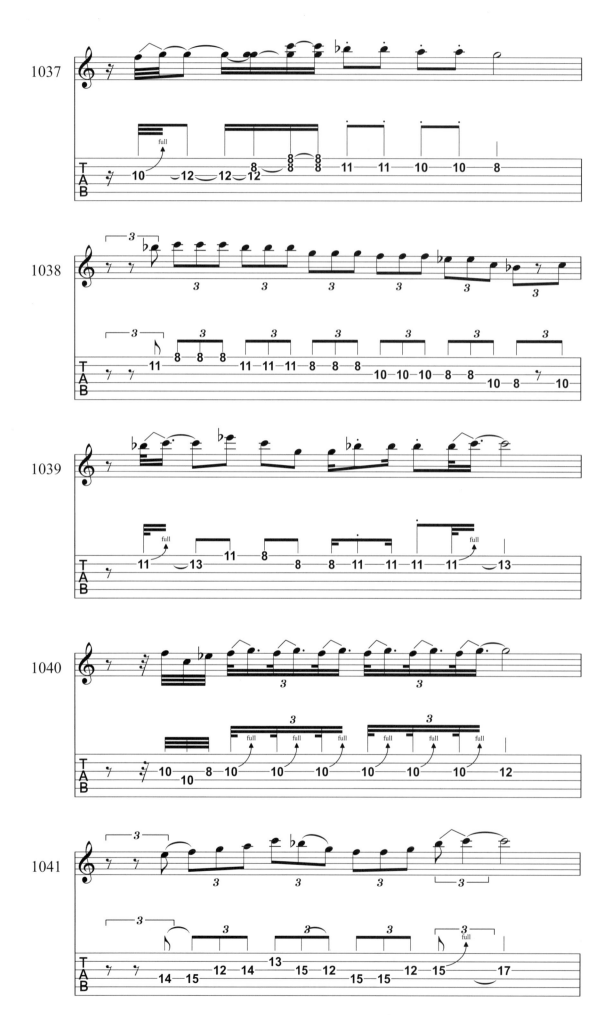

213

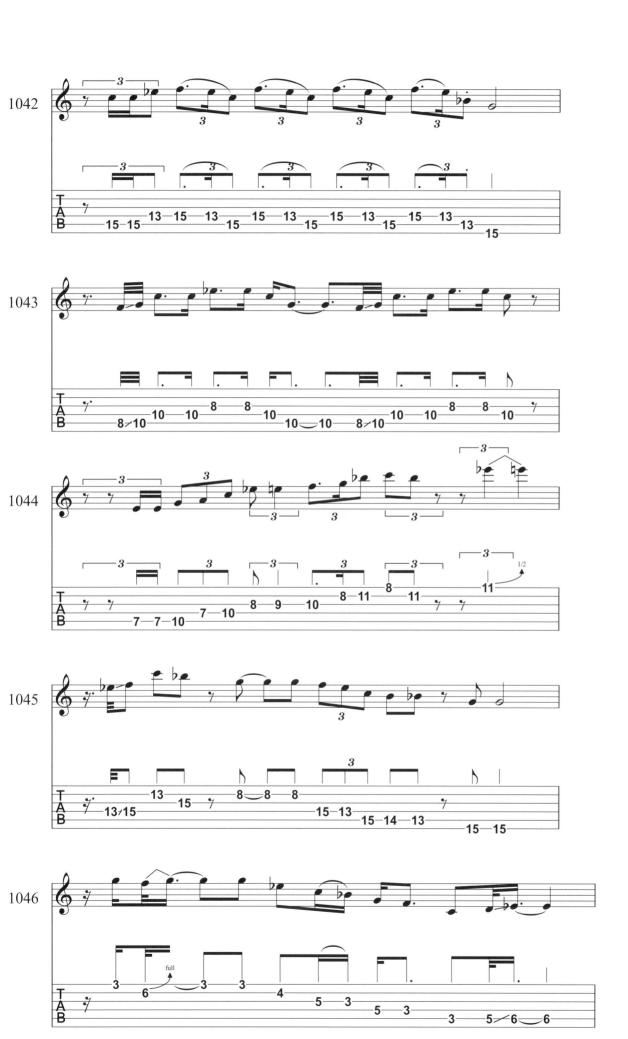

214

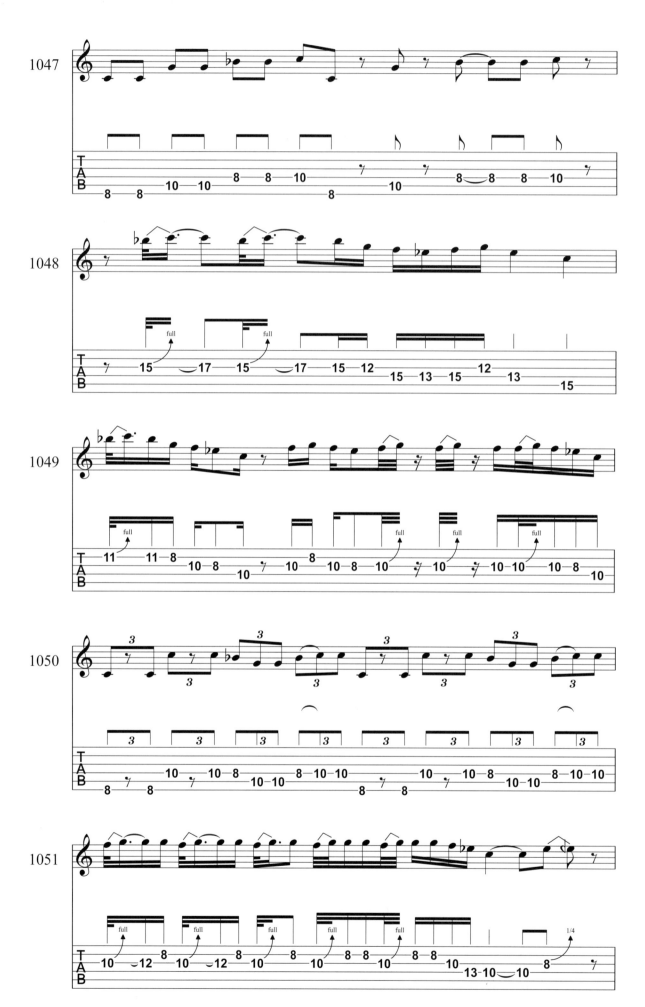

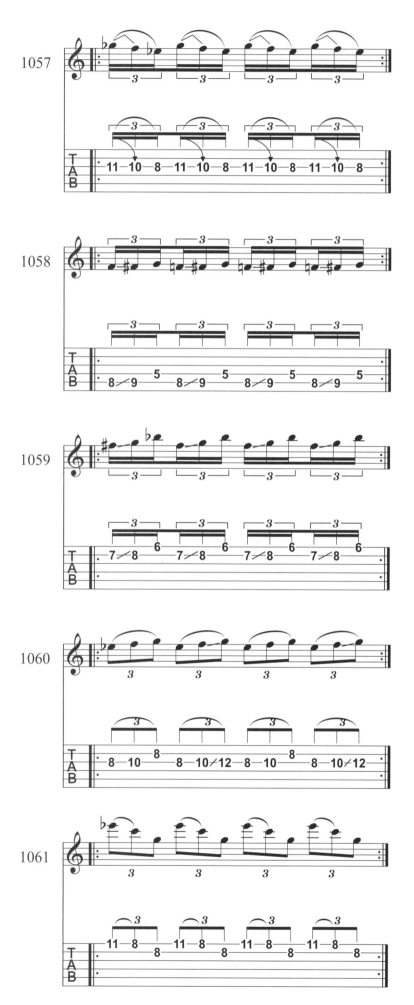

Chapter 19: Repeated Figures

One of the most unique stylistic conventions in music is the rapidly repeating melodic figures found in blues and blues-influenced rock guitar solos. Repeated figures, such as the ones found in this chapter, are very effective ways of building and maintaining moments of great intensity. Albert Collins, Eric Clapton, and Stevie Ray Vaughan are among the most renowned guitarists using this particular phrasing technique.

1062

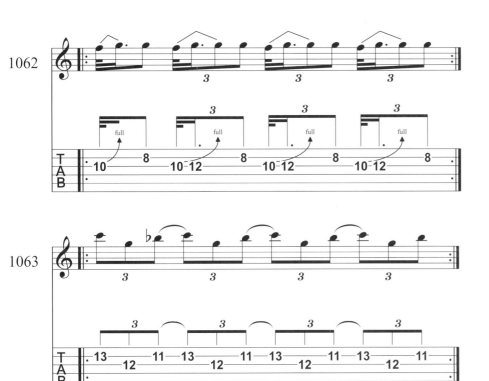

Lonnie Brooks

1063

1064

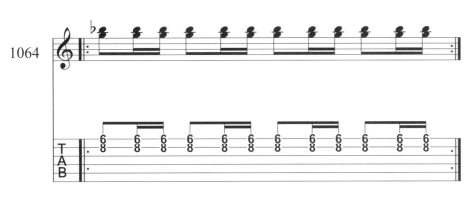

1065

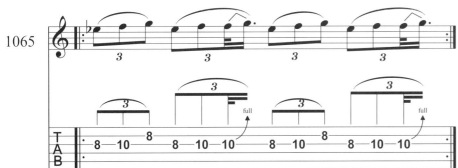

1066

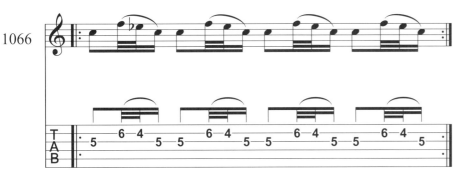

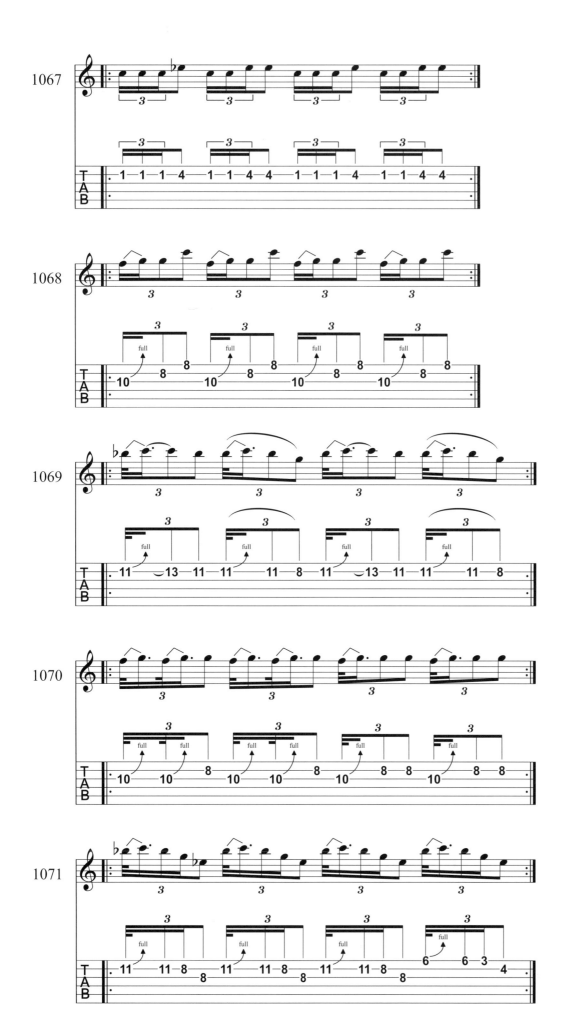

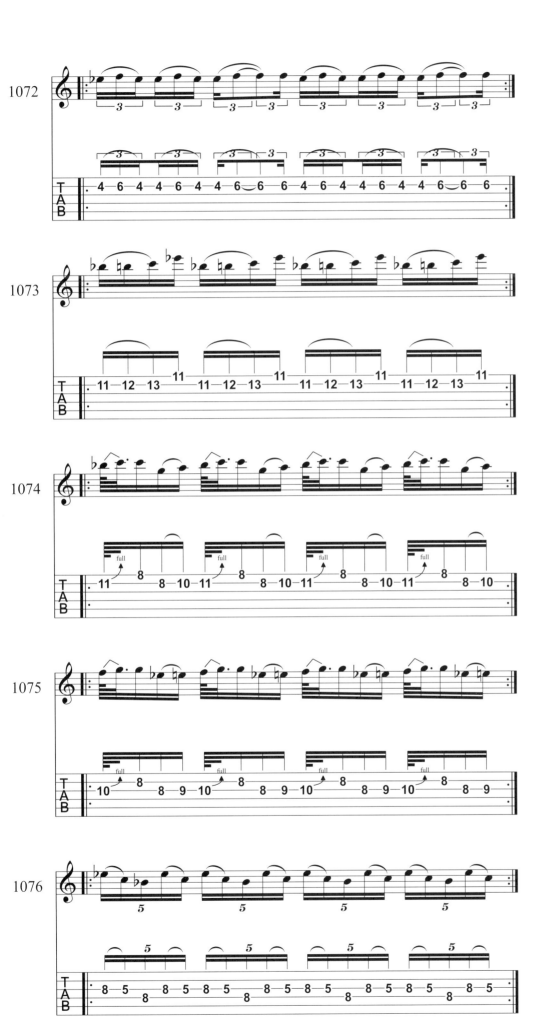

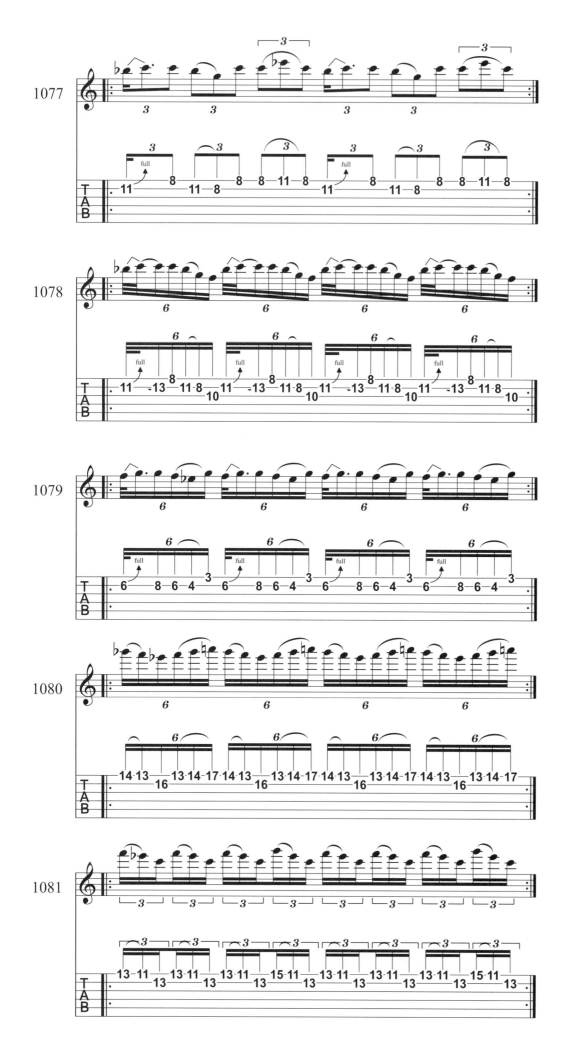

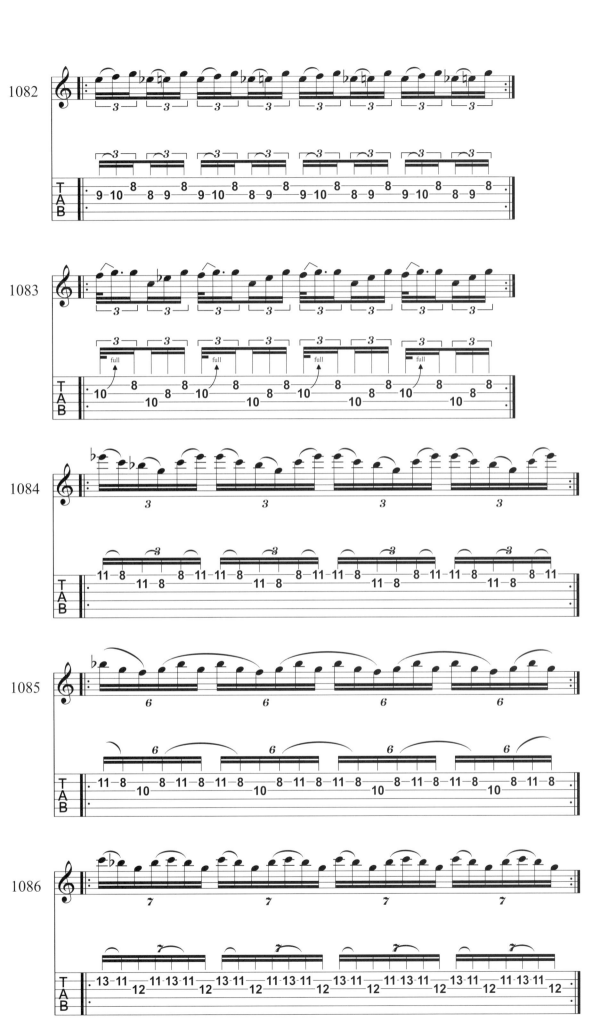

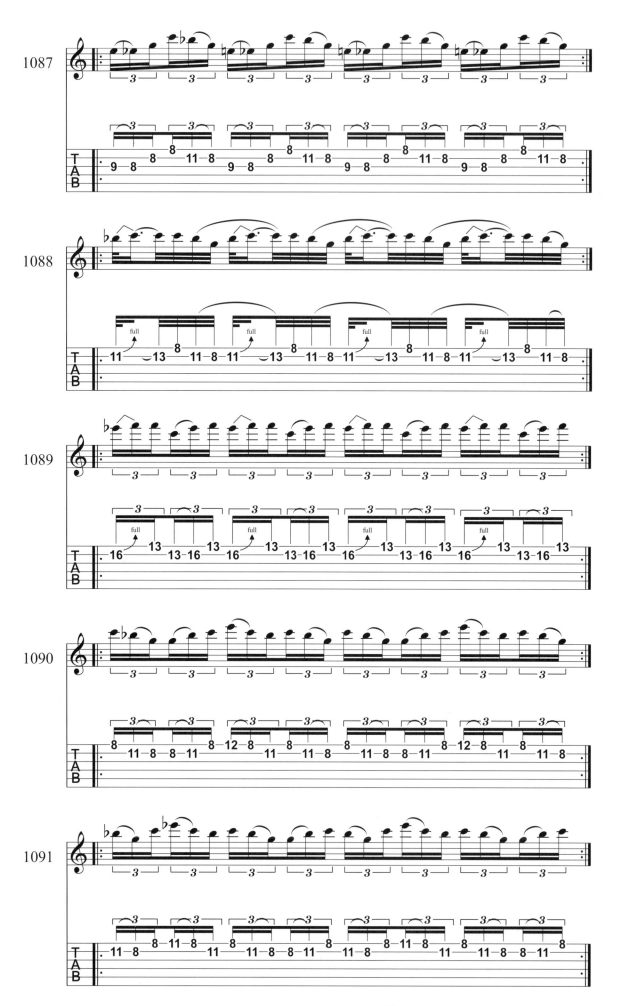

223

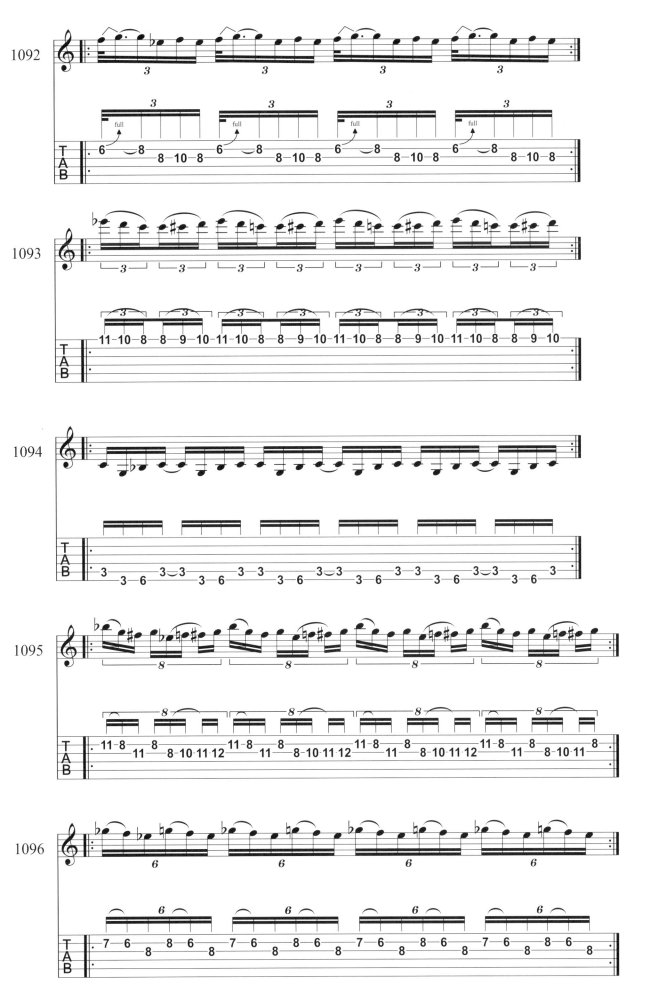

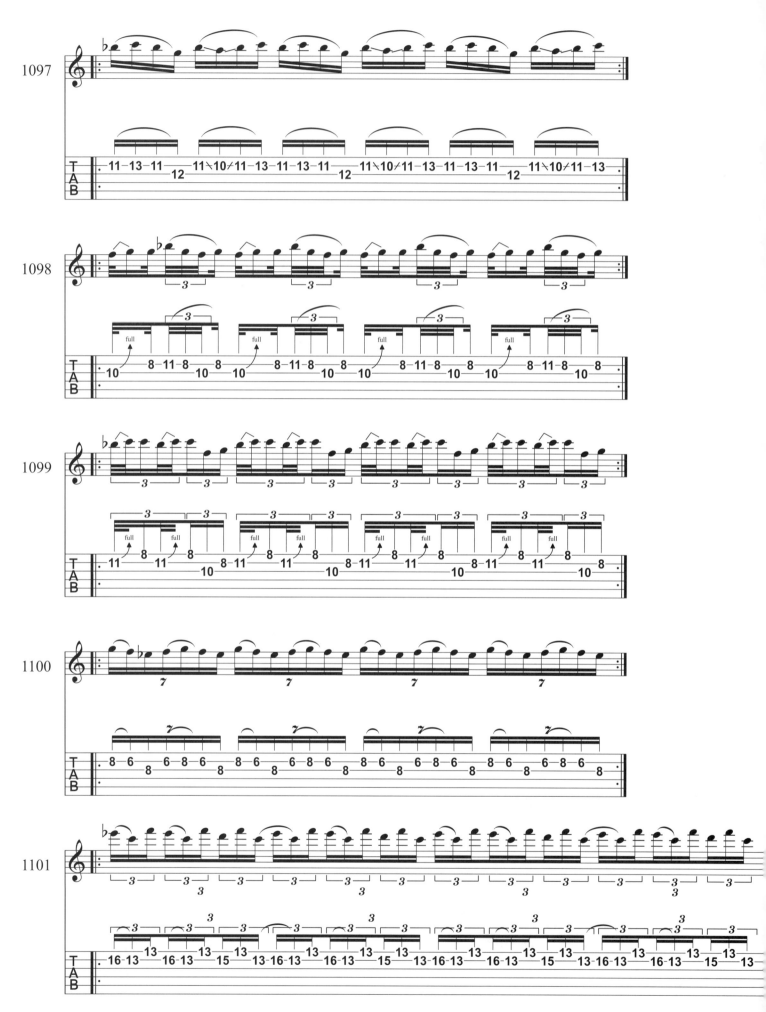

225

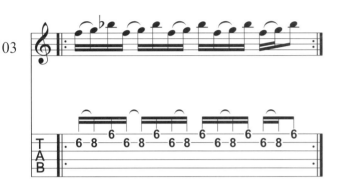

1102

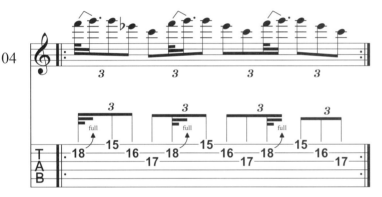

1103

Chapter 20: Cross-Rhythms

A cross-rhythm is a figure rhythmic values, articulations, slurs, or accents are in conflict with its pitch patterns. This occurs, for example, when a pattern of sixteenth-notes, which divide a beat into 4 equal parts, is played with 3 pitches, repeated over a given number of beats. Cross-rhythms like these are often used to boost the energy level of a solo, while being not especially technically demanding for the guitarist.

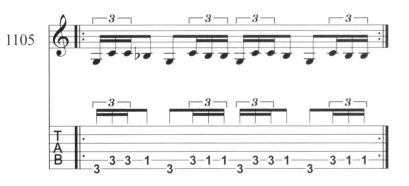

1104

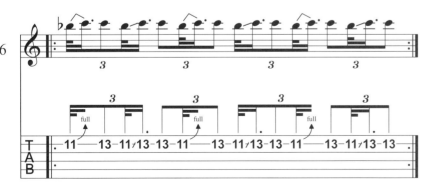

1105

1106

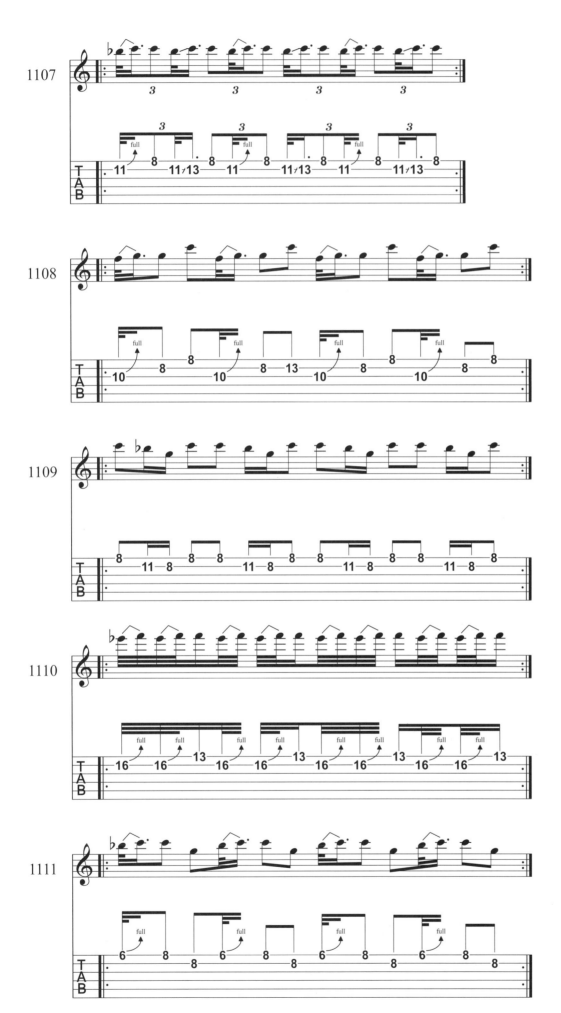

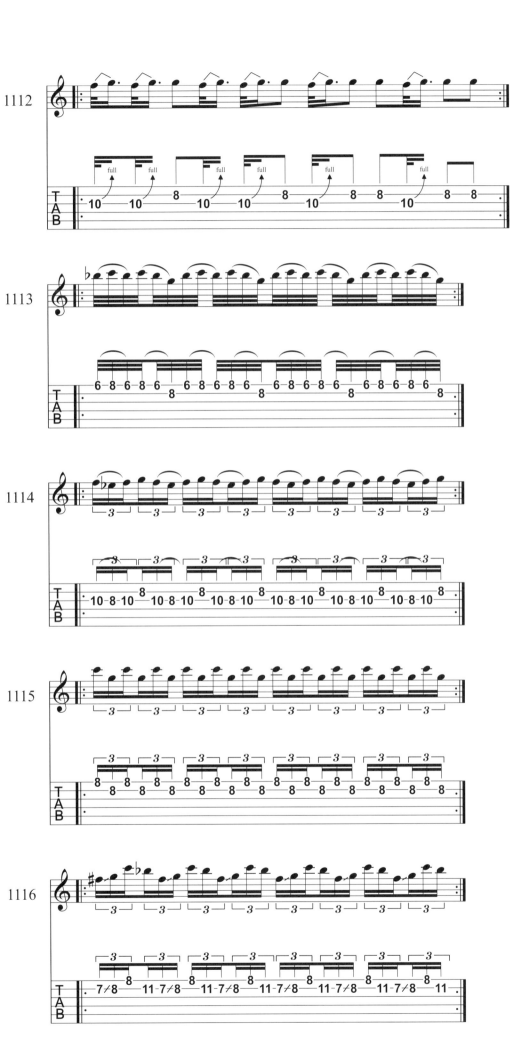

228

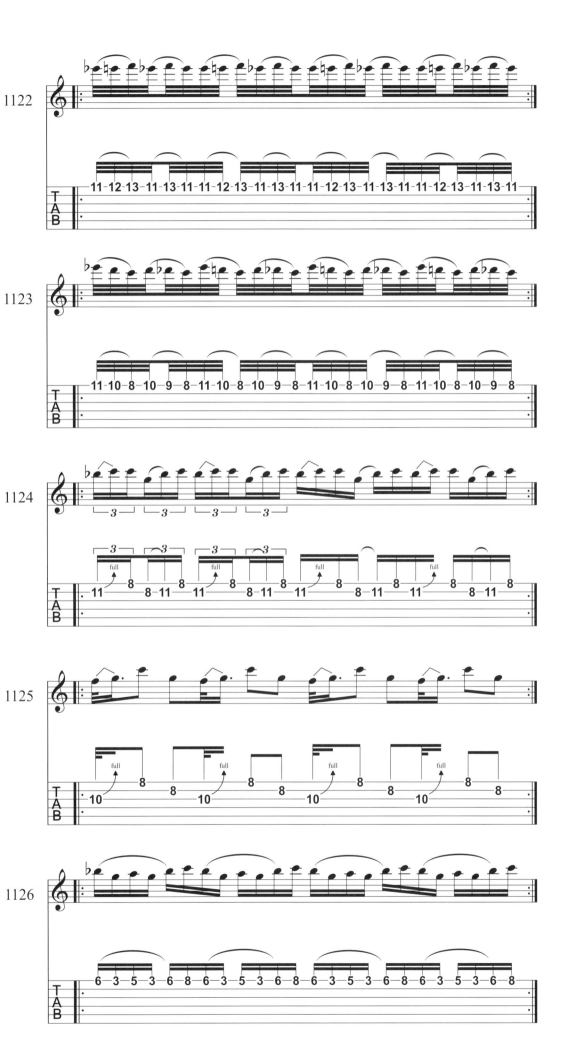

230

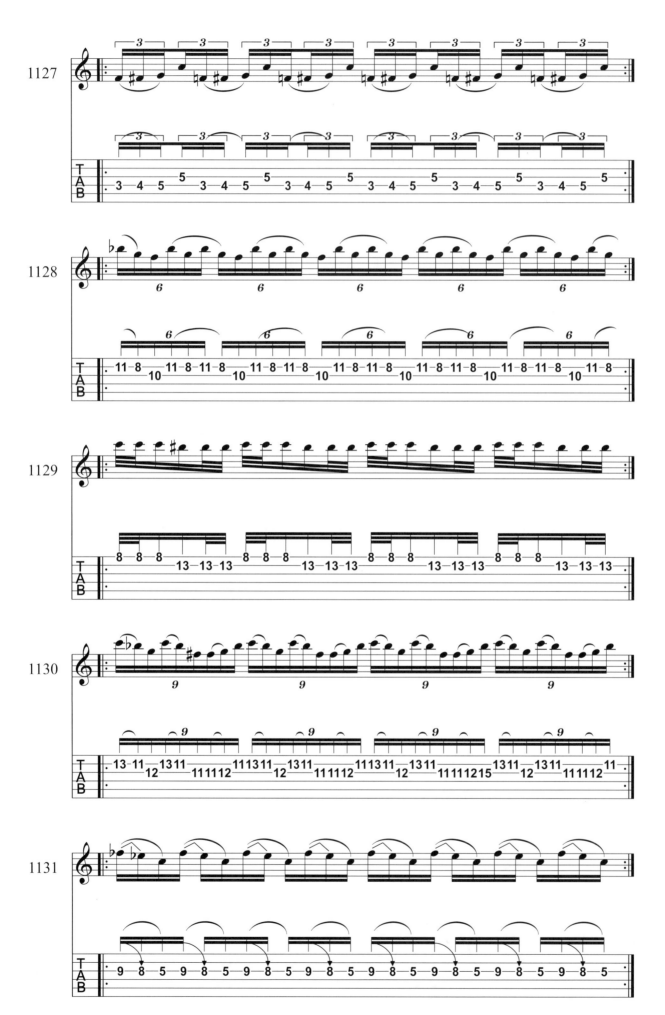

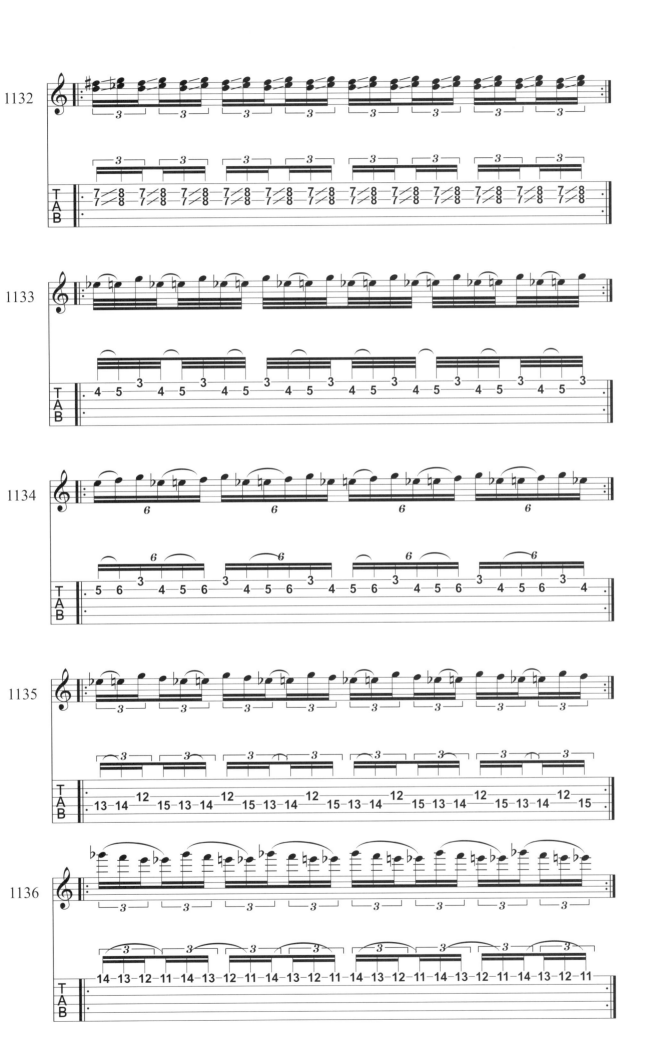

233

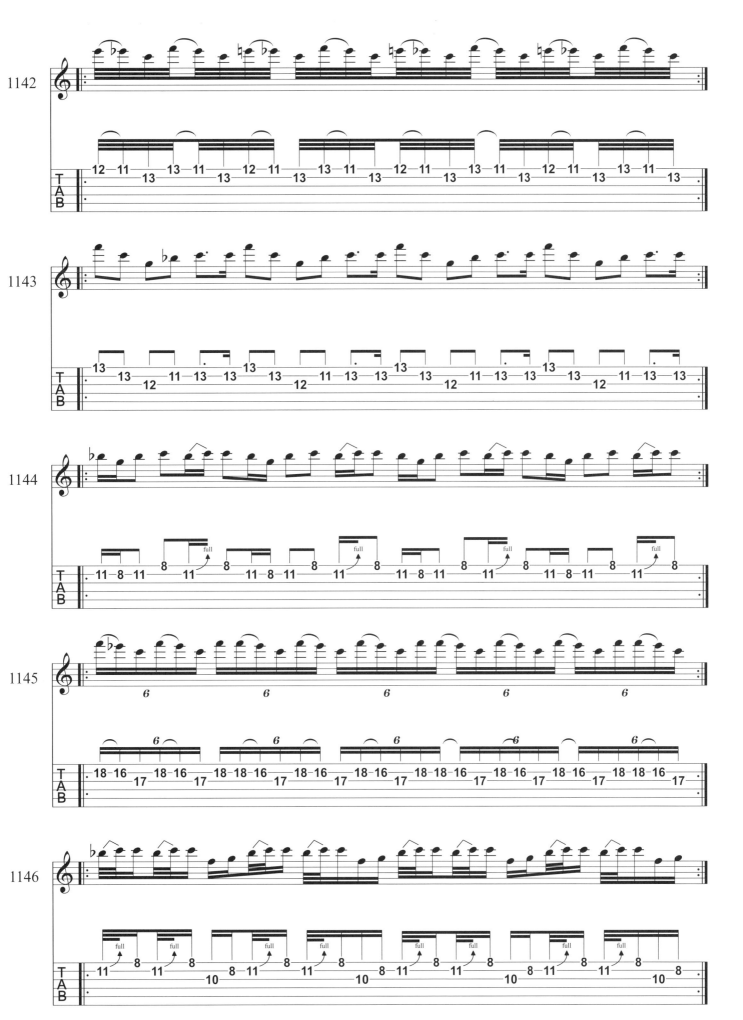

234

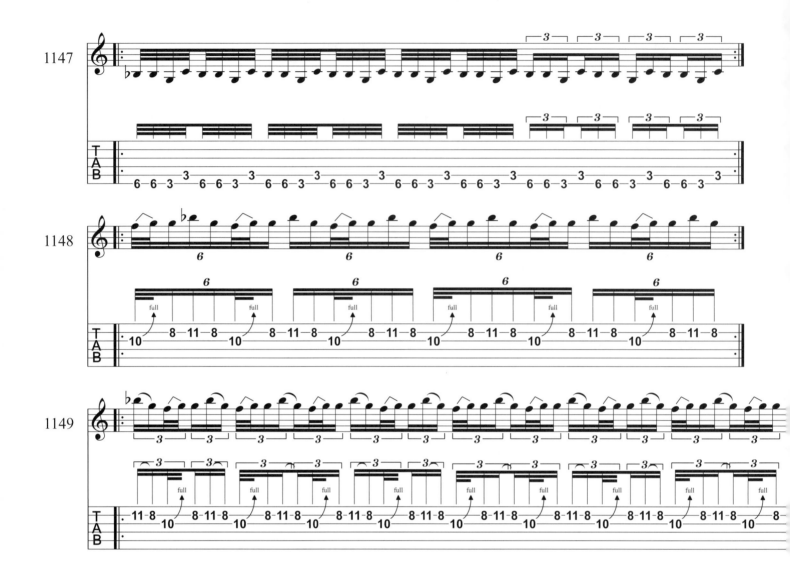

235

1150

1151

1152

1153

1154

Chapter 21: Equal Rhythmic Values

Blues melodies are often quite varied, rhythmically. Therefore, when playing a guitar solo in a blues song, it can be a refreshing change of pace to include phrases that are made of equal rhythmic durations. The guitarist should be mindful that long phrases in equal note values can evoke other styles, especially classical, Baroque, jazz, prog-rock, and metal shredding. Even-note phrases of one bar or less can be used very effectively to release energy which has been building up during a solo. This allows the listener to relax for a moment before the solo starts building more tension and excitement.

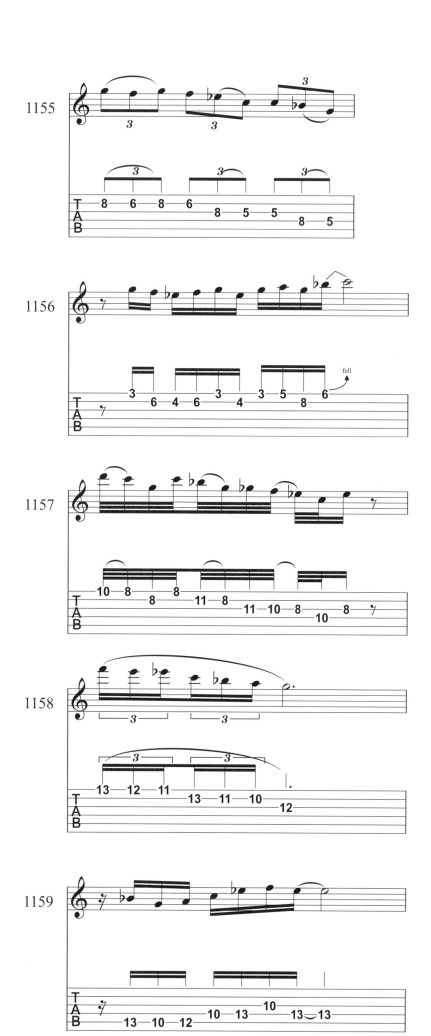

R. Leadbelly

237

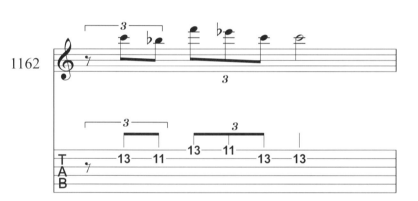

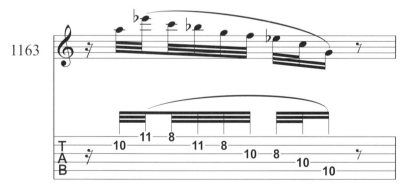

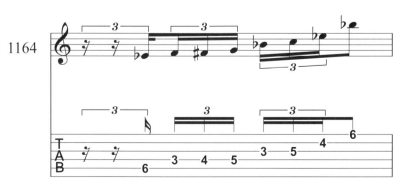

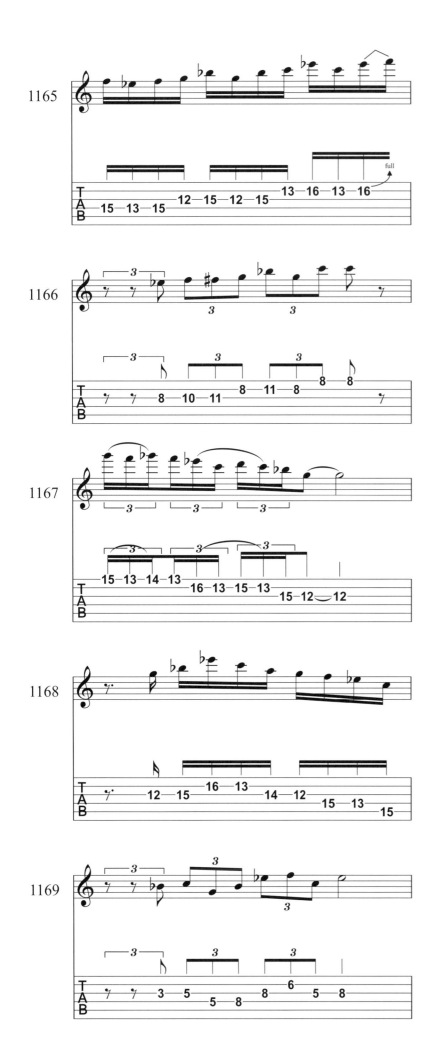

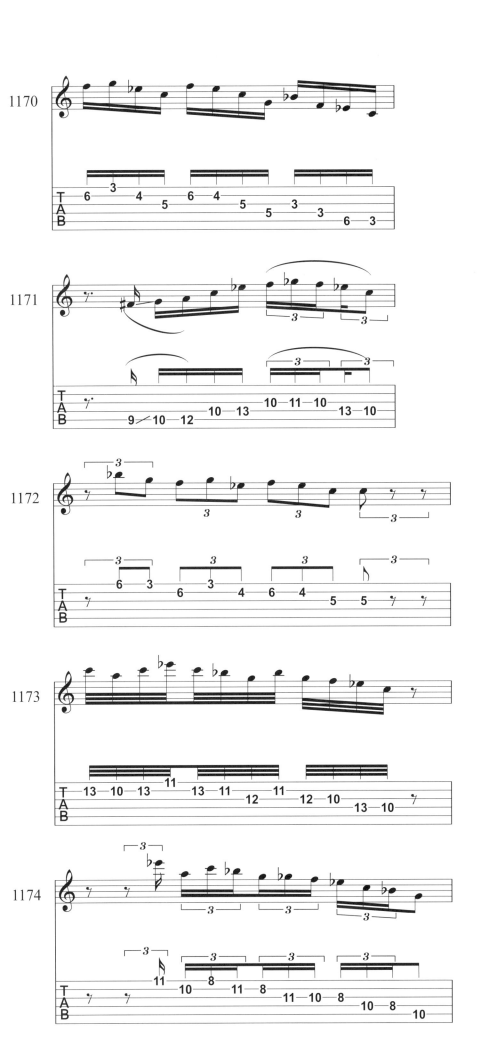

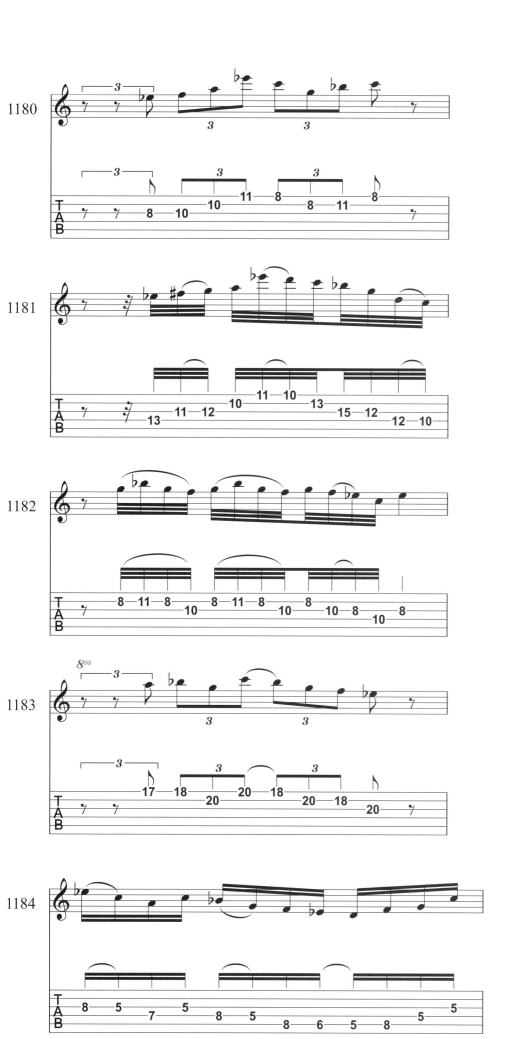

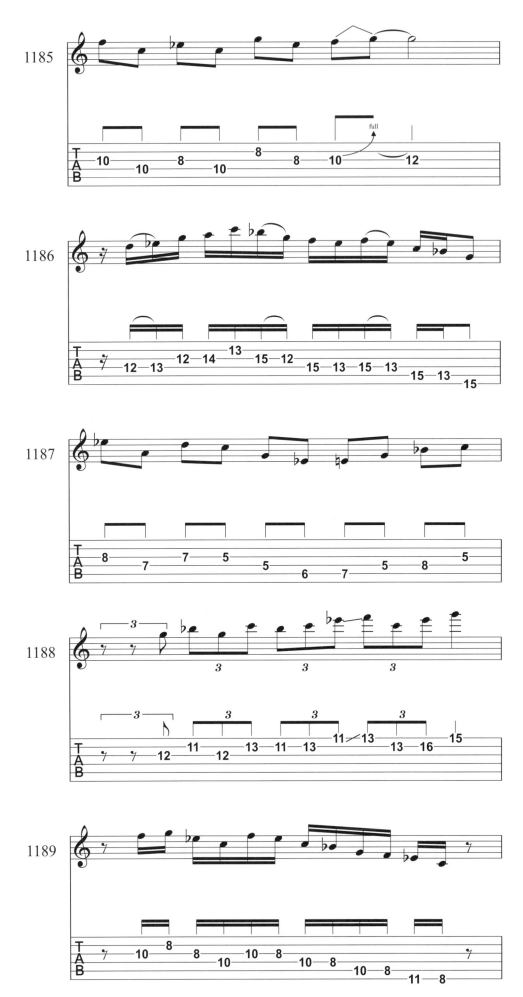

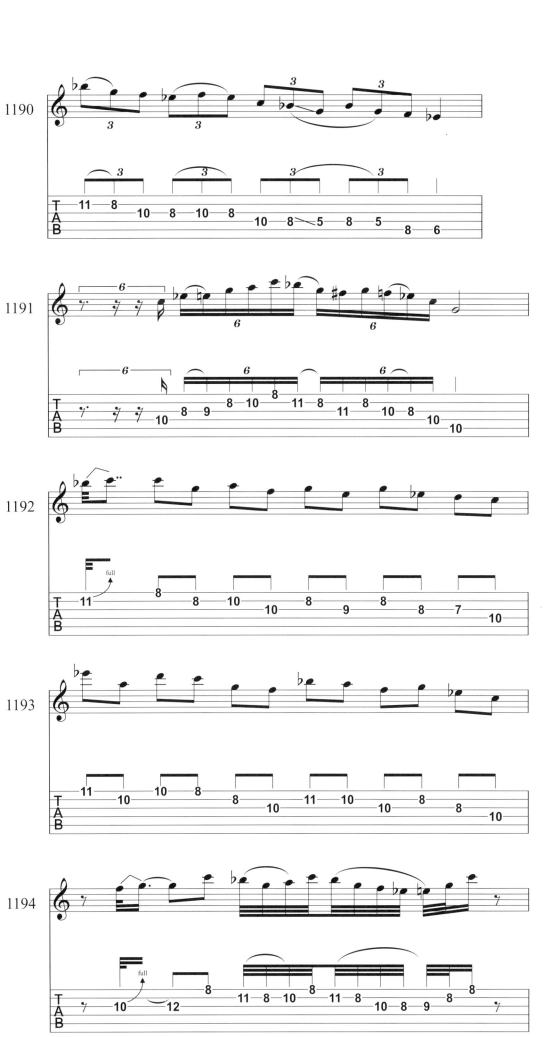

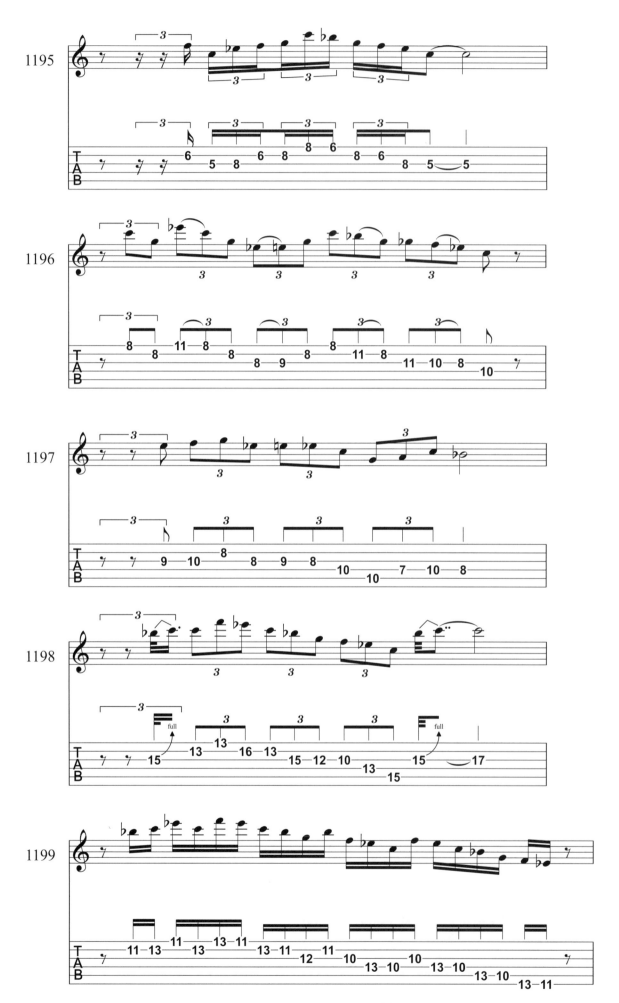

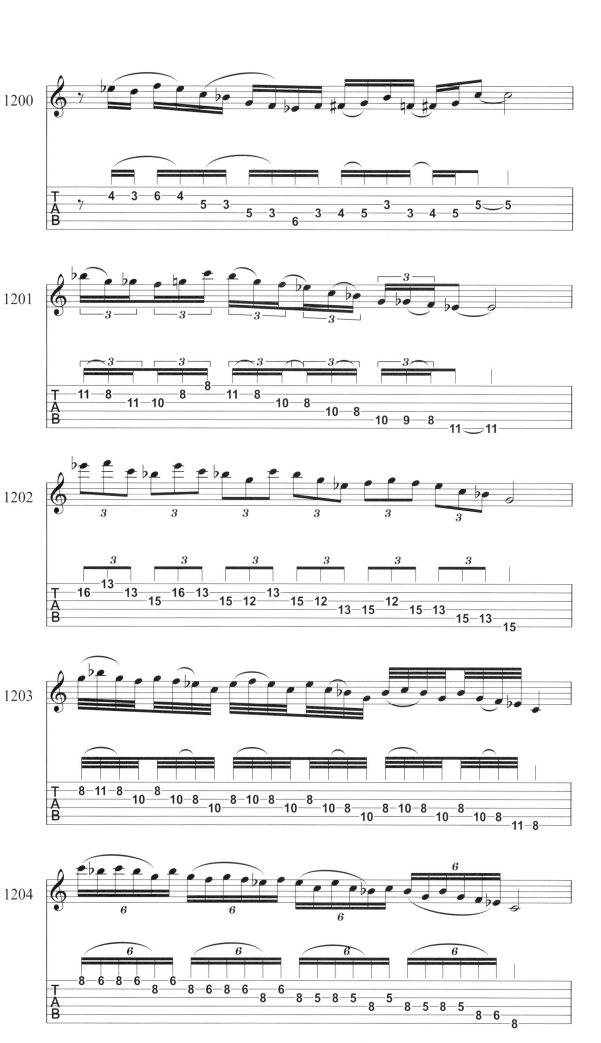

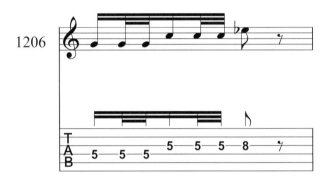

1205

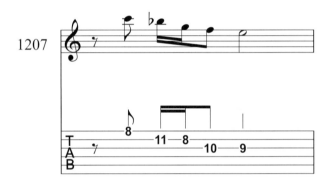

1206

Chapter 22:
Rhythmic Pairs

Melodies of blues songs generally emphasize rhythm over pitch. Some of the most driving and energetic rhythms are comprised of two short notes and one long note. Common examples are an eighth-note and two sixteenths, either as long-short-short or short-short-long. In triplet form, one finds long-long-short-short and long-short-short-long. Both of these rhythms are very common in blues guitar solos, especially the second pattern, which can be deceptively challenging to play. Any of the patterns above can be played two or more times in succession, with or without different pitches. In either case, the rhythmic figure can act as an important unifying element of a guitar solo. These kinds of patterns are a hallmark of Albert King's vocal-derived guitar playing.

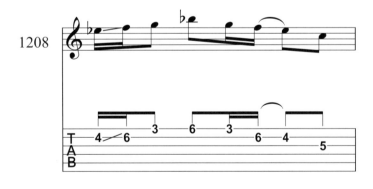

1207

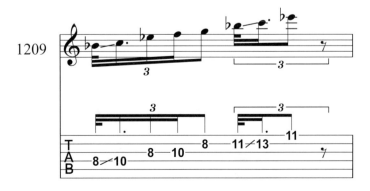

1208

1209

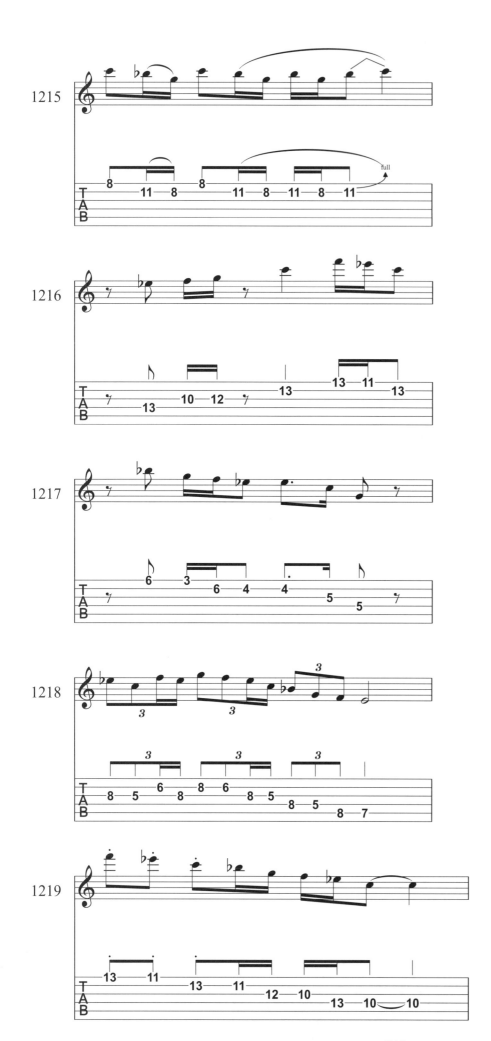

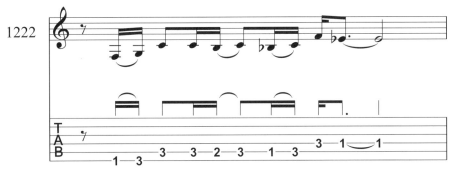

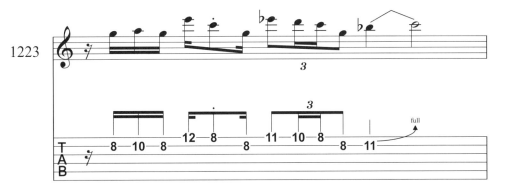

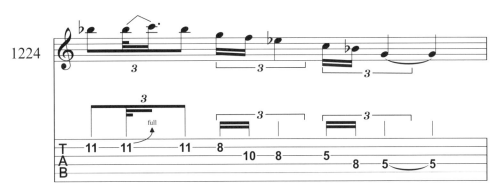

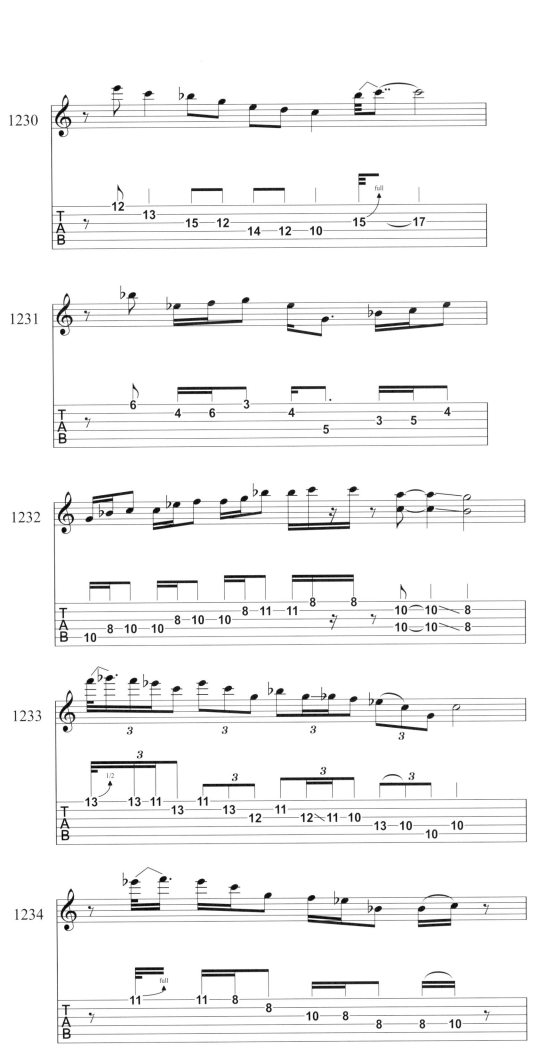

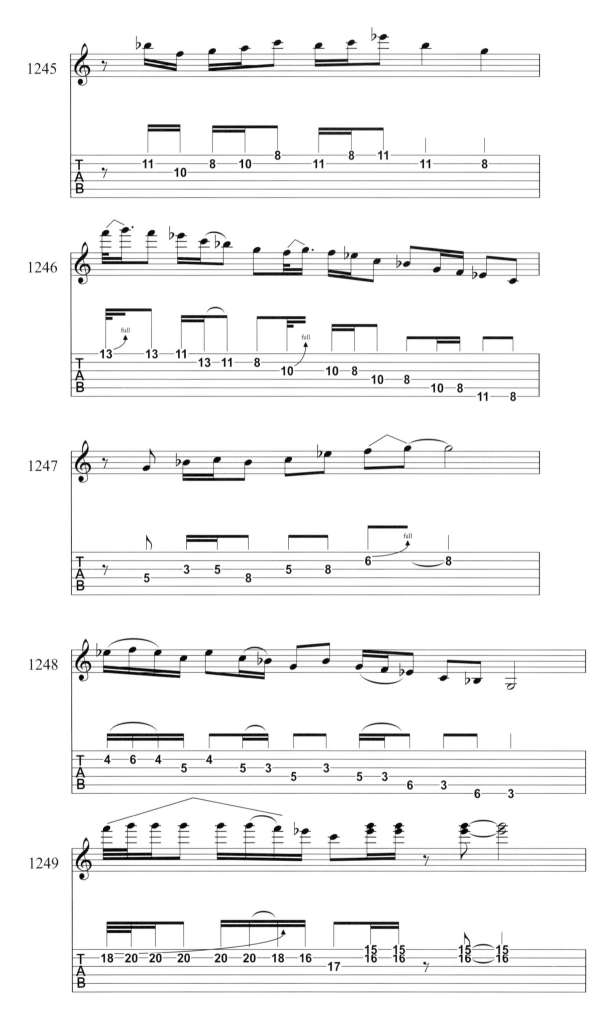

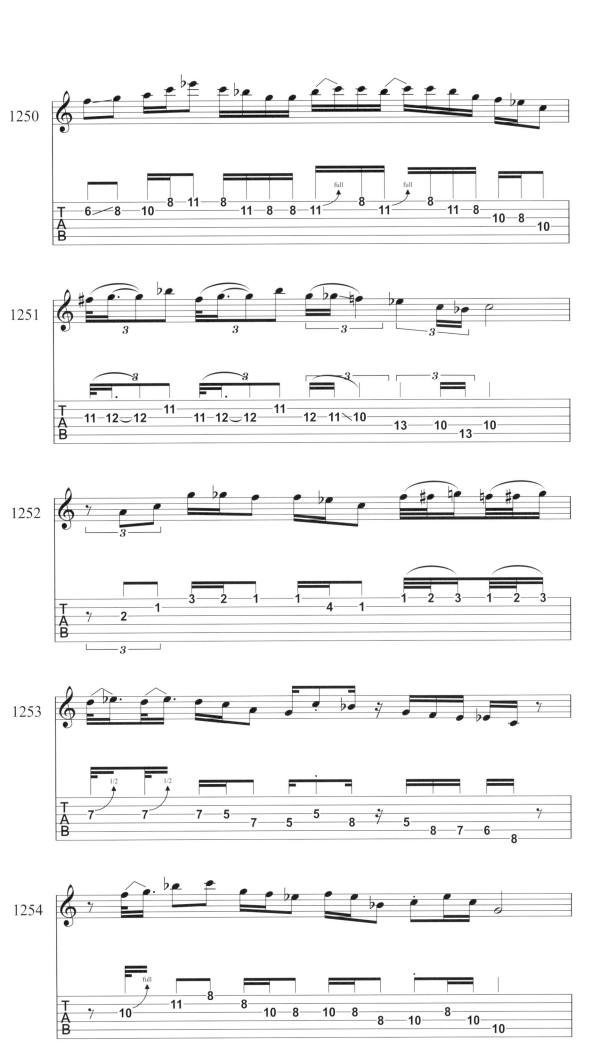

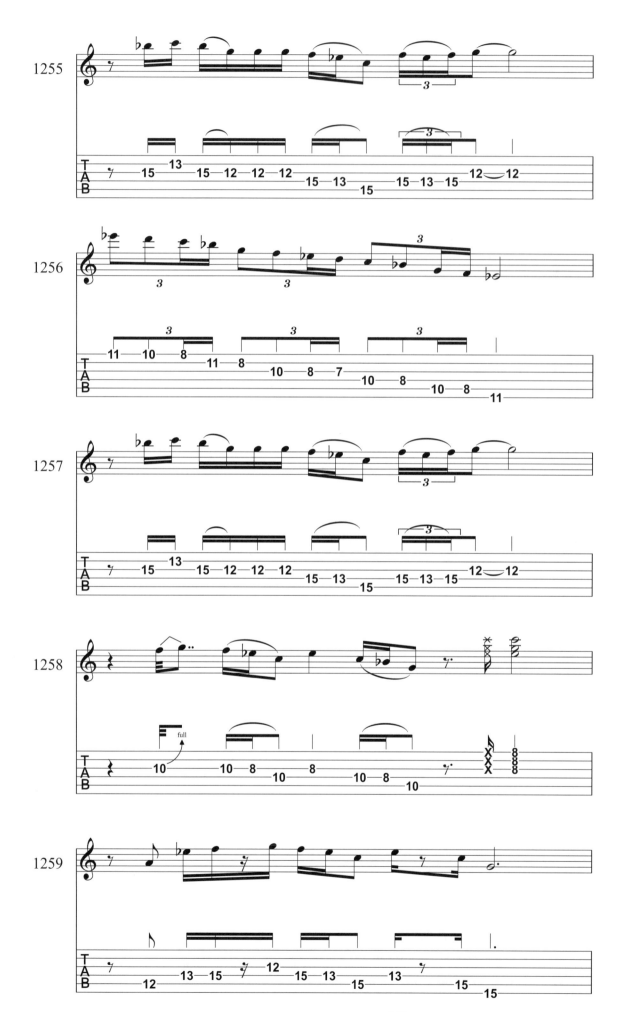

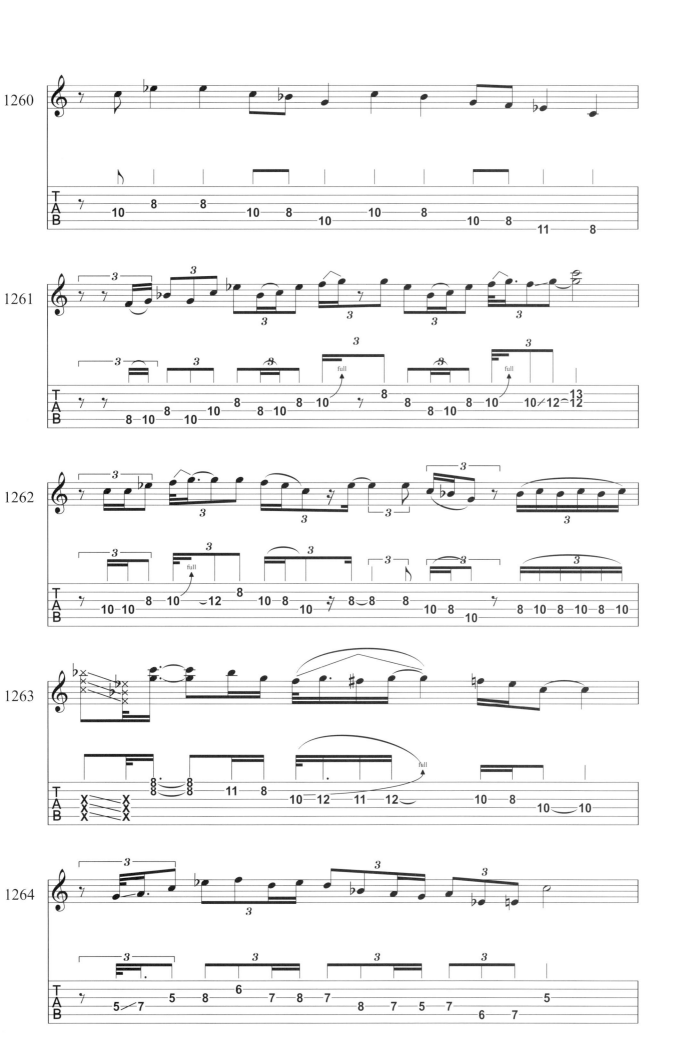

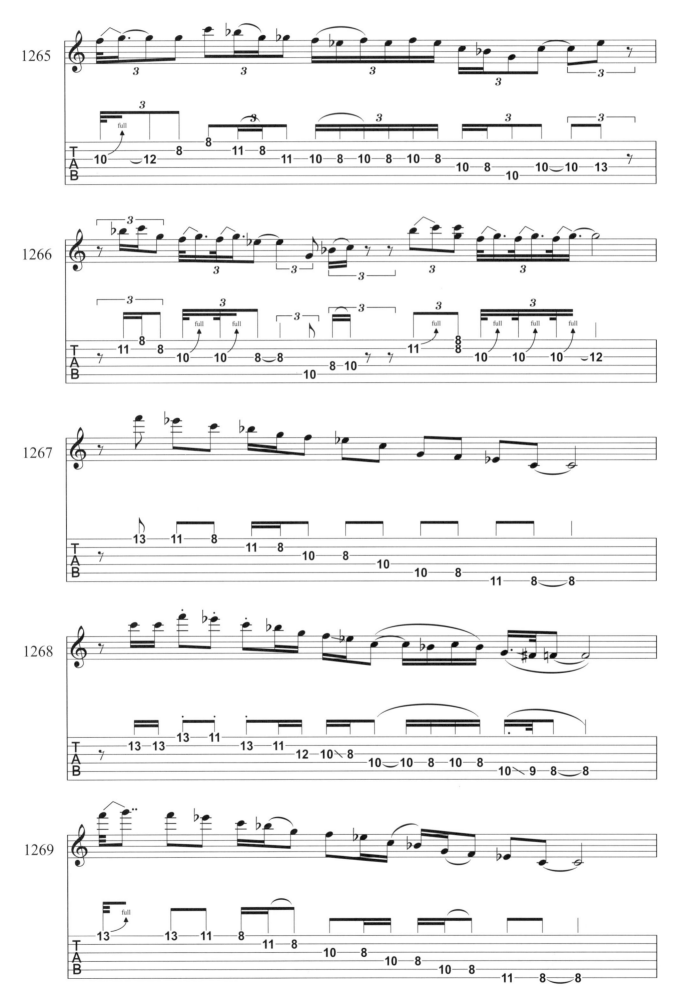

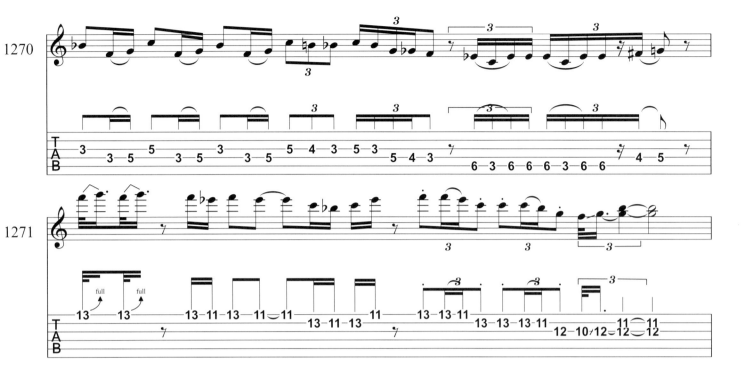

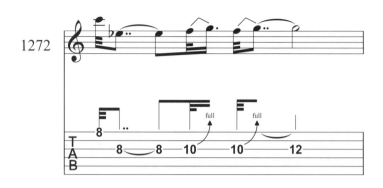

1272

Chapter 23: Snap Rhythms

A snap rhythm is a two-note pattern of strong-weak or weak-strong subdivisions, played in very quick succession. It is widely used by Chicago blues guitarists, most notably Otis Rush, Magic Sam, and Buddy Guy. Eric Clapton often used this figure as a kind of announcement in guitar solos in his Mayall and early Cream era.

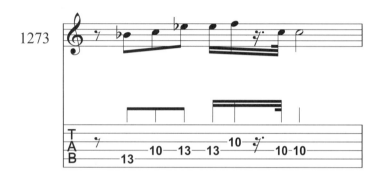

1273

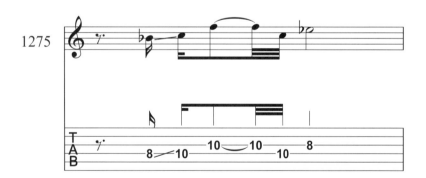

1274

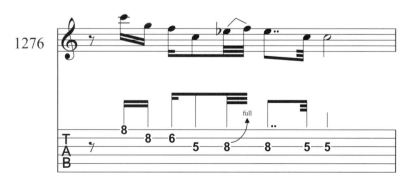

1275

1276

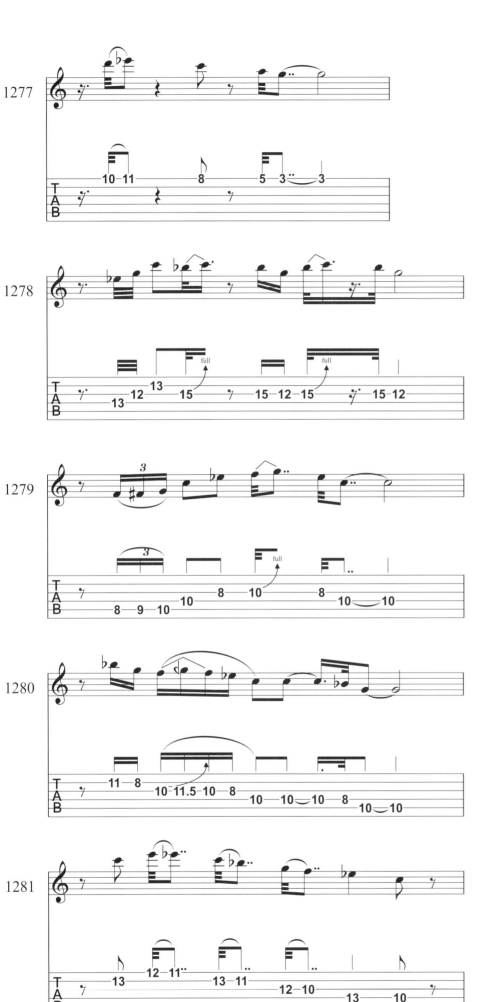

Buddy Guy

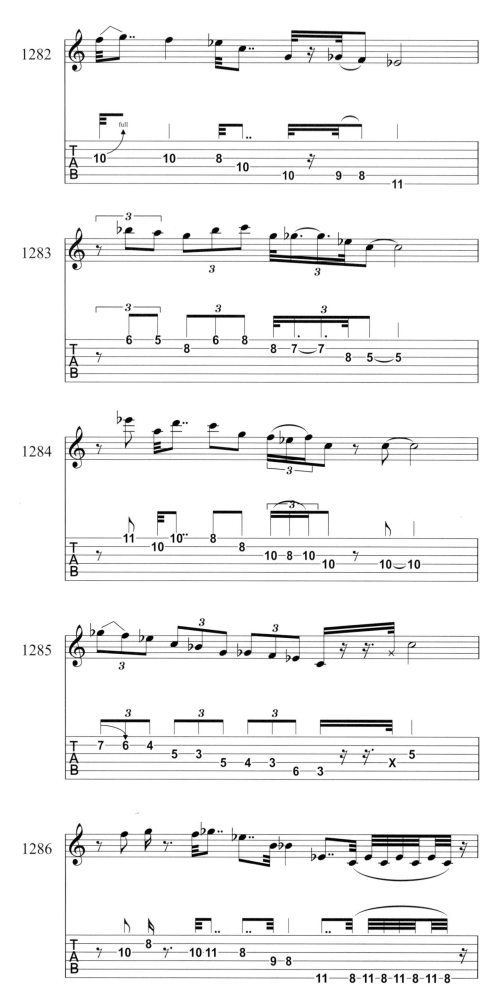

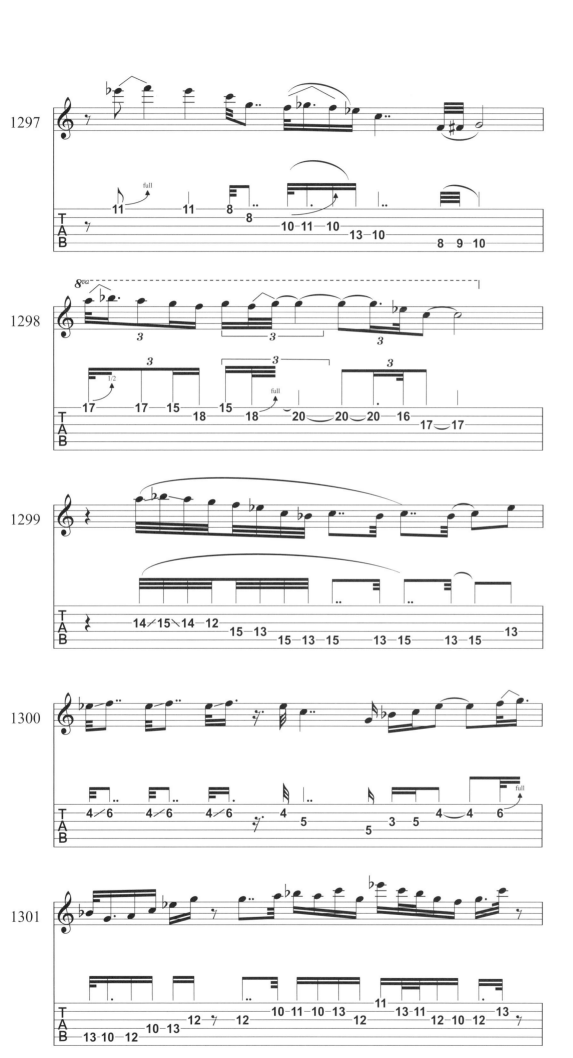

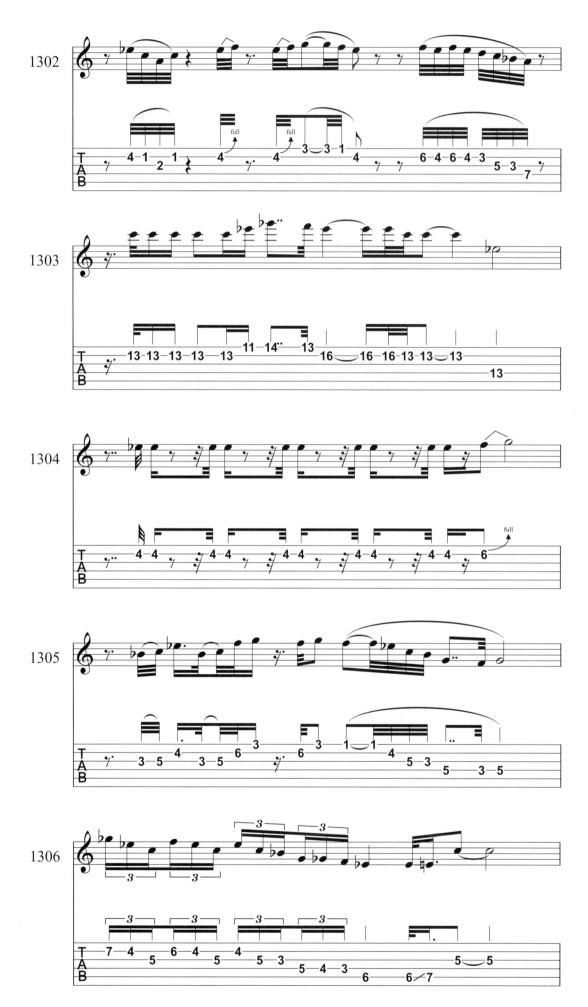

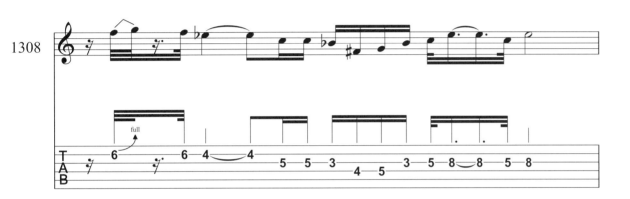

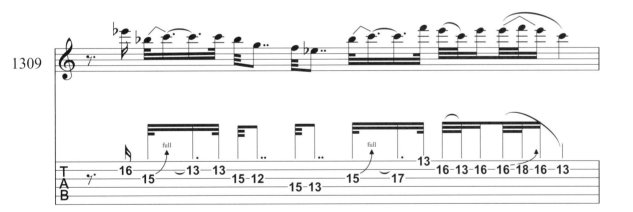

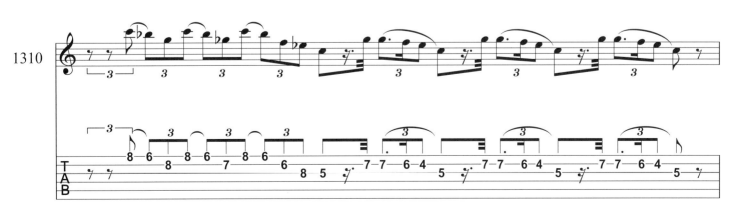

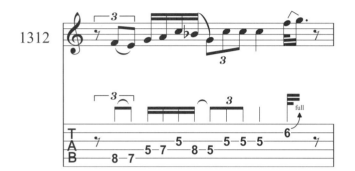

1311

Chapter 24:
Combined Duples and Triplets

When playing in a fast and florid blues style, it is important to control the relative speed and density of the rhythmic flow. This is achieved to great effect by such virtuosic players as Roy Buchanan, Joe Bonamassa, and Robben Ford by the very simple device of changing from straight sixteenth-notes to eighth-note triplets. Changing the pulse of the subdivisions of a quarter-note or eighth-note from four to three, or vice versa, alternately intensifies or reduces the energy levels of a phrase or solo.

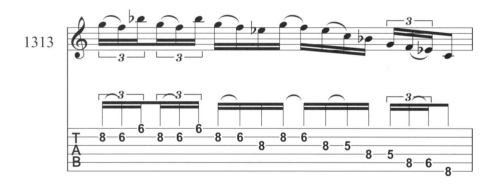

1312

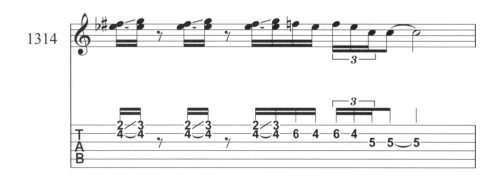

1313

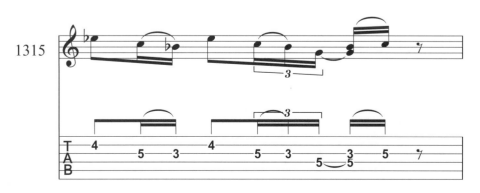

1314

1315

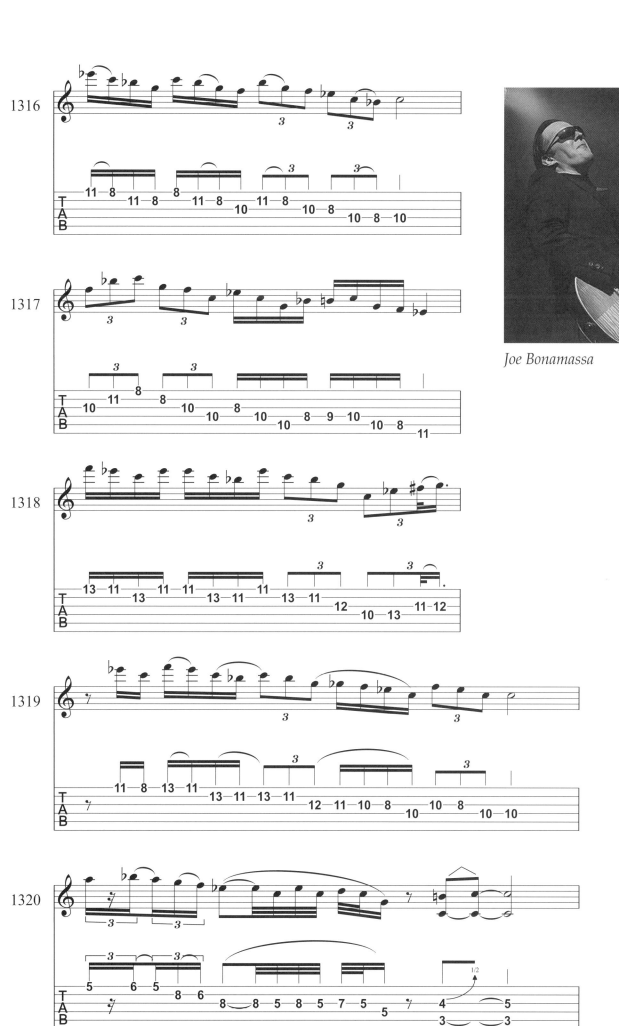

Joe Bonamassa

270

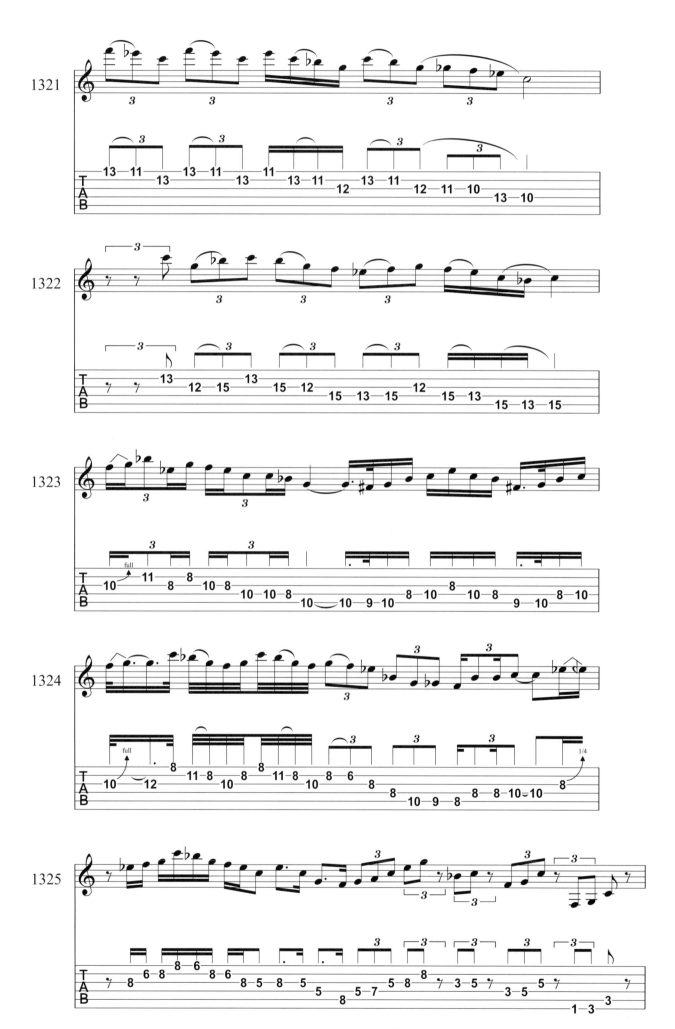

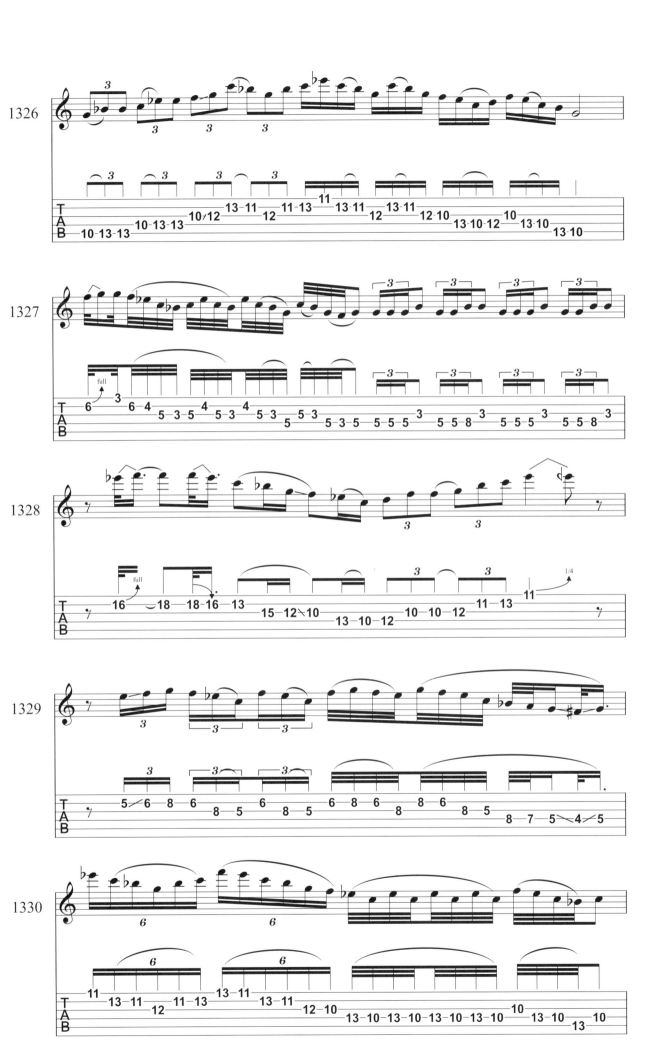

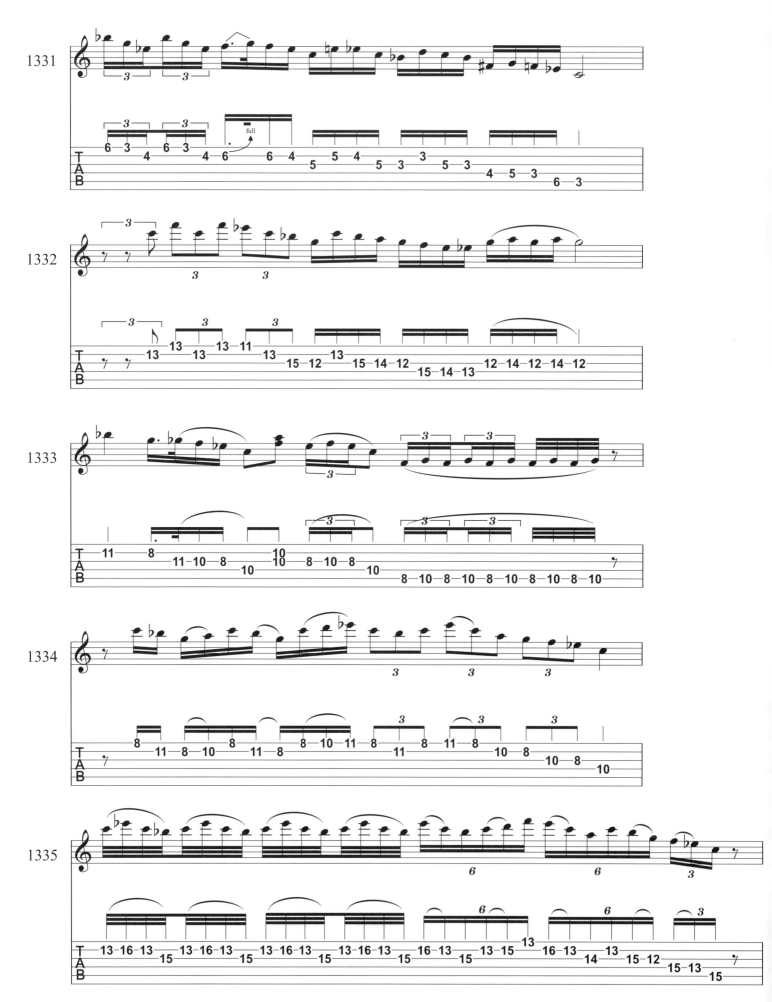

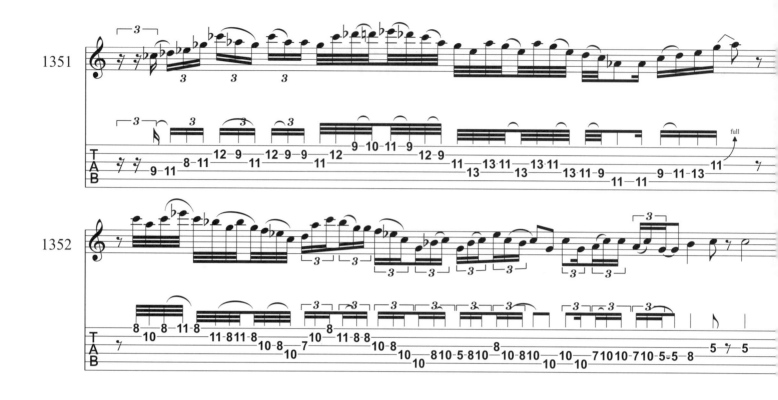

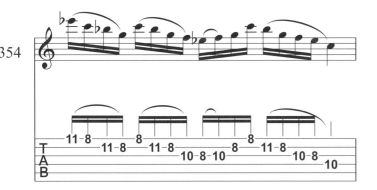

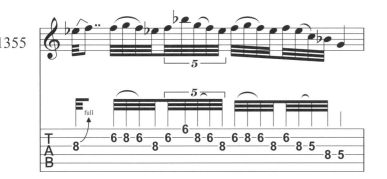

Chapter 25: Passagework

Blues guitar solos are often built out of short, fragmented, and incomplete ideas. Tension is produced when these are separated by silence, then repeated or varied. Albert Collins, Freddie King, and Jimmie Vaughan are masters of this approach. This kind of approach to phrasing builds tension over time and can be thought of as stored energy. Guitarists such as Buddy Guy and Walter Trout will sometimes release this energy in a cathartic, if histrionic, way by playing fast, virtuosic passages in streams of equal-note rhythms like those shown in this chapter.

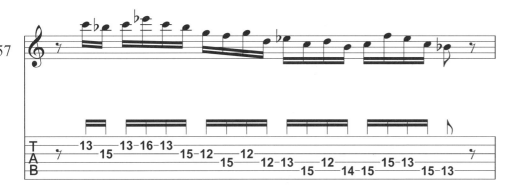

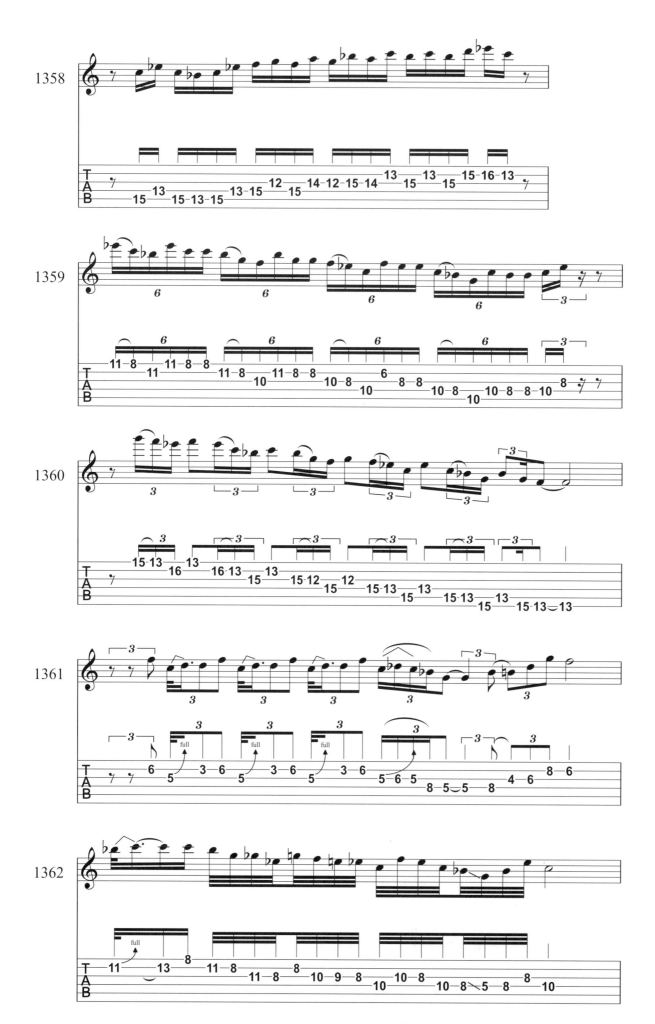

279

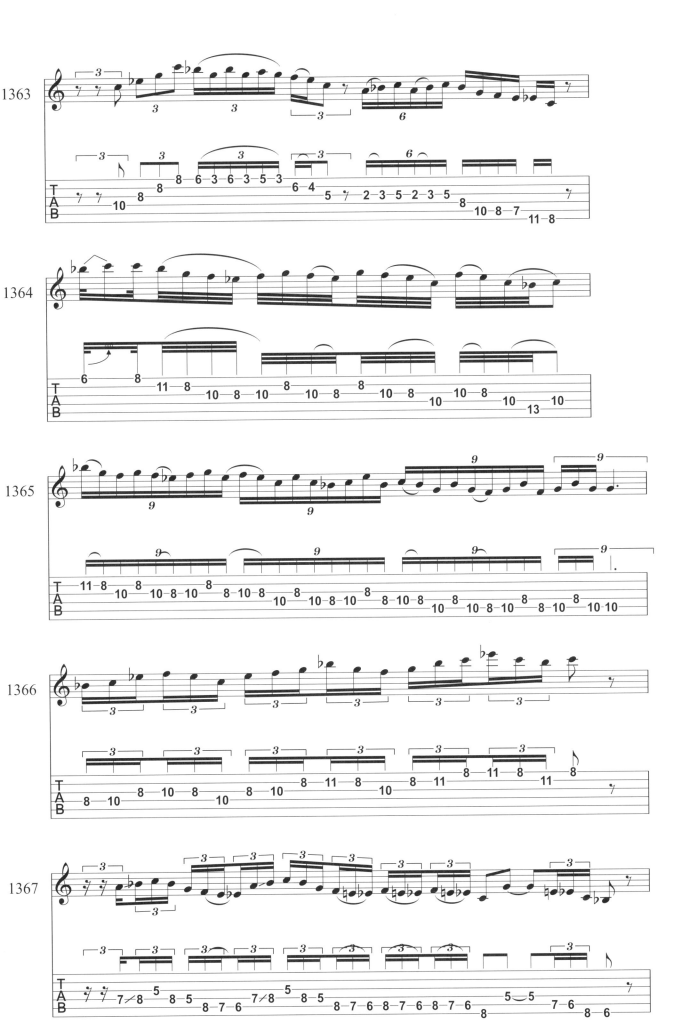

284

Chapter 26: Picking Motions

The licks in this chapter are produced by picking and hammering notes on different strong and weak beat subdivisions. These are sometimes combined with repeated notes, bends, slides, and string skips to produce highly energetic, syncopated rhythms.

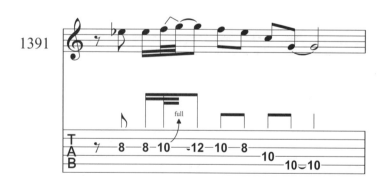

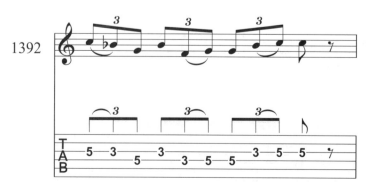

1393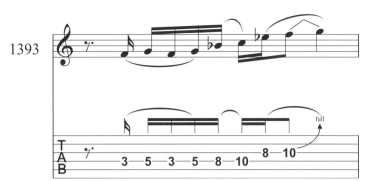

1394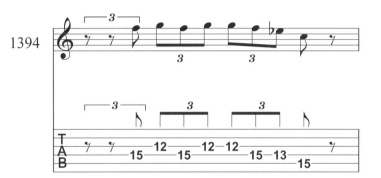

1395

1396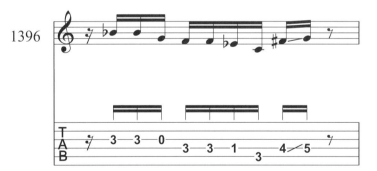

1397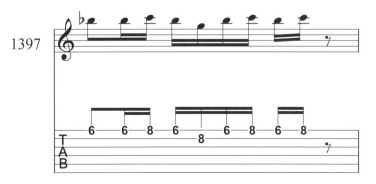

Roy Rogers

286

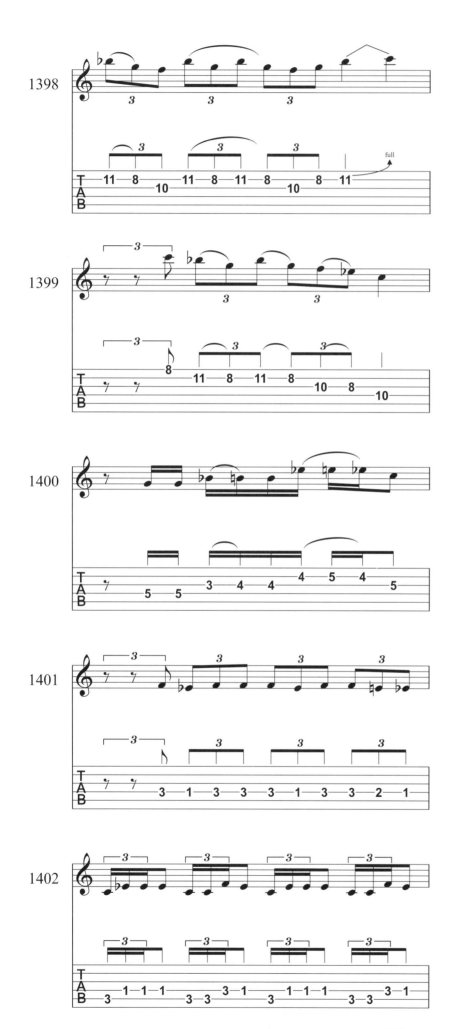

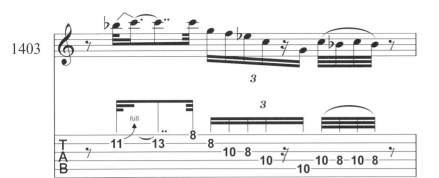

1403

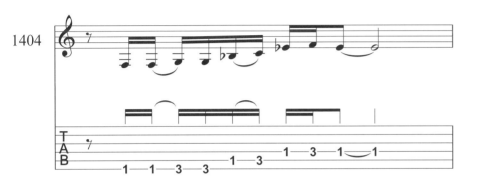

1404

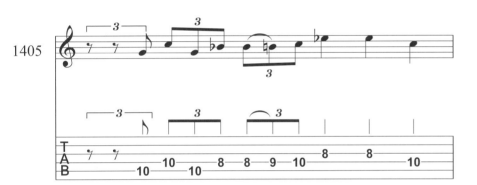

1405

1406

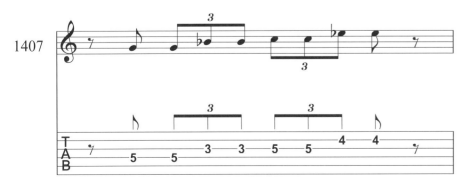

1407

288

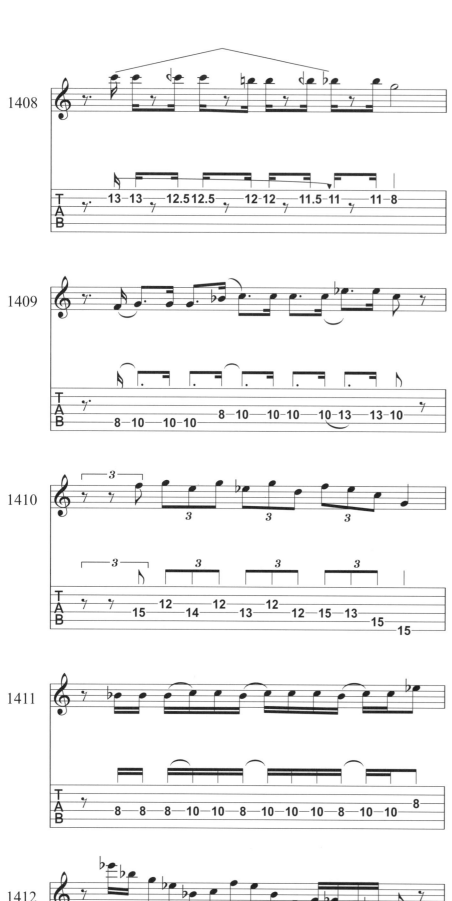

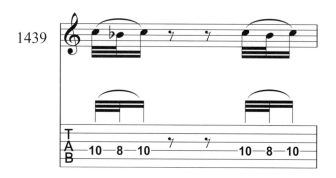

Chapter 27:
Punctuations

Punctuations are short, incisive figures that can be used as fills between vocal phrases. Albert Collins, B.B. King, and other singer-guitarists use punctuations in this way. They can also be used within a guitar solo to announce the beginning of a new phrase or to punctuate the conclusion of an existing phrase.

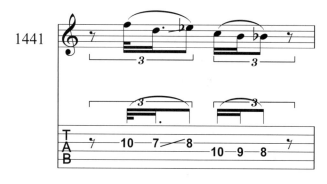

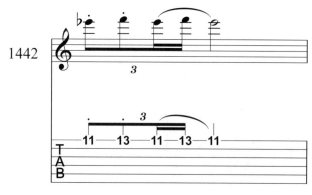

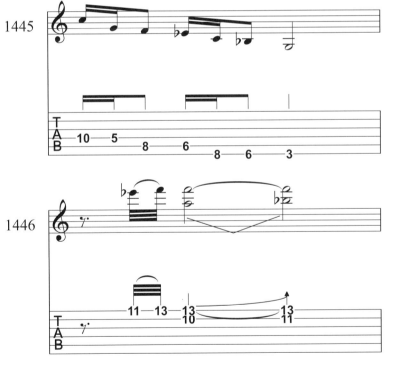

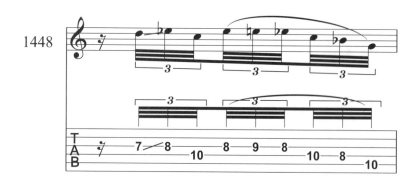

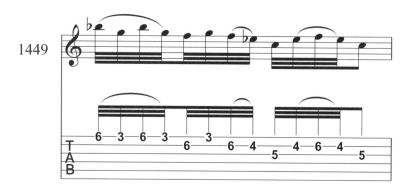

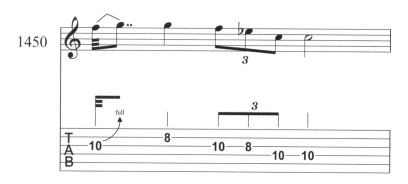

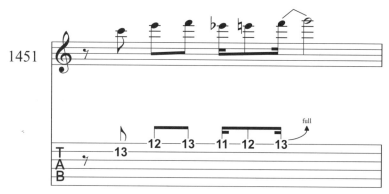

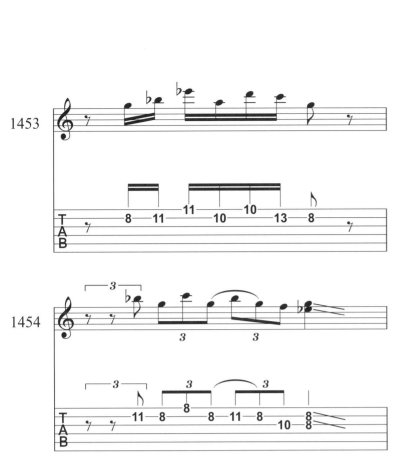

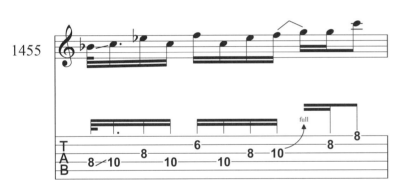

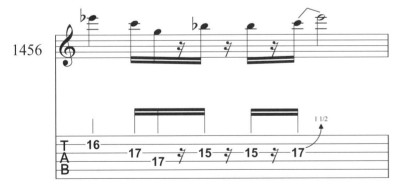

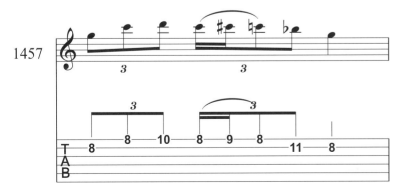

1458

1459

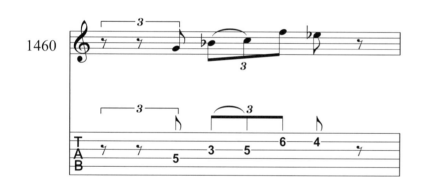

1460

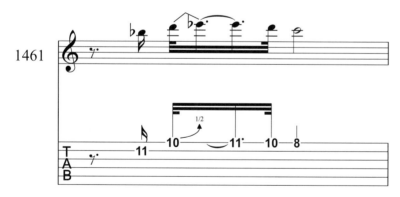

1461

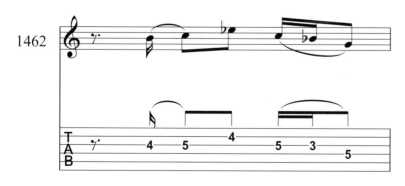

1462

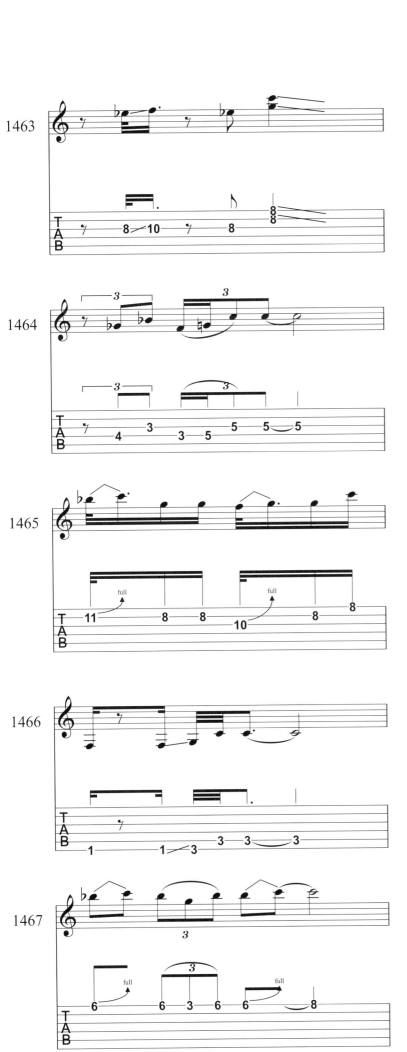

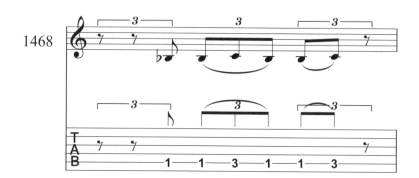

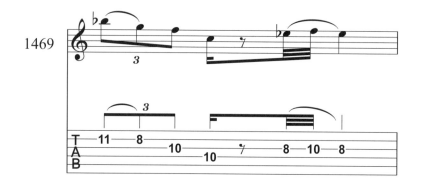

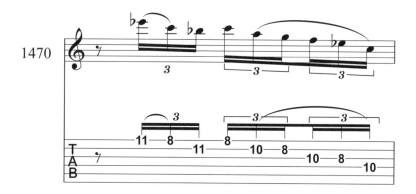

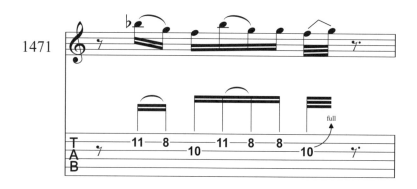

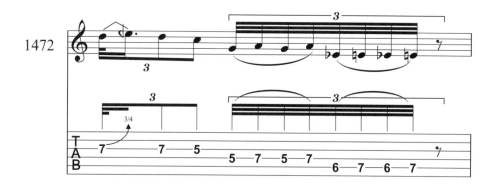

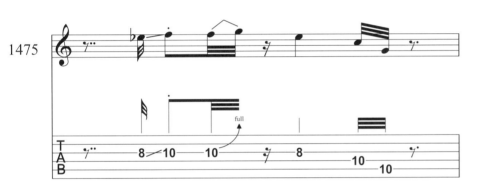

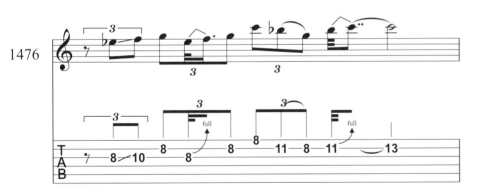

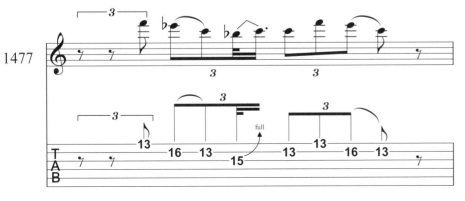

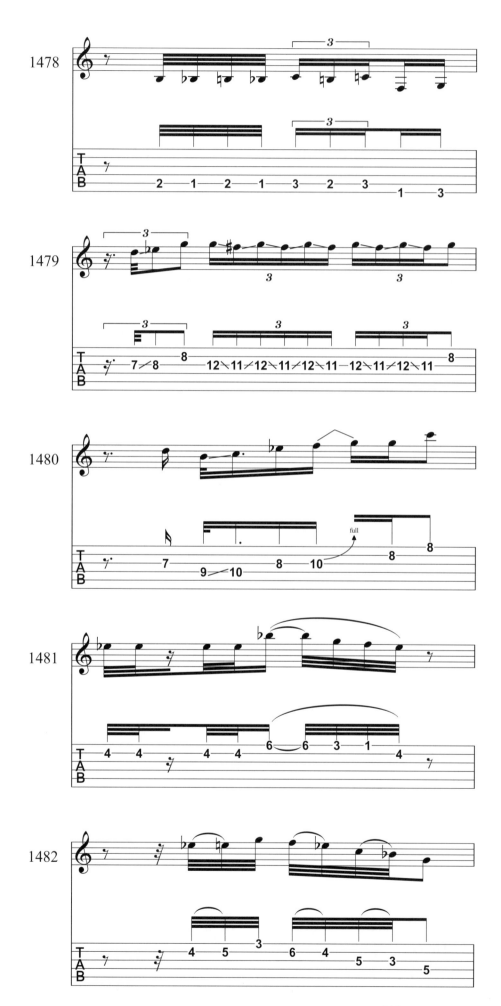

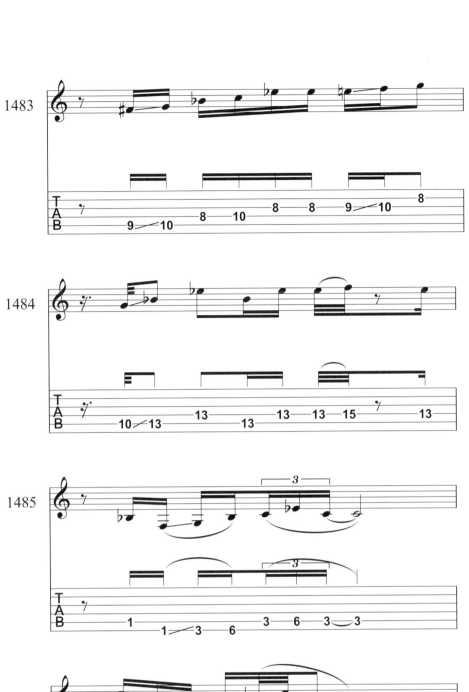

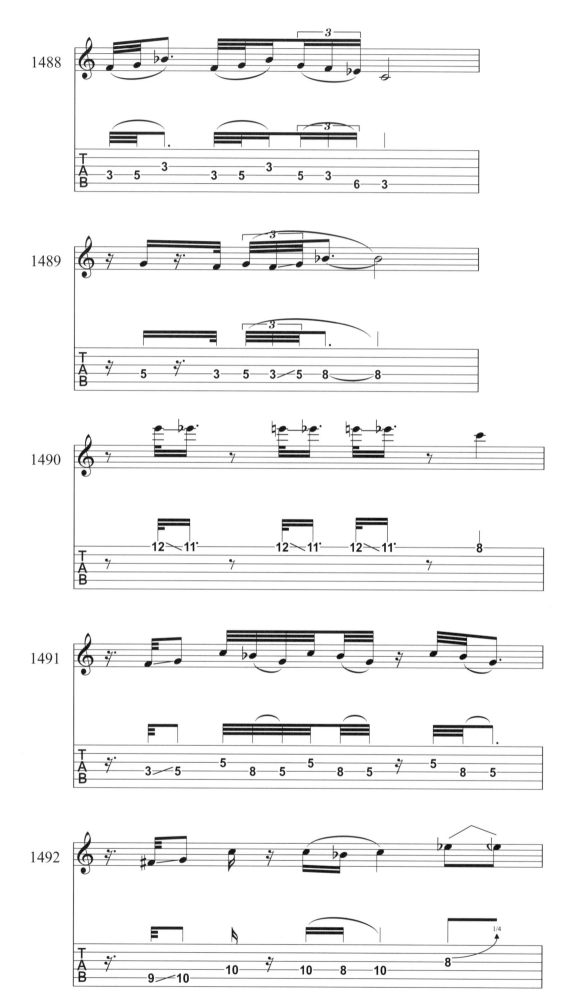

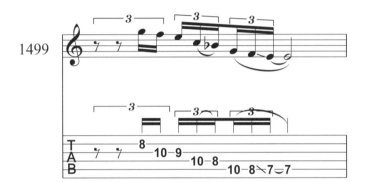

1498

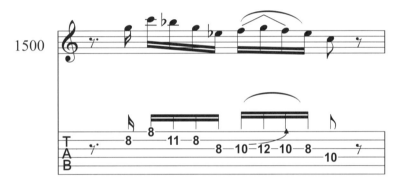

1499

Chapter 28: Descending Lines

One of the most common conventions of blues guitar solos concerns the direction and contour of pitch material. When the solo is moving higher in pitch, it does this in short, repeated patterns. Expressively, it seems like the solo is working against gravity, and exerts a great deal of energy to reach the pinnacle of the highest note. Once the peak has been reached, the musician seems to become overwhelmed by the force of gravity and the notes come cascading down smoothly, effortlessly, and with great speed. One of the main distinctions between blues guitar solos and those in jazz, rock, and metal is that those other styles incorporate rapid passages that both ascend and descend.

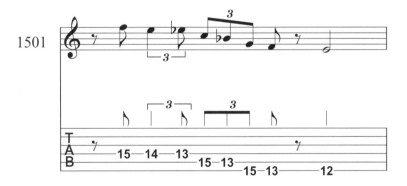

1500

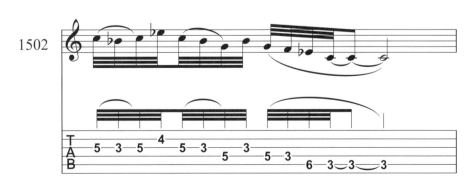

1501

1502

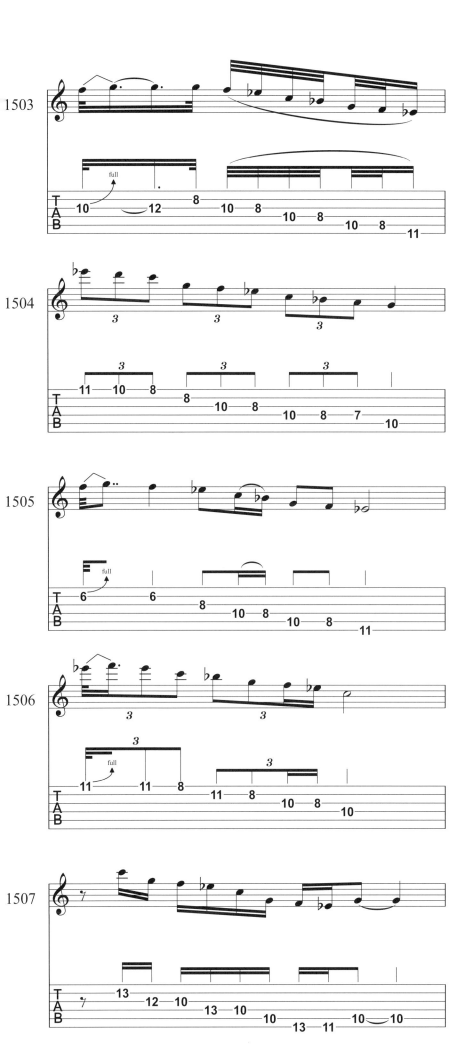

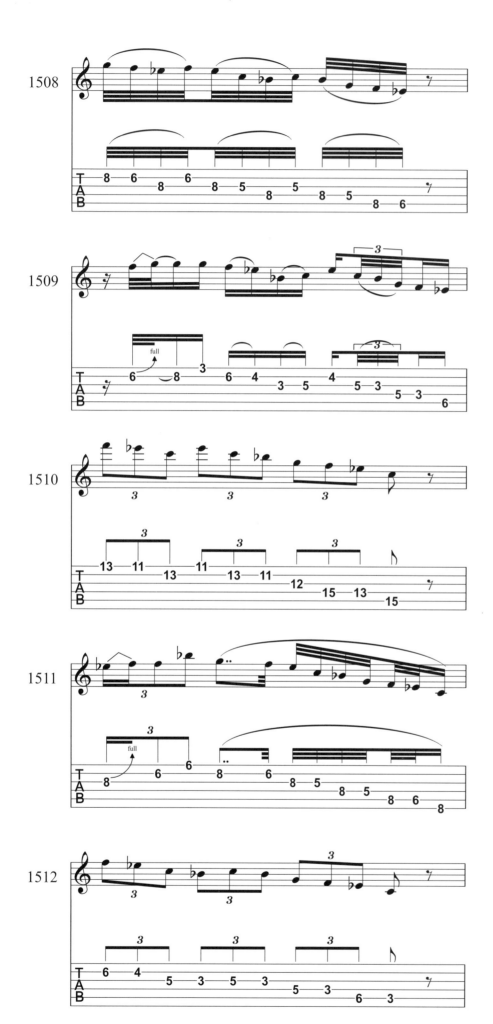

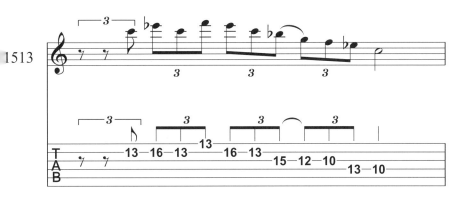

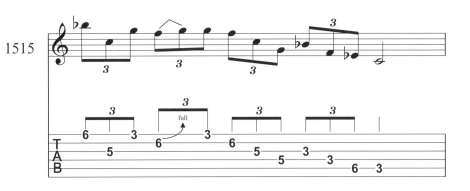

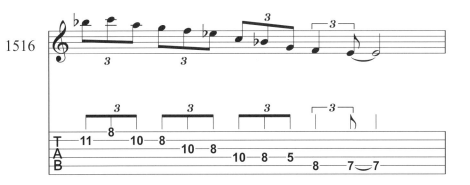

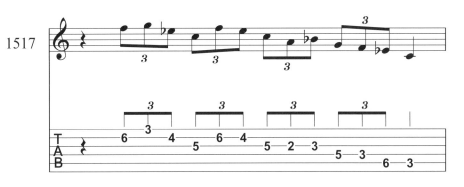

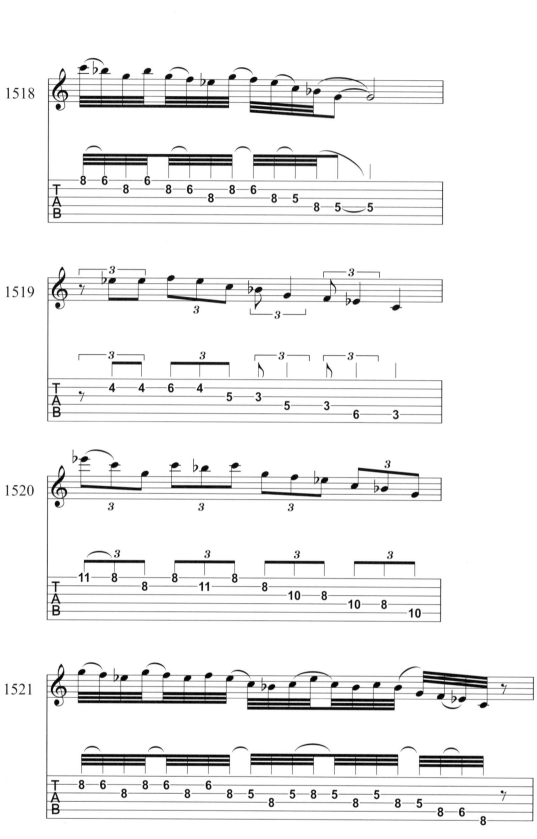

311

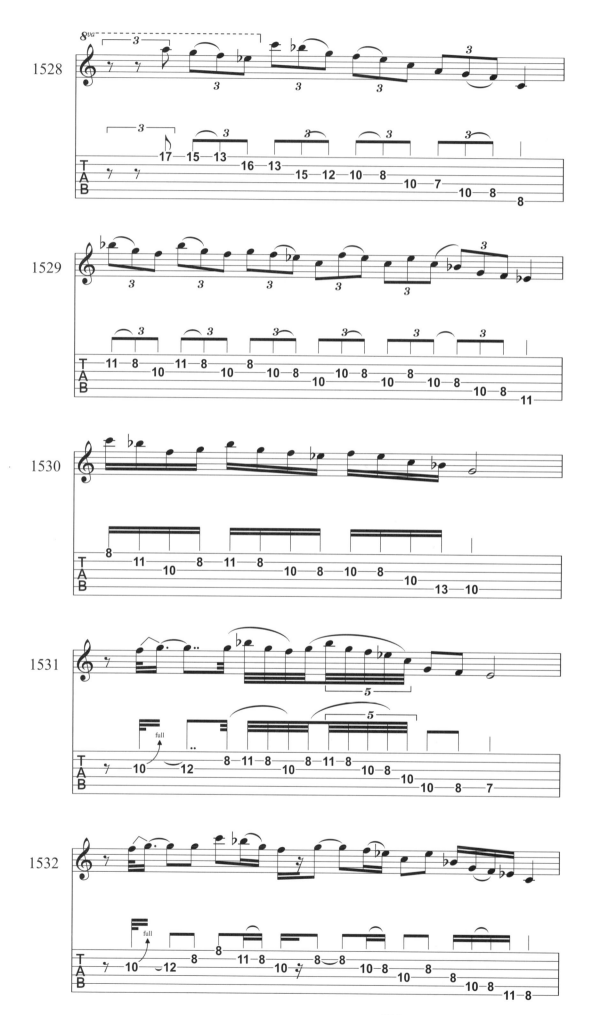

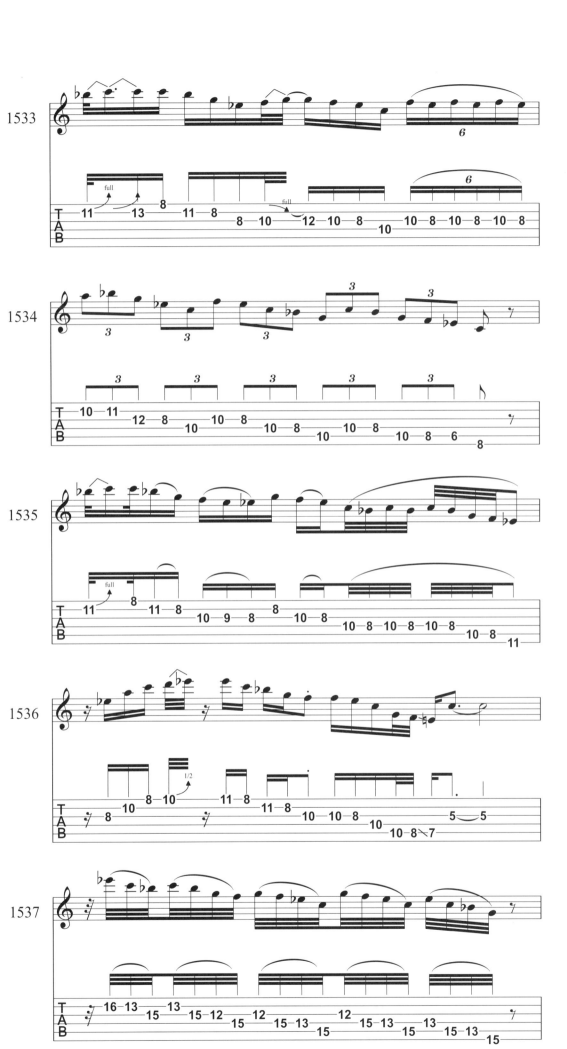

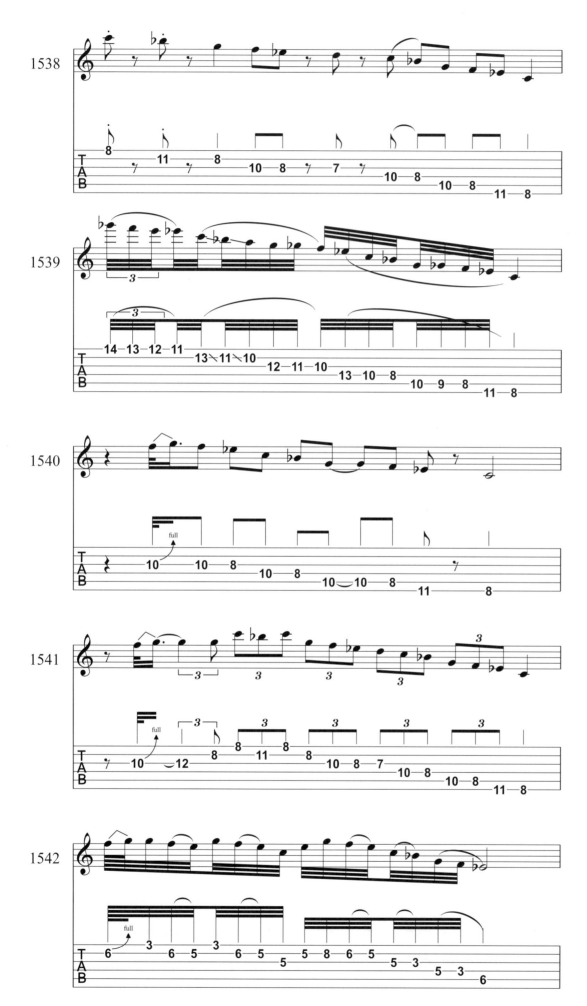

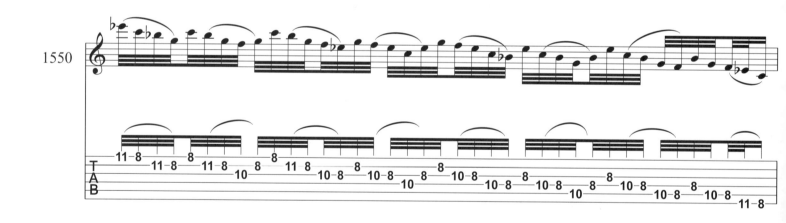

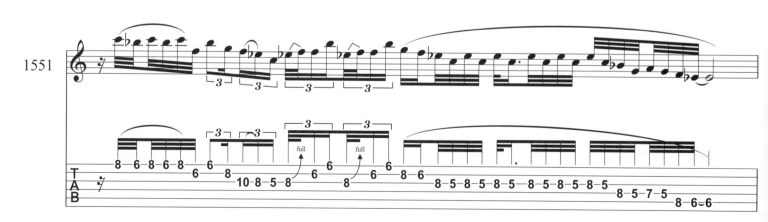

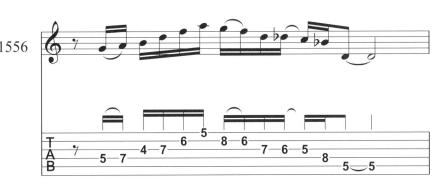

Chapter 29: Melodic Arpeggiation

Arpeggios are chords whose notes are played successively, rather than strummed. While arpeggios can be played as part of an accompaniment pattern, they can also be used melodically. As the licks in this chapter show, melodic arpeggios are often preceded by and are followed by stepwise motion, and thus are integrated into phrases. While it is quite common to melodically arpeggiate the chord that is sounding in the accompaniment of a song, or 12-bar blues progression, it is also possible to melodically arpeggiate a different chord in a solo than is sounding in the accompaniment. This is one of many examples of how blues guitarists sometimes emphasize notes in a solo that are not necessarily supported by the underlying chordal structure of a song. This explains how certain phrases seem unmoored and float above the backing instruments in the blues, contributing to the feeling of freedom from the status quo. Melodic arpeggios are frequently heard in the music of T-Bone Walker, Pee Wee Crayton, Hollywood Fats, Duke Robillard, and Junior Watson. In addition to west coast, jump, and swing, arpeggios figure prominently in early rock and rockabilly styles.

318

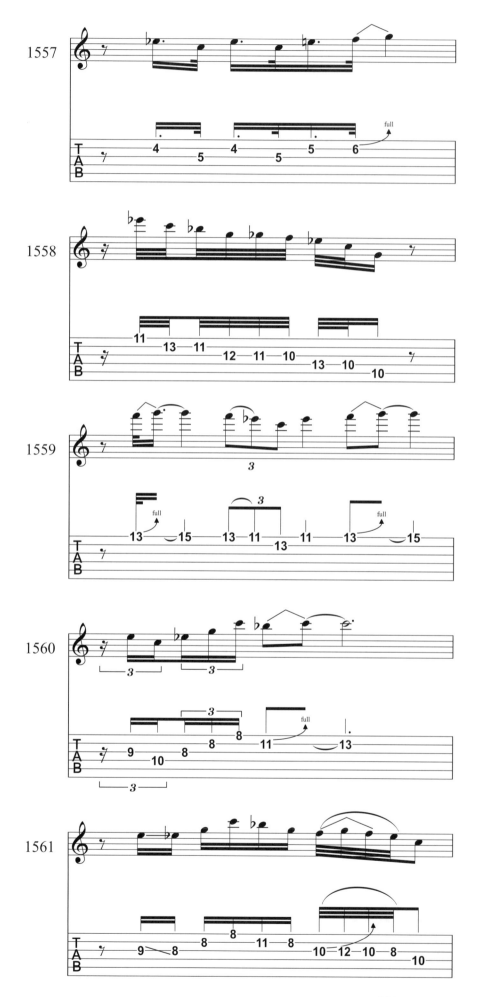

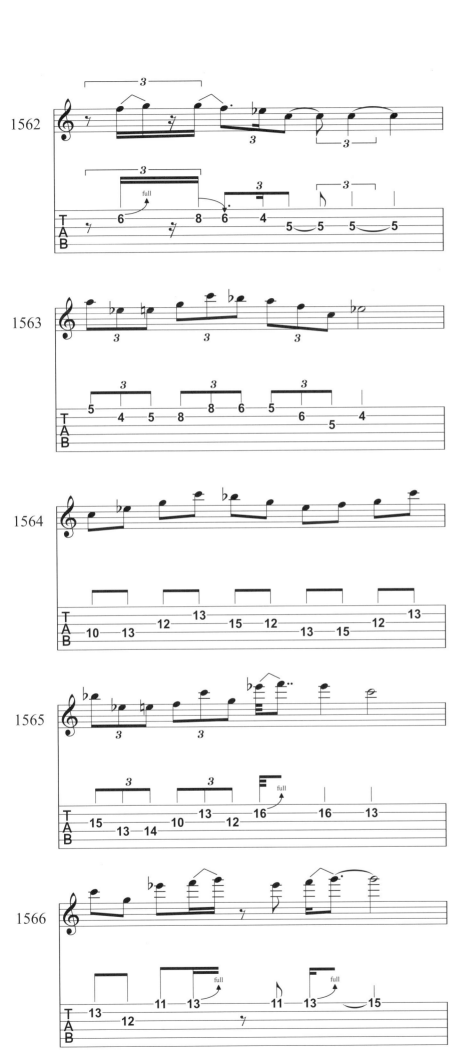

320

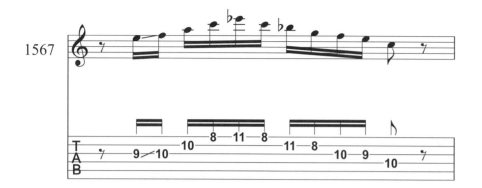

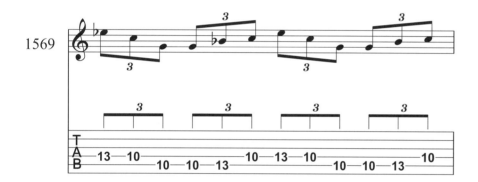

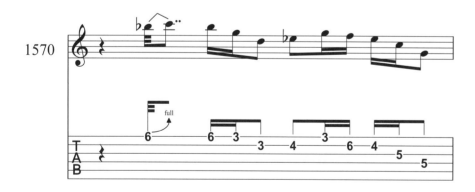

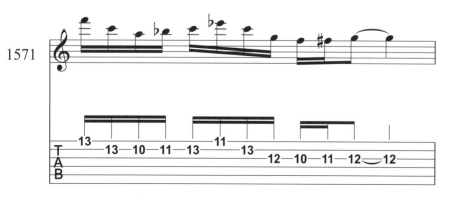

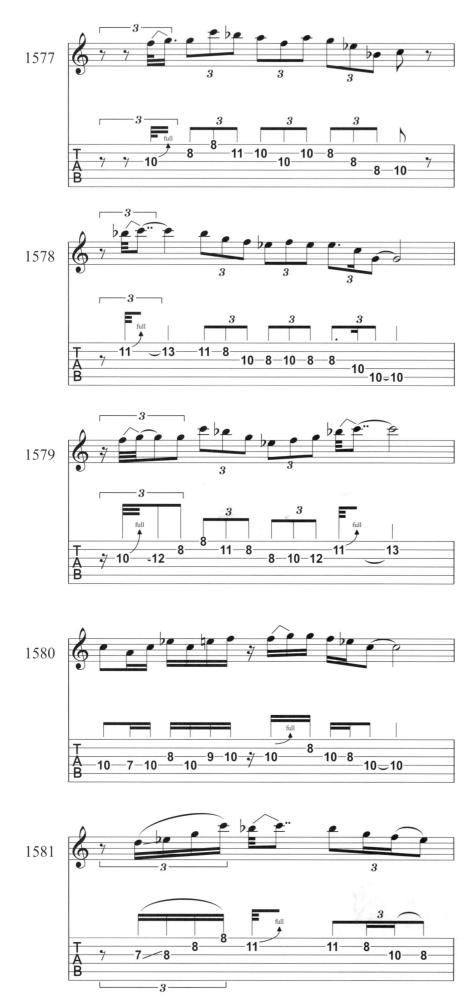

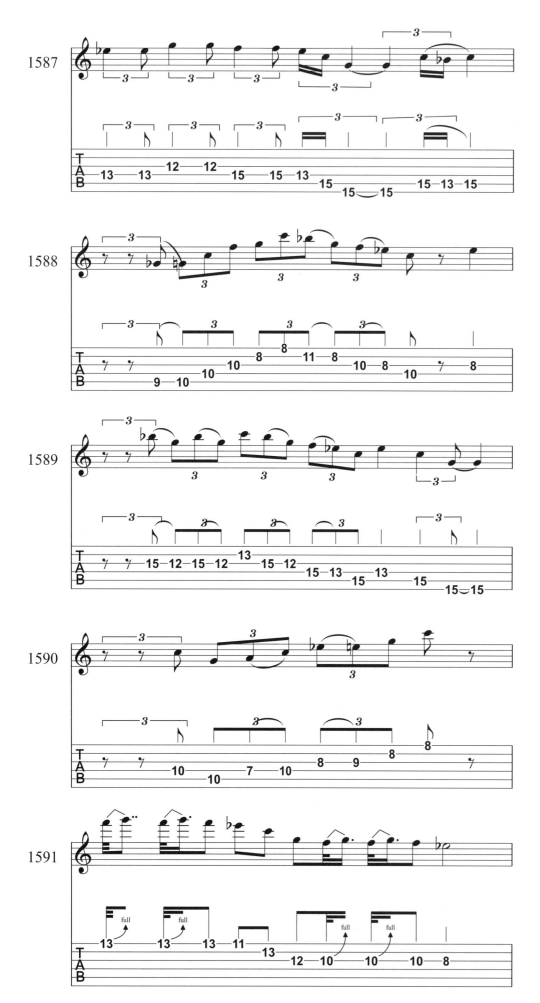

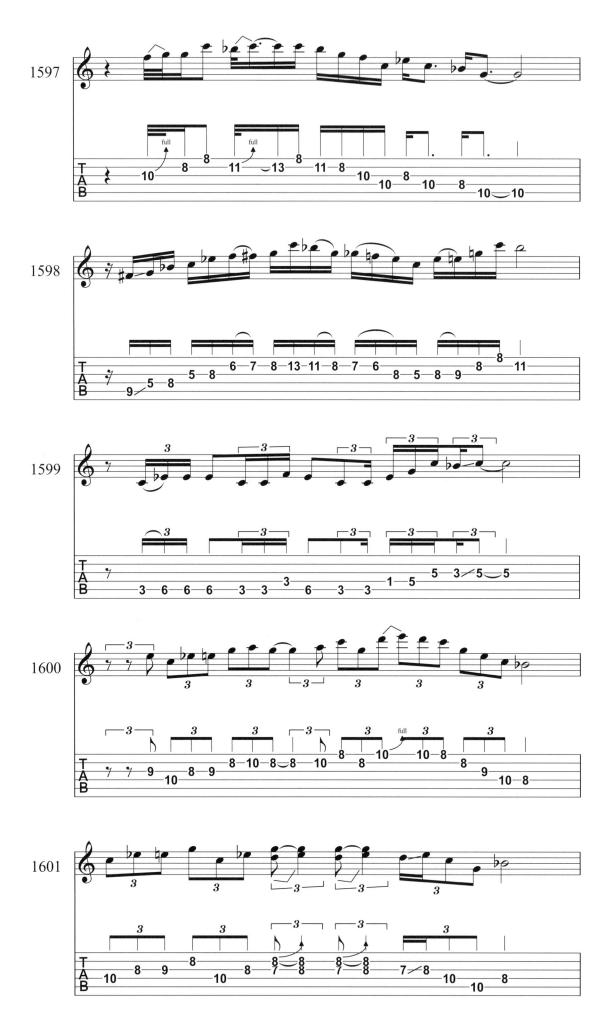

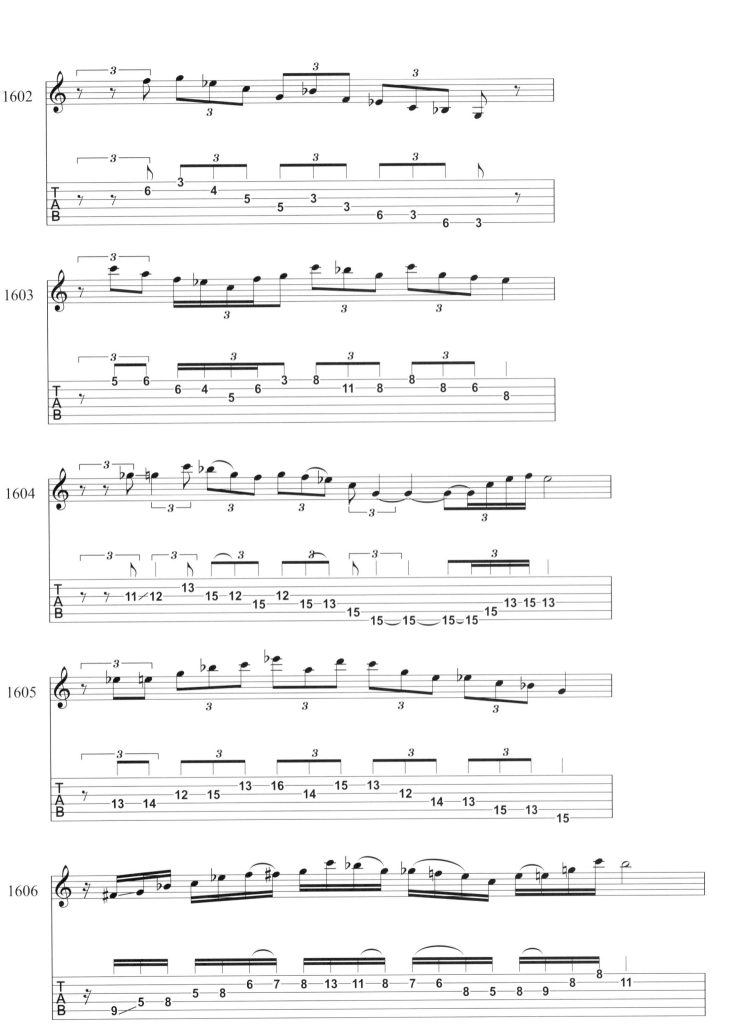

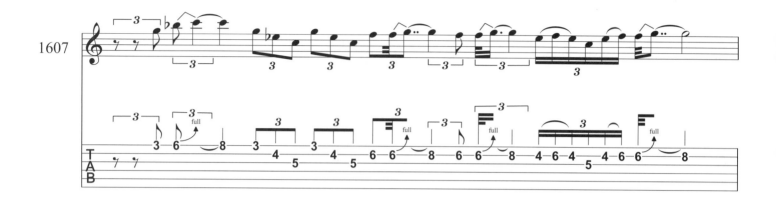

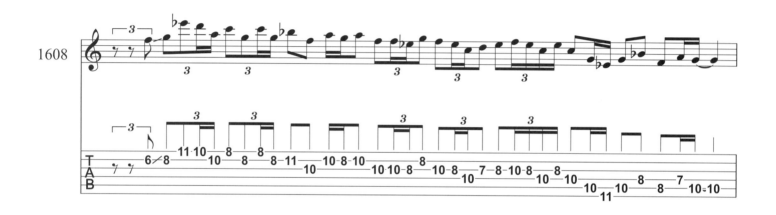

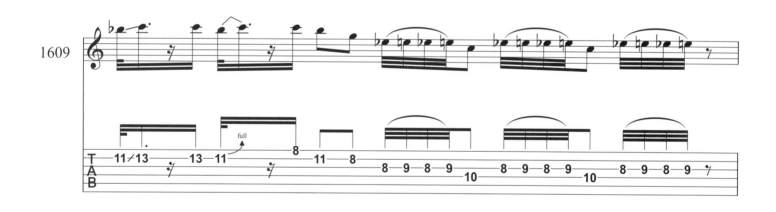

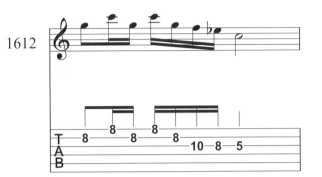

1611

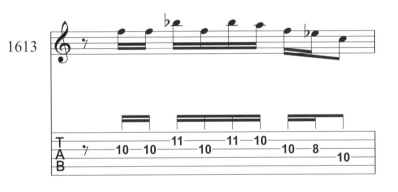

1612

Chapter 30:
Alternating Notes

This chapter focuses on the phrasing technique of alternating between two notes. Used extensively by Albert King, Otis Rush, and Billy Boy Arnold, it is generally played in fourths, starting on a weak beat at the beginning of a phrase that often descends. It is sometimes played by sliding up to the first note and letting it hold over the second note, before returning to the first note. This manner of playing is reminiscent of a slide guitar sound.

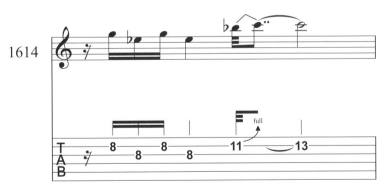

1613

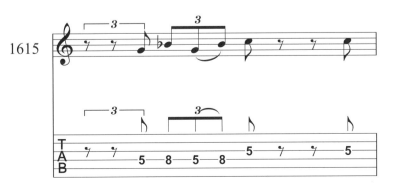

1614

1615

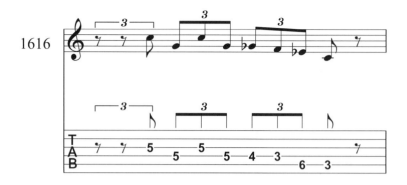

1616

1617

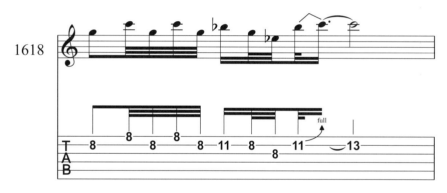

1618

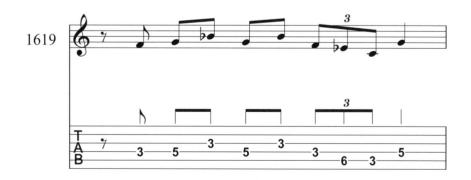

1619

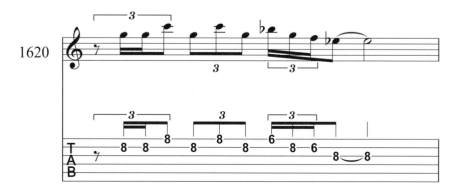

1620

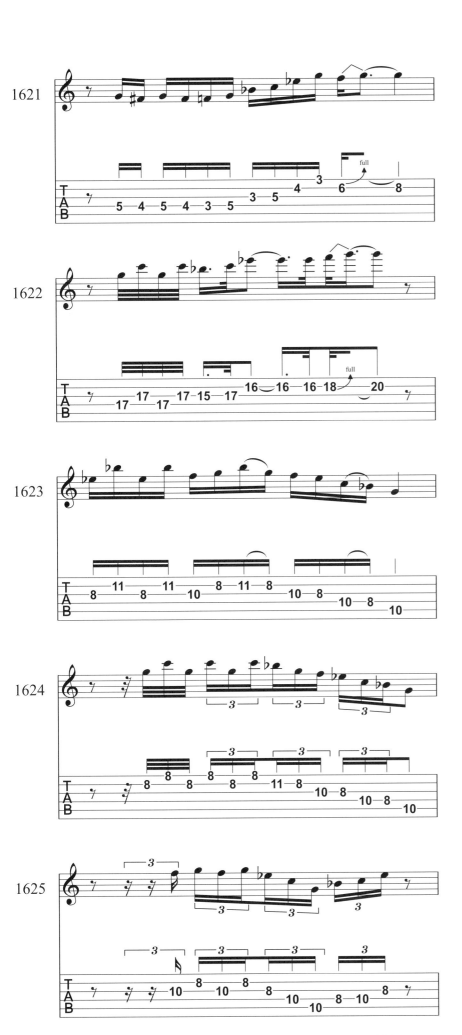

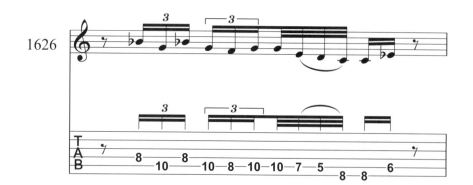

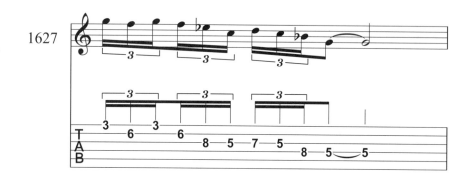

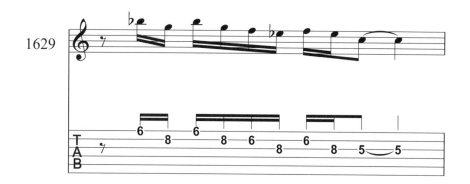

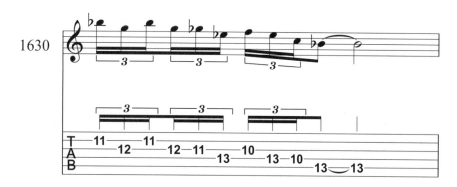

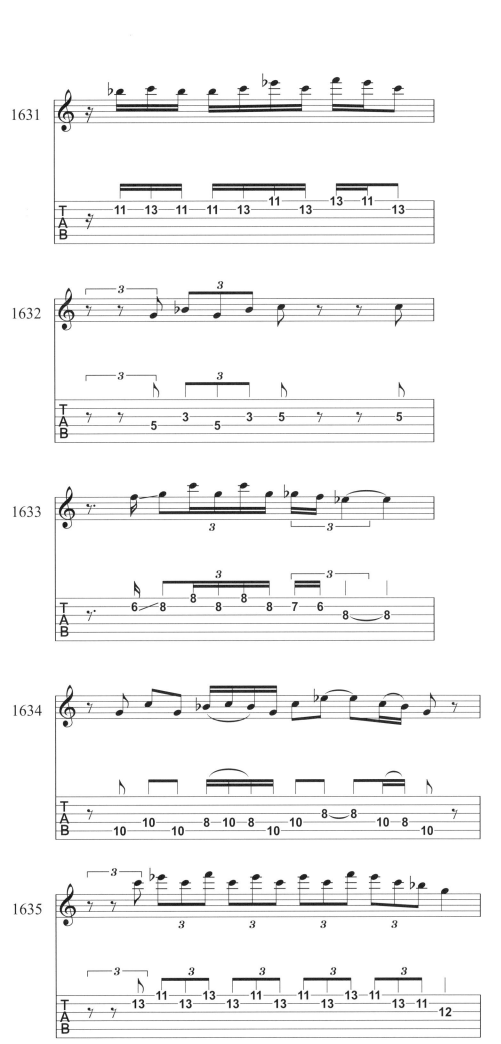

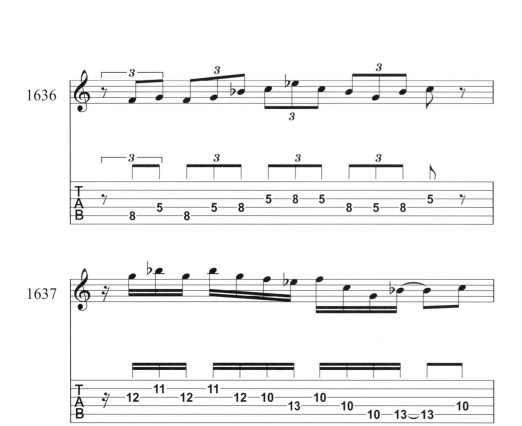

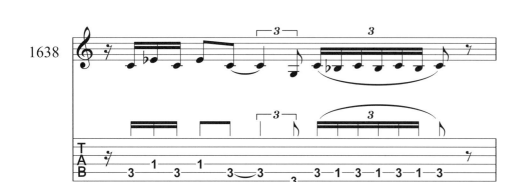

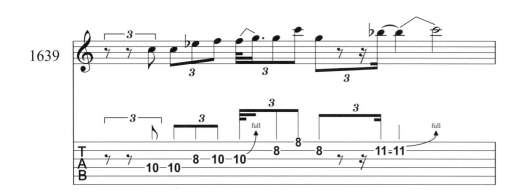

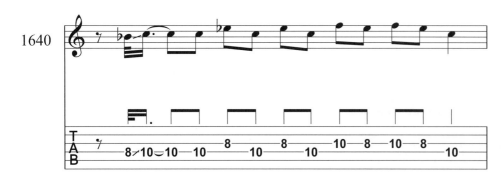

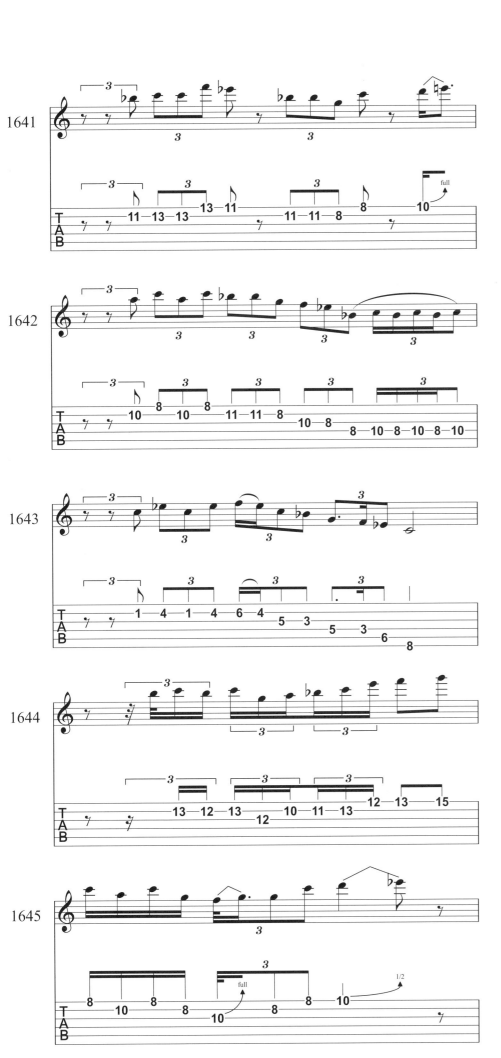

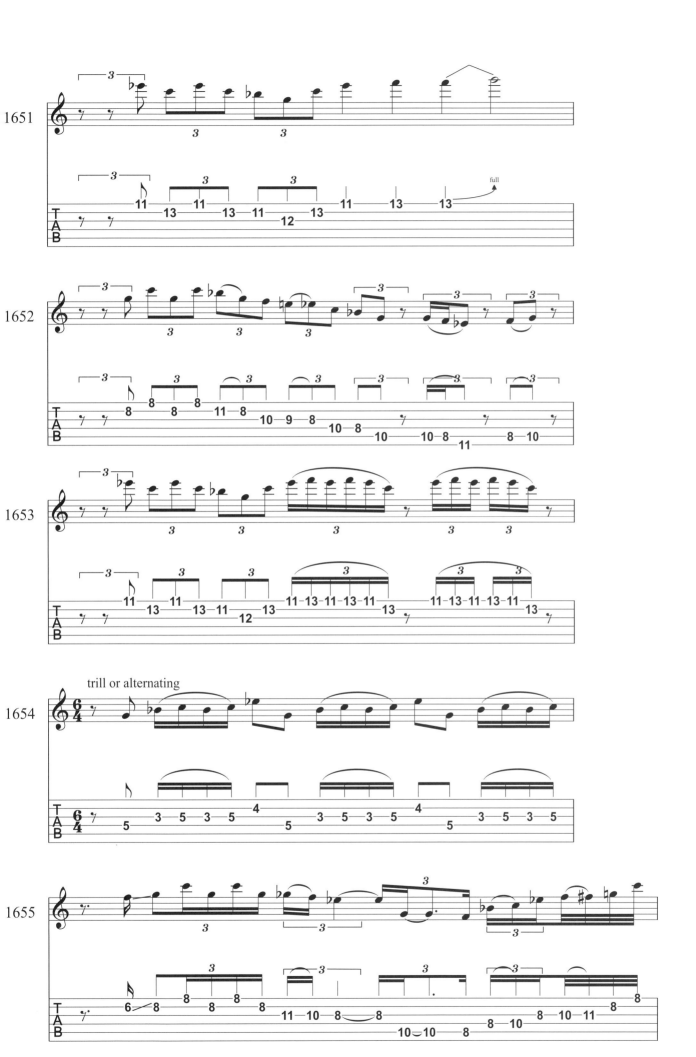

338

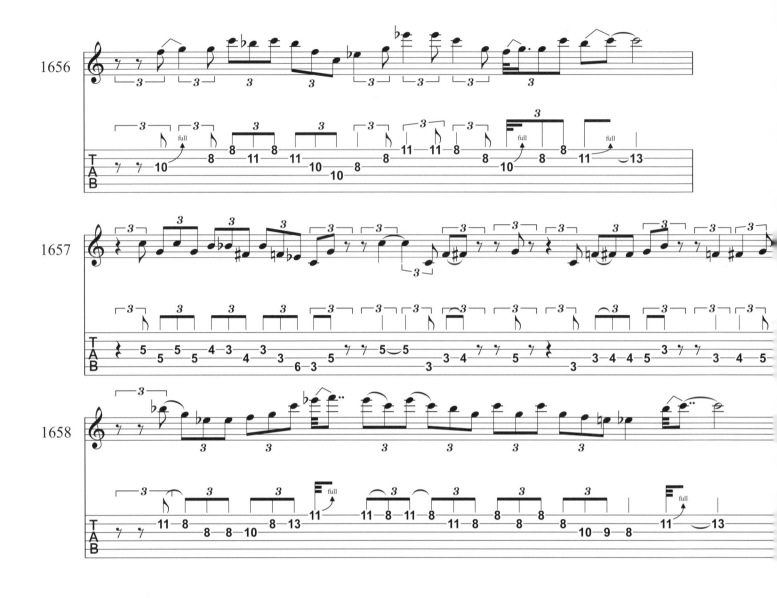

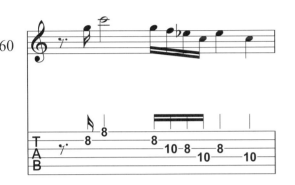

659

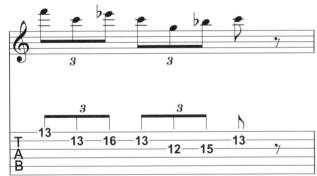

660

Chapter 31: Melodic Gaps

In western music in general, a melodic skip or gap is an interval of a third or greater. In blues structured on the minor pentatonic scale, a gap is an interval of a fourth or greater. This is because the successive notes C-Eb and G-Bb function as steps, even though they are the interval of a third. A gap in most western music is generally followed by a step in the opposite direction. In blues, this tendency is sometimes thwarted by such guitarists as Stevie Ray Vaughan and Jimi Hendrix, who will follow a gap with a step in the same direction, which has the effect of opening up a phrase into a higher or lower register.

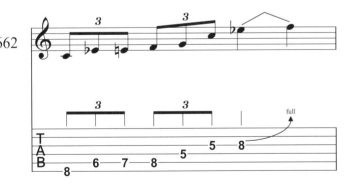

1661

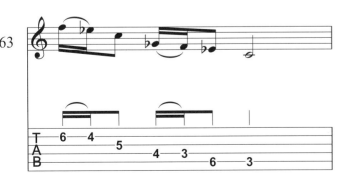

1662

1663

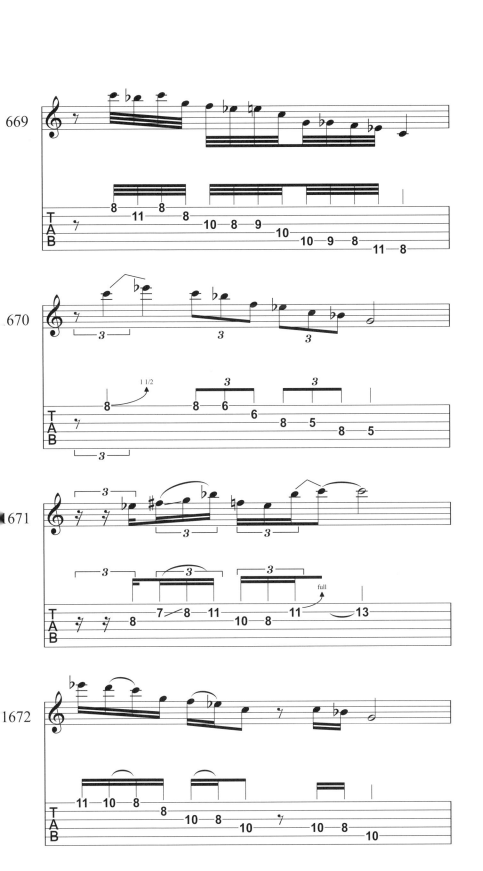
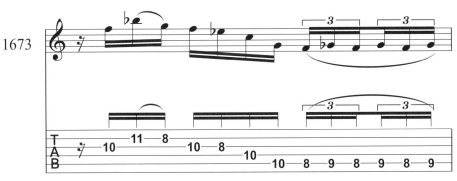

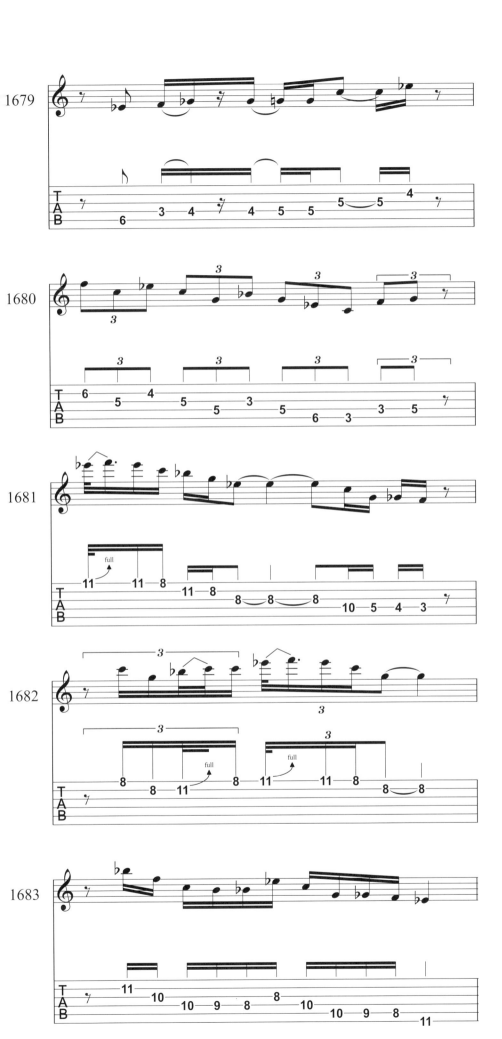

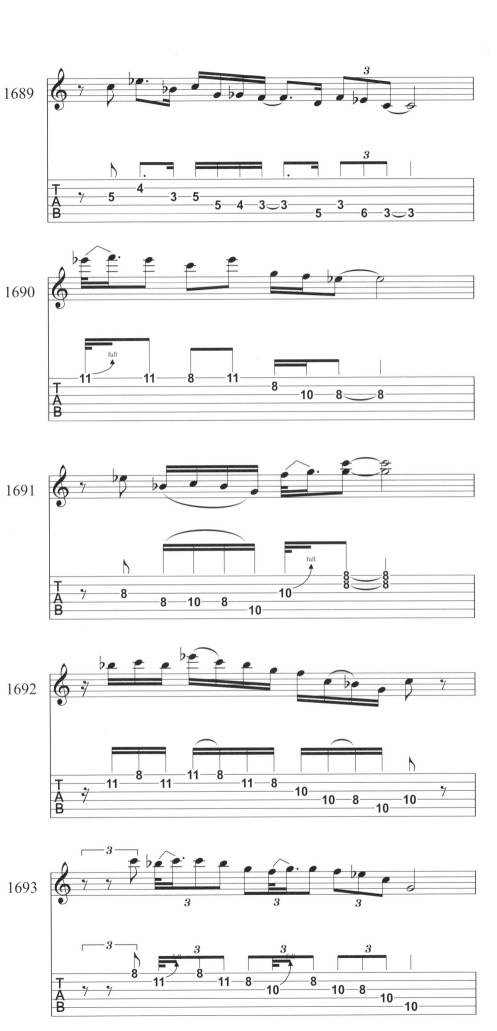

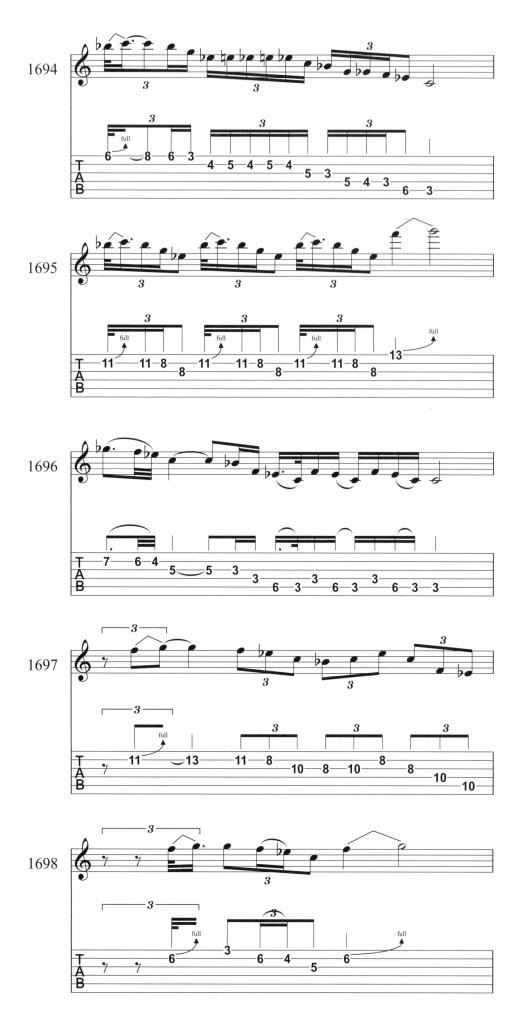

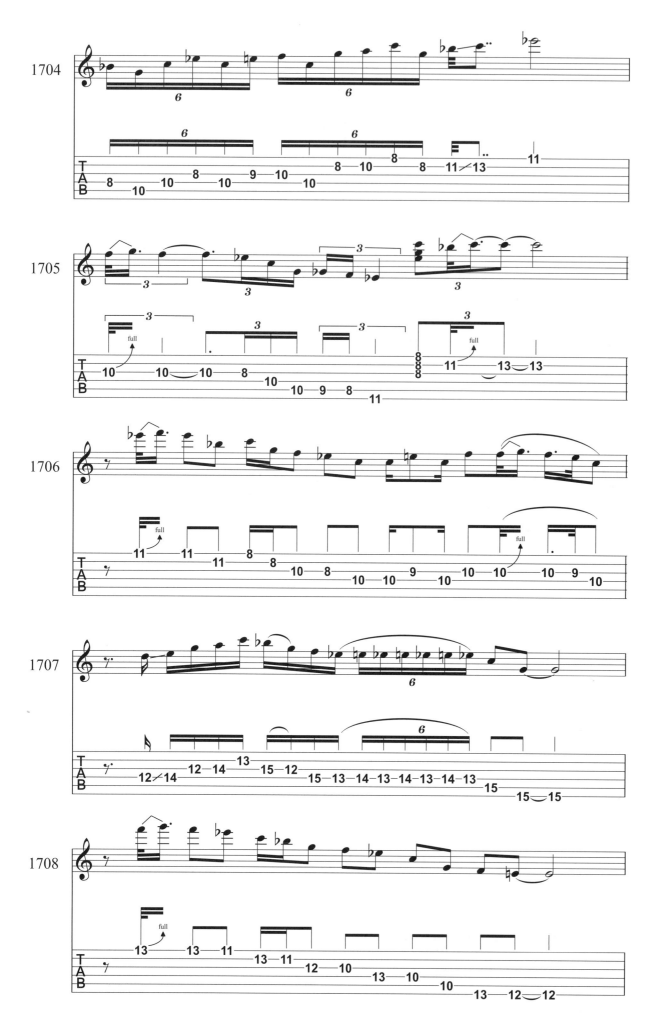

349

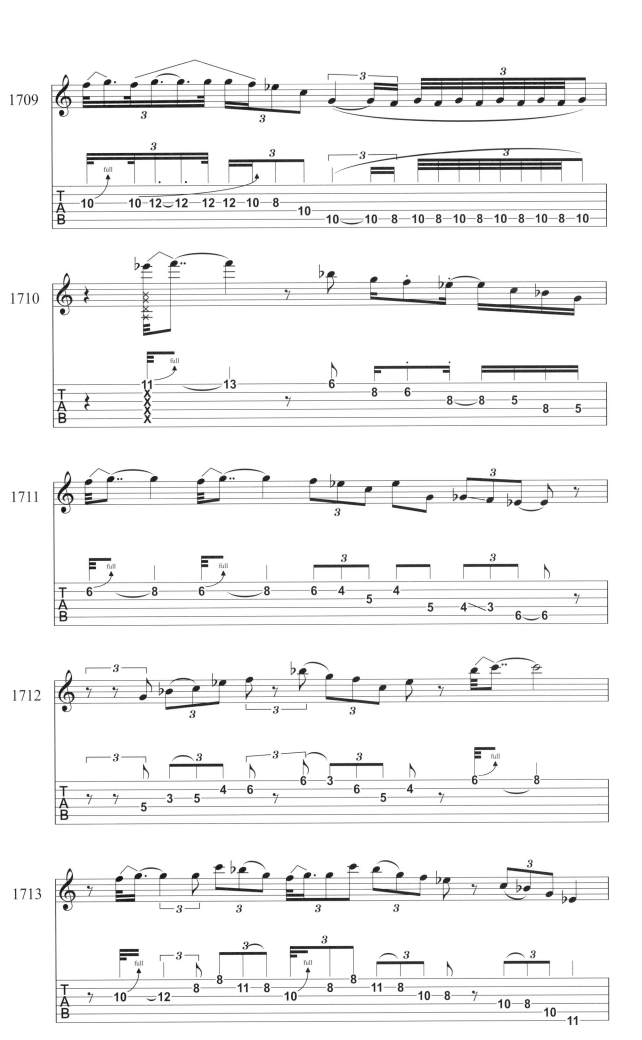

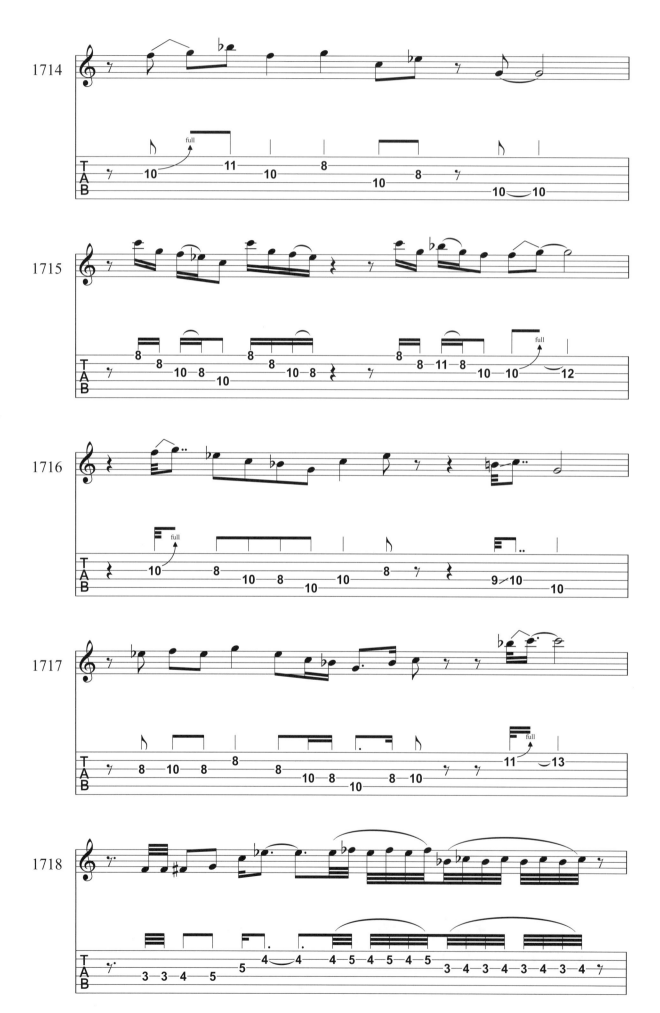

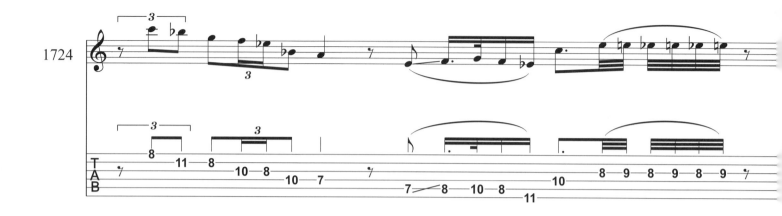

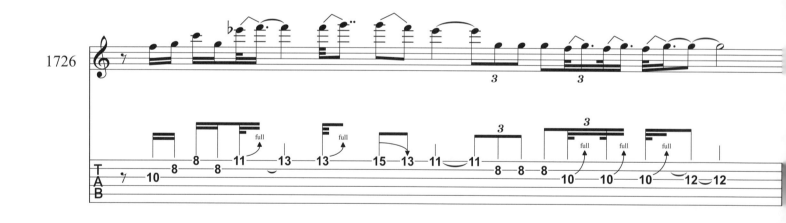

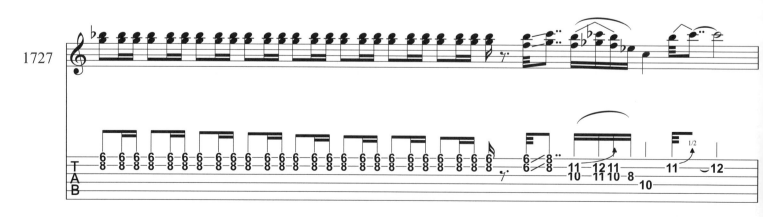

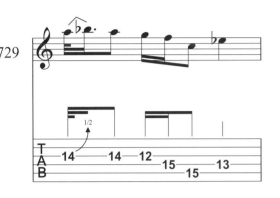

1728

Chapter 32:
Melodic Gap-Fills

The concept of melodic gaps was introduced in Chapter 31. The licks in this chapter illustrate the principle of gap-fill. Here, leap of a fourth or larger creates a gap in the melody. For many generations of listeners, a melodic gap creates a psychological need for the following notes to fill in that gap. Researchers believe that filling in such a gap gives the process a sense of completion, making the melody seem inevitable and natural. In a guitar solo, there exists a tension between the need to fulfill the listener's expectations and desires, and denying or thwarting them. The musician's skill and artistry lies in his or her ability to mediate between these two conflicting outcomes.

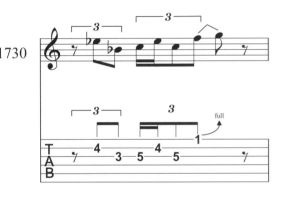

1729

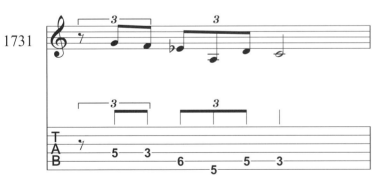

1730

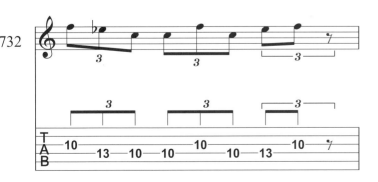

1731

1732

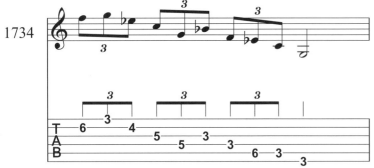

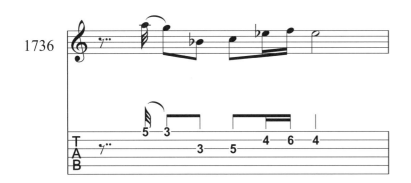

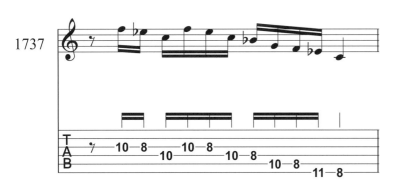

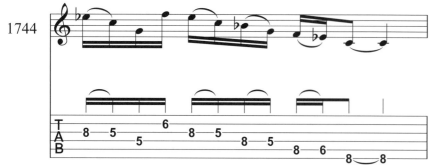

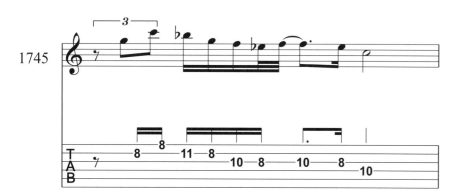

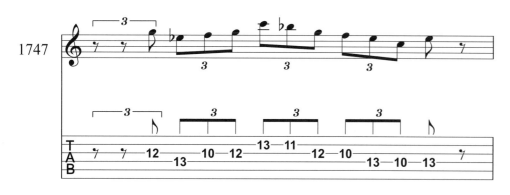

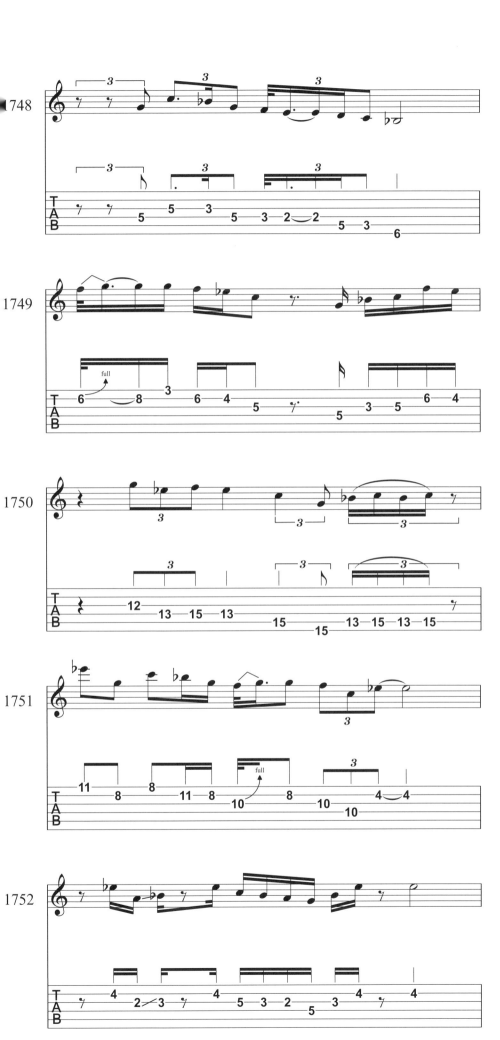

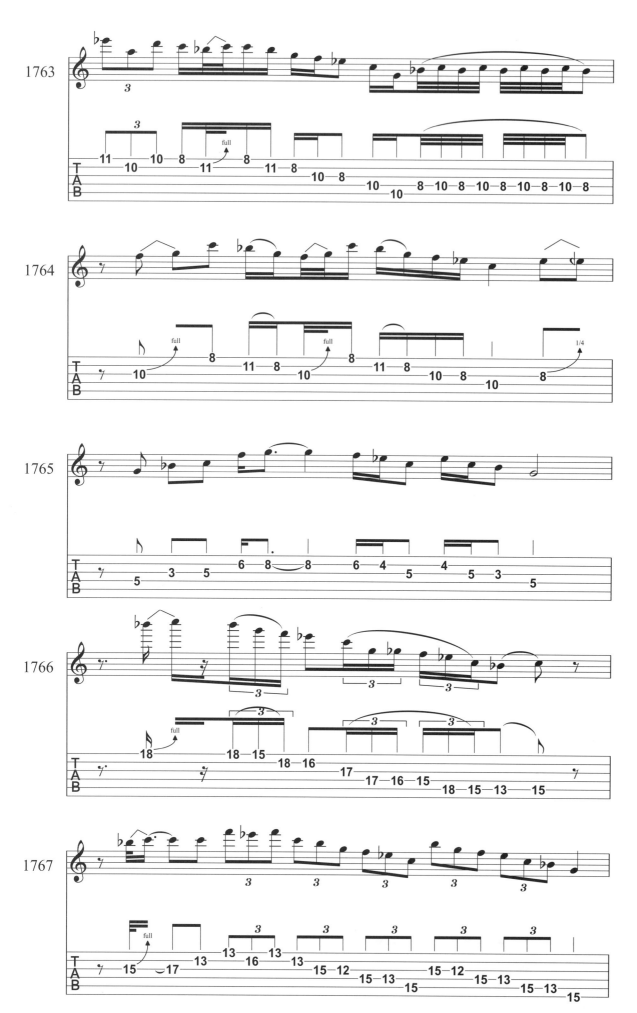

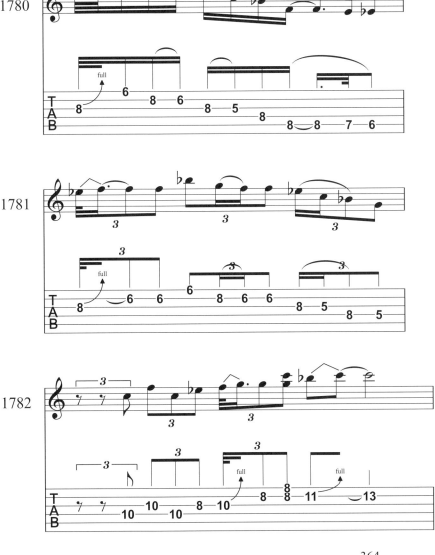

Chapter 33:
Bends to Unisons and Fourths

This chapter focuses on a very common idiomatic blues guitar gesture that does not appear to have a name, even though it has been widely used since being introduced by T-Bone Walker, popularized by Chuck Berry adopted by countless blues, blues-rock, and rock musicians. Often heard at the beginning of a phrase, it can also be played repeatedly throughout an entire phrase to build tension and excitement.

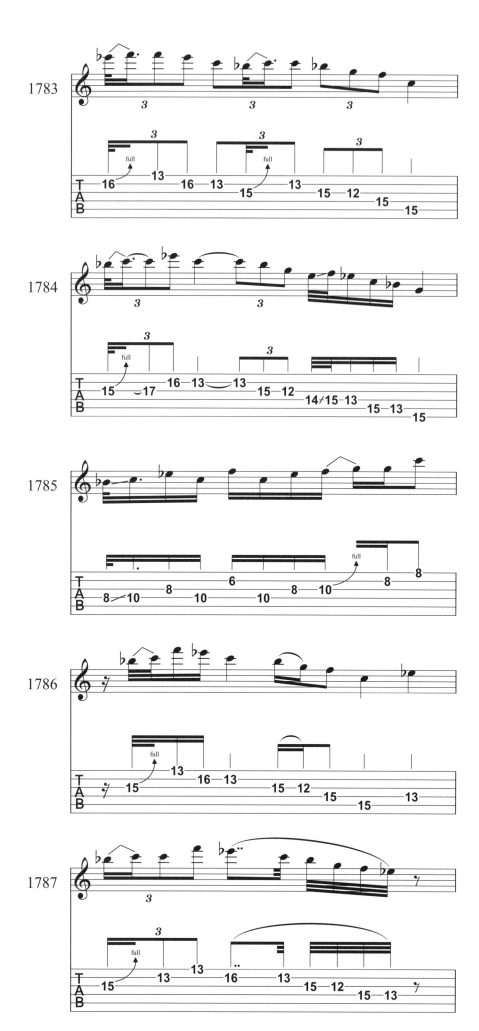

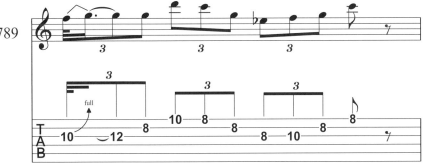

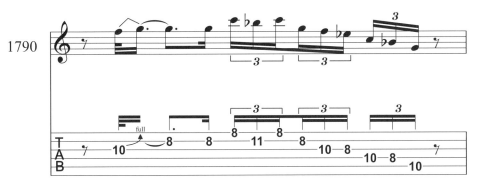

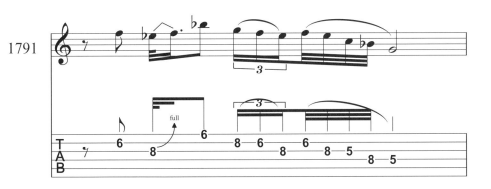

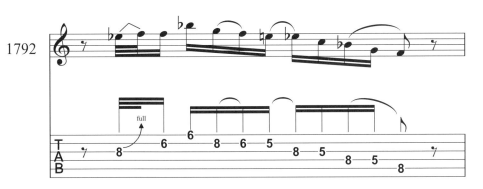

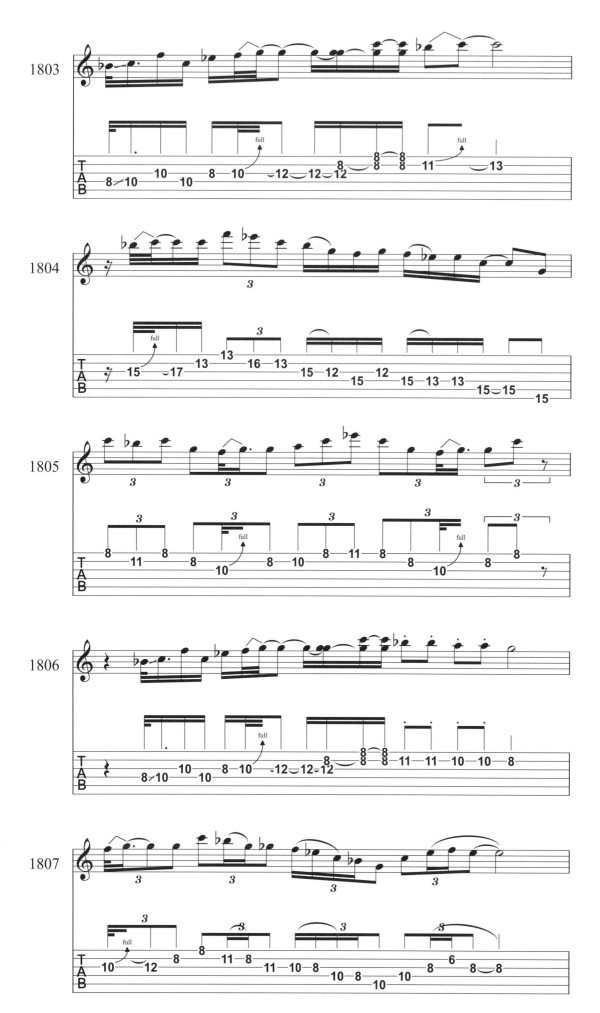

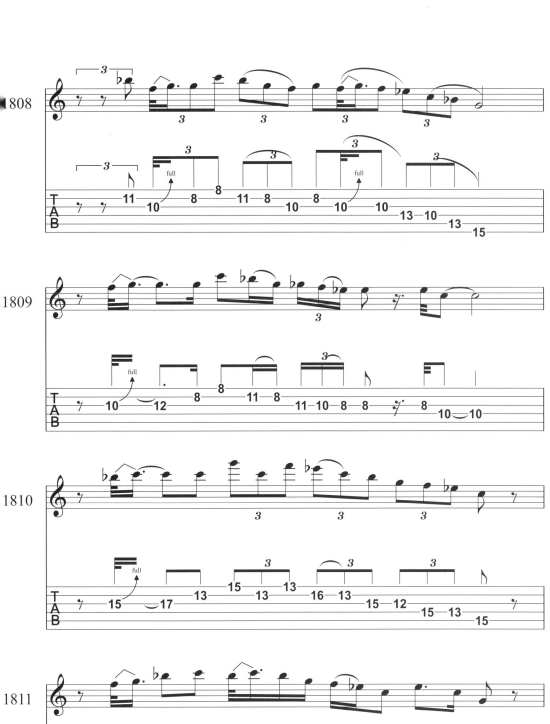
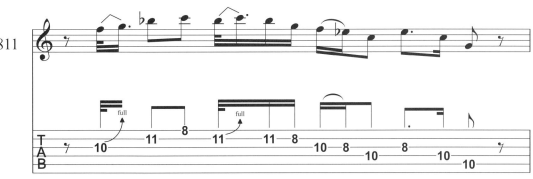
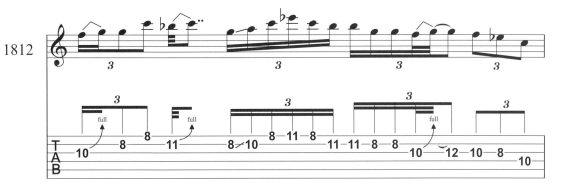

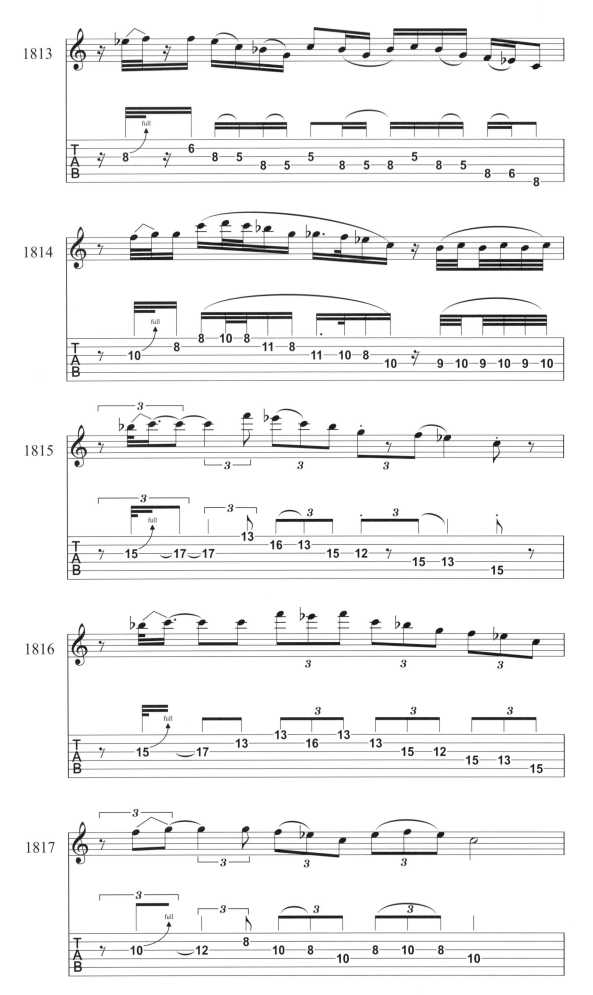

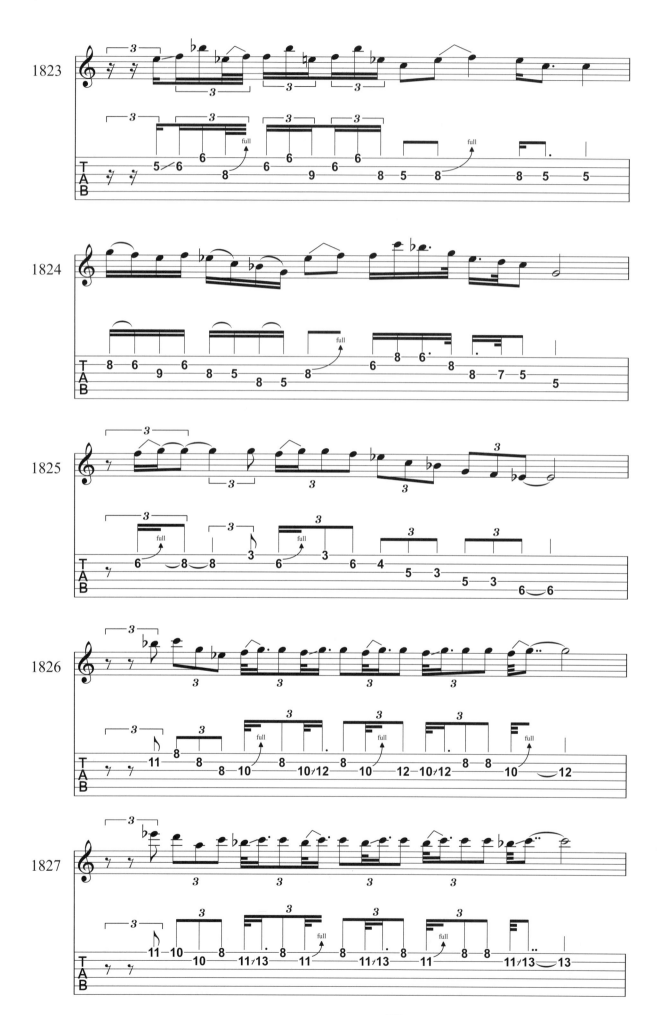

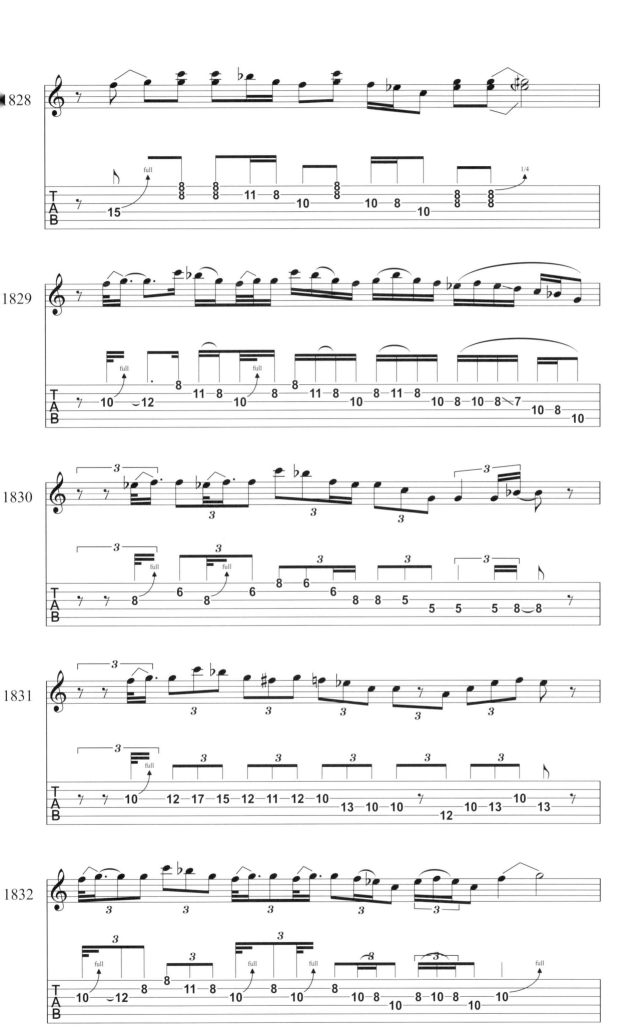

375

Chapter 34:
Melodic Sequences

A sequence is a melodic figure that is repeated at a different pitch level than the original figure. They are very useful tools providing coherence without literal repetition. They should be used with caution, however, since because they can easily sound dry and mechanical.

Because of this, sequences can be very effective when stability and an emotional cooling down period are needed. This gives the listener a chance to recharge and prepare for what will follow.

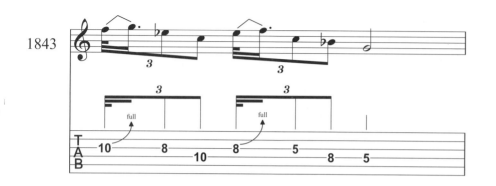

377

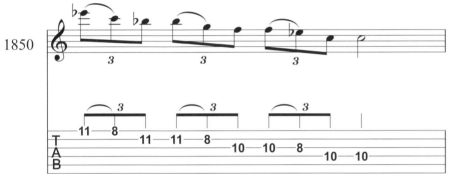

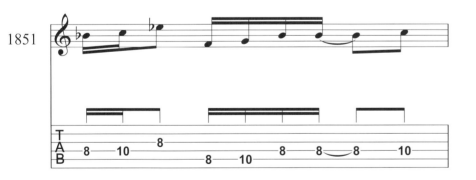

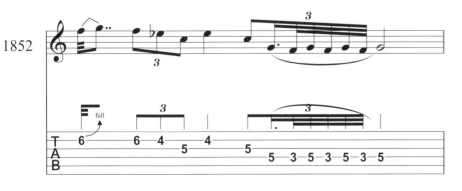

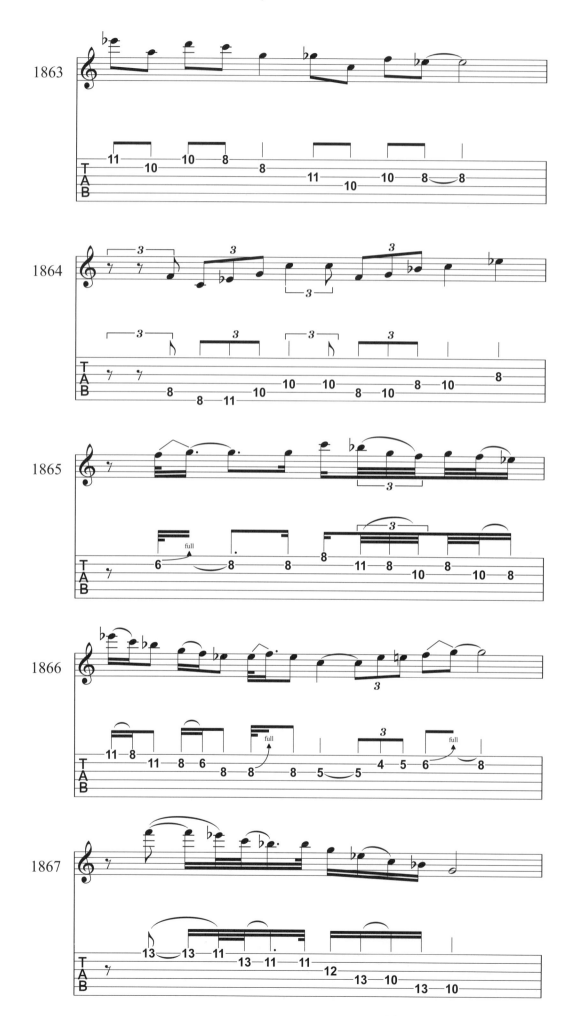

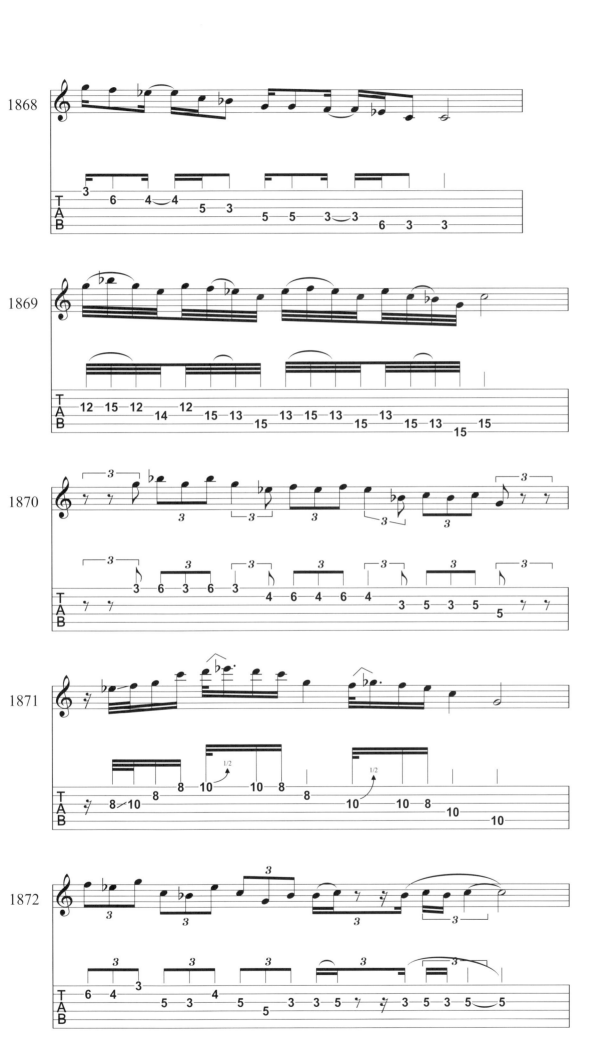

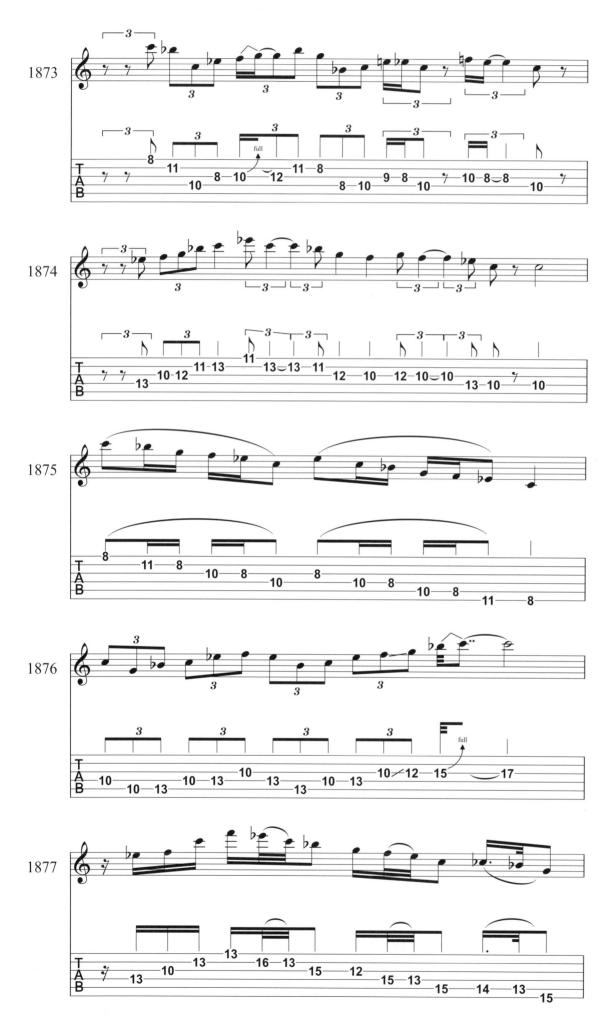

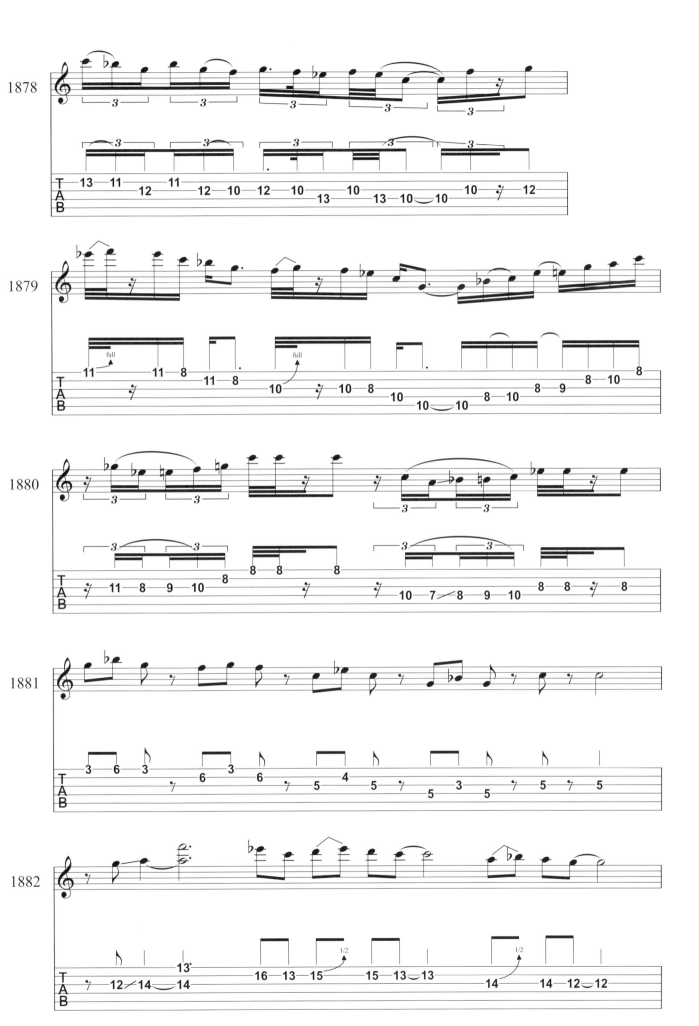

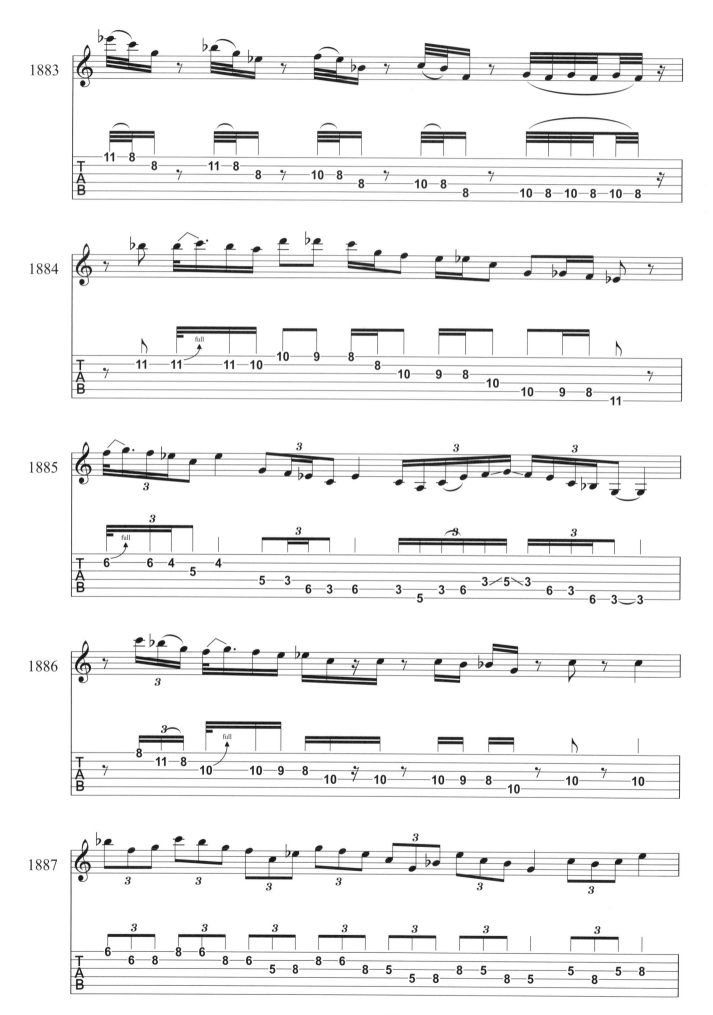

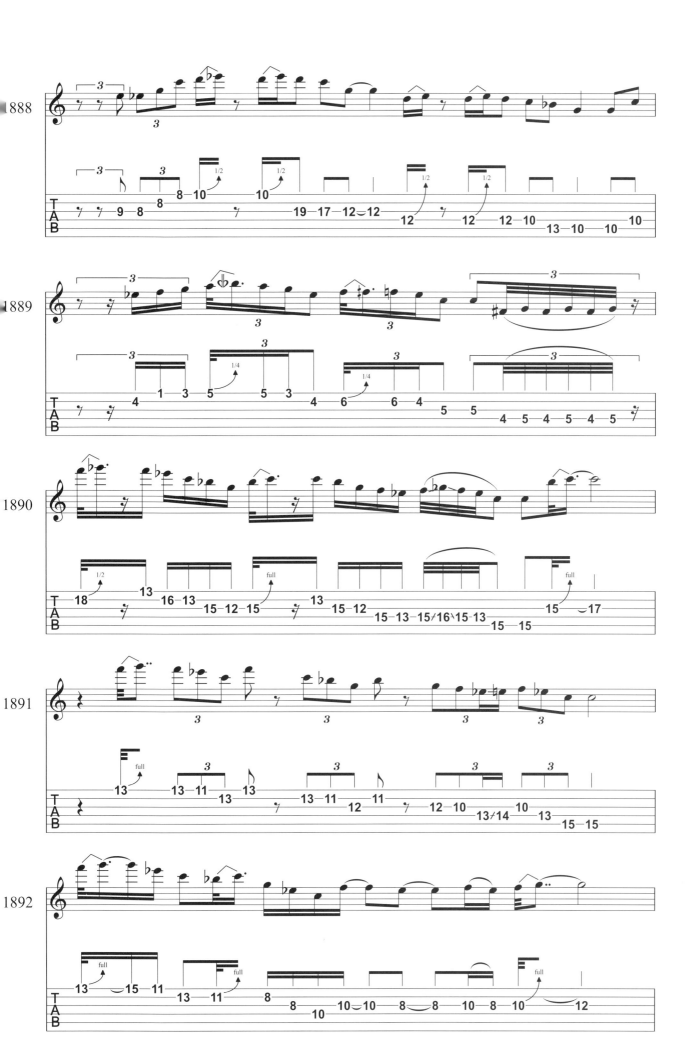

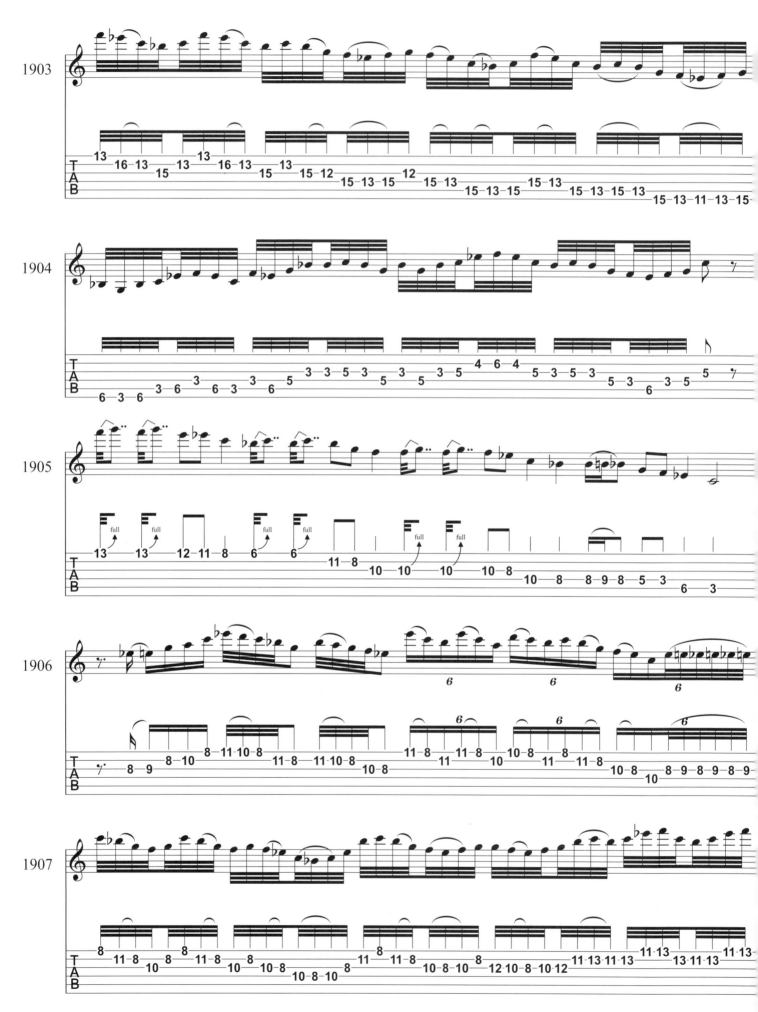

389

908

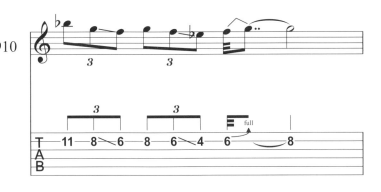

909

Chapter 35: Position Shifts

This chapter explores the technique of fingerboard position shifts. By moving along the length of the fingerboard instead of across it in one position, the guitarist is able to use the tonal quality of individual strings in a unified melodic voice. Mike Bloomfield uses the fingerboard in this way to create a very vocal and linear playing style, as contrasted with someone like B.B. King who tends to stay in one position throughout a phrase. Another consideration is that a guitarist sometimes uses position shifts to set up string bends, trills, slides, dyadic motion, and other string-dependent techniques.

1910

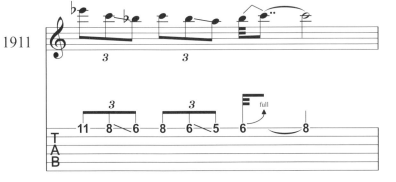

1911

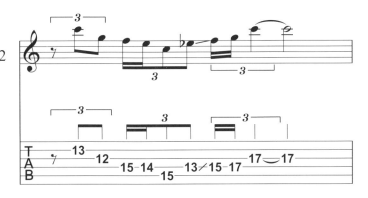

1912

1913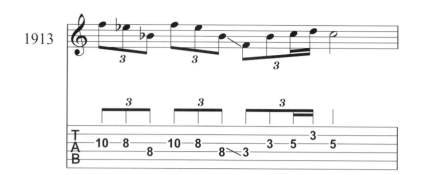

1914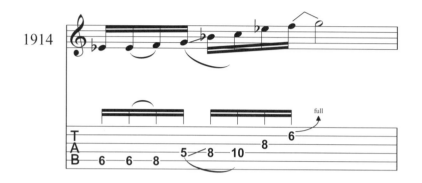

1915

1916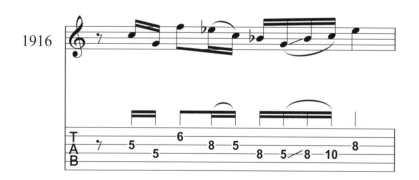

1917

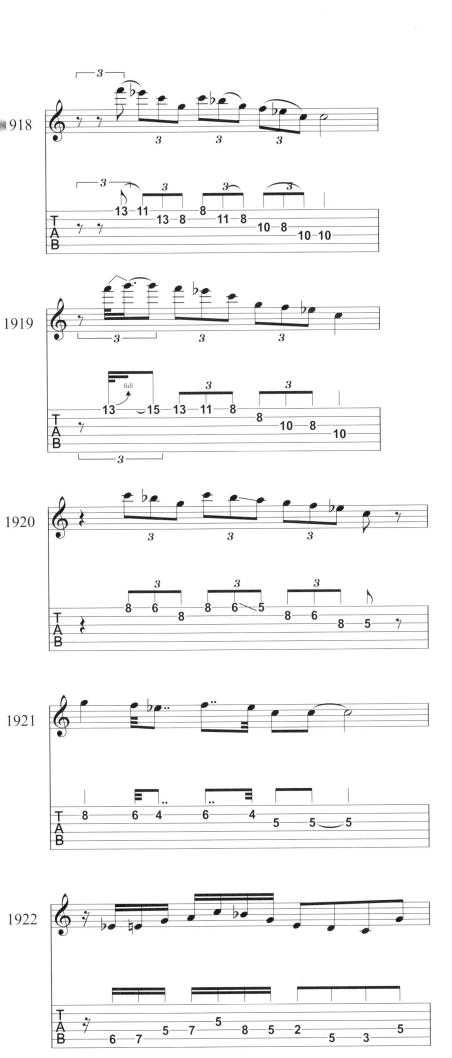

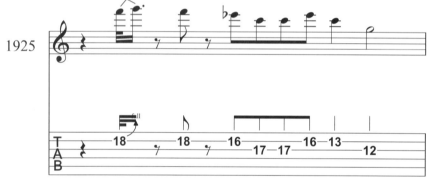

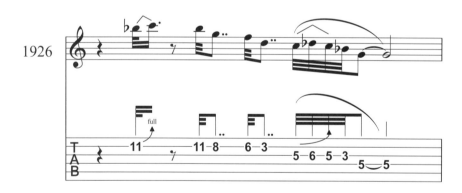

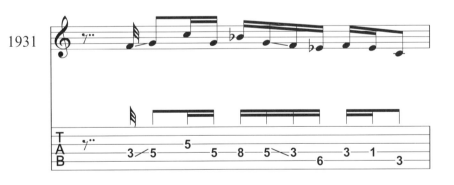

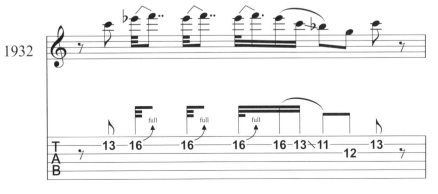

394

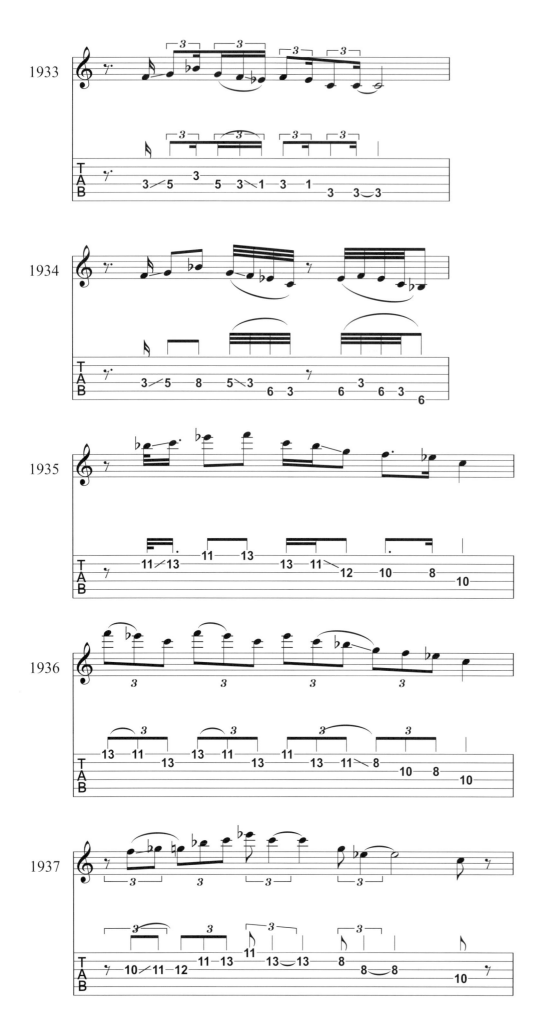

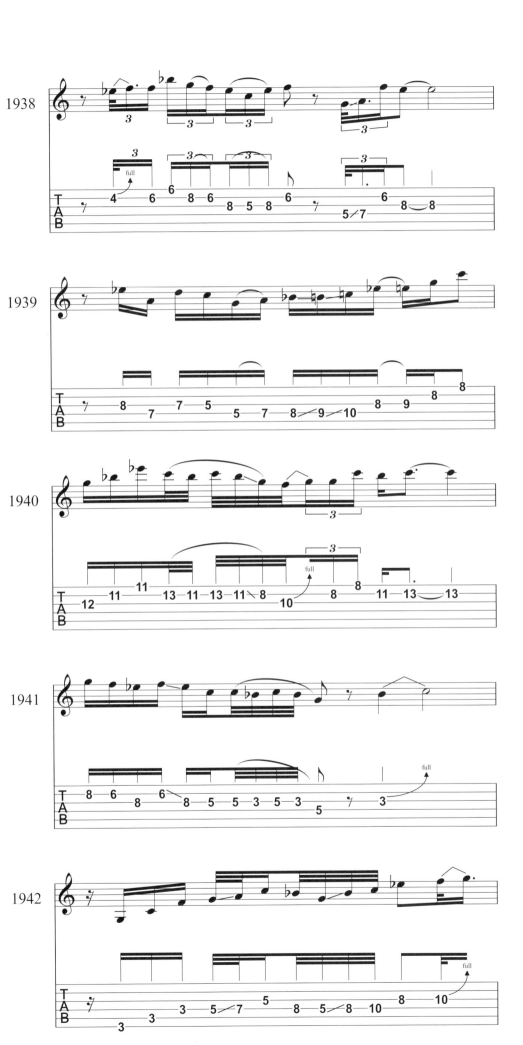

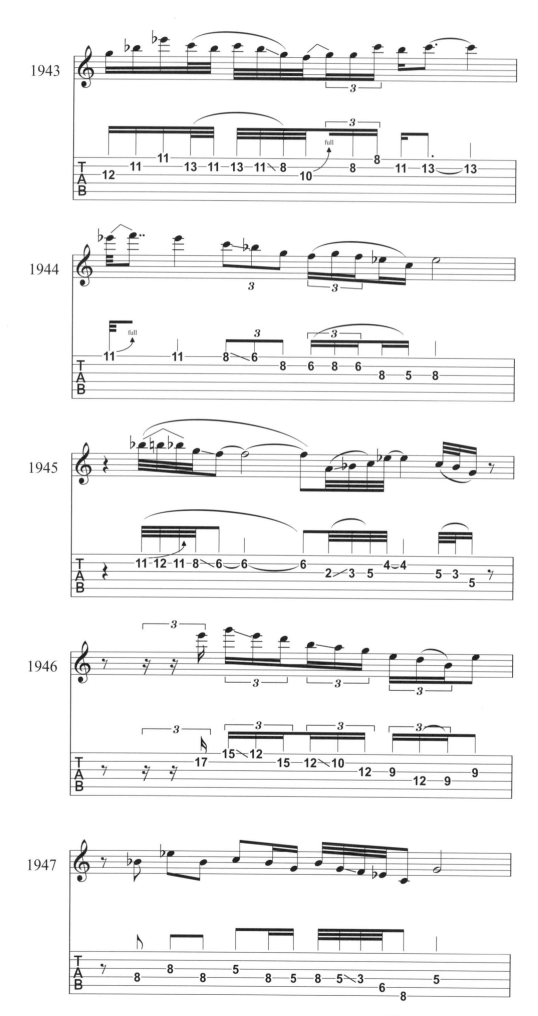

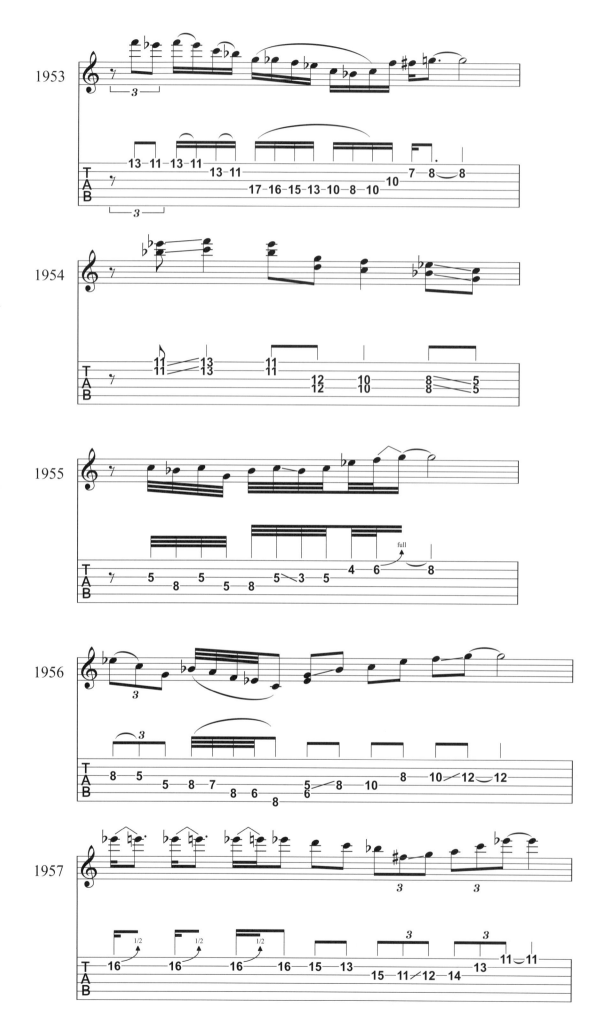

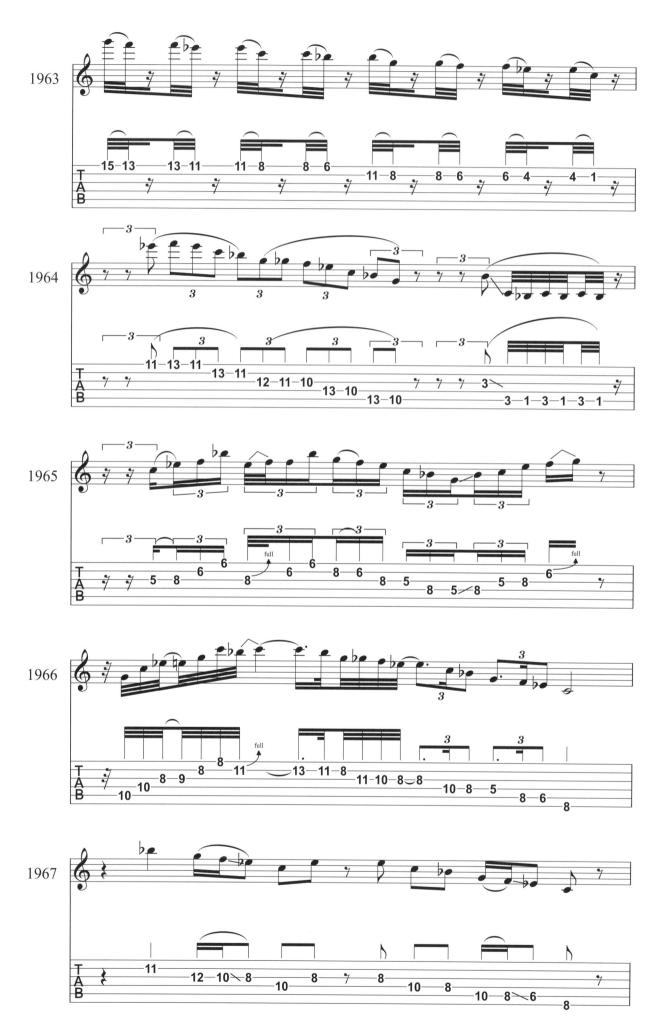

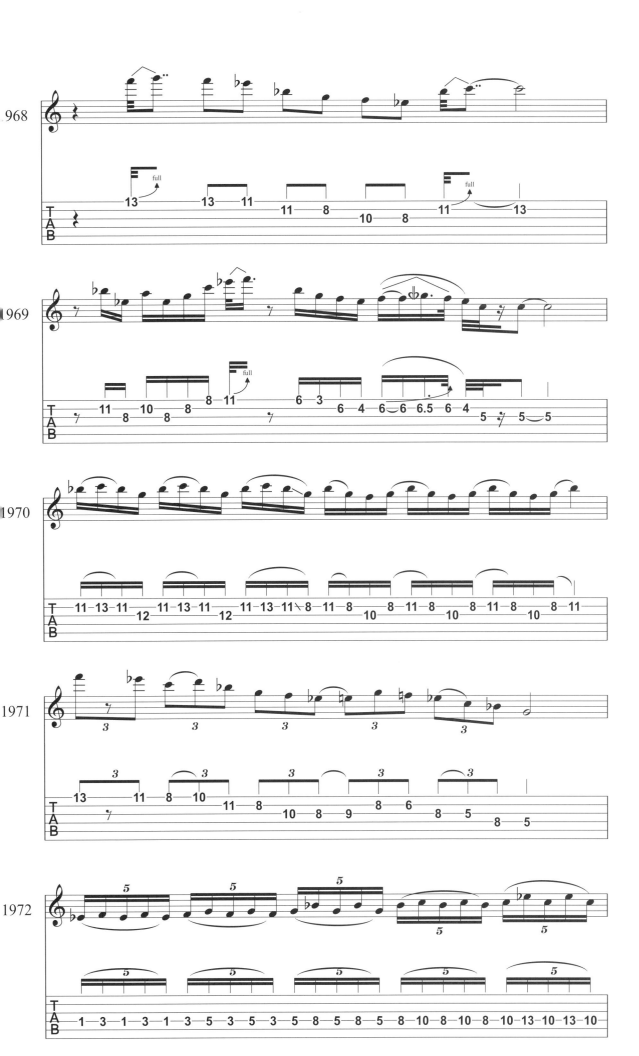

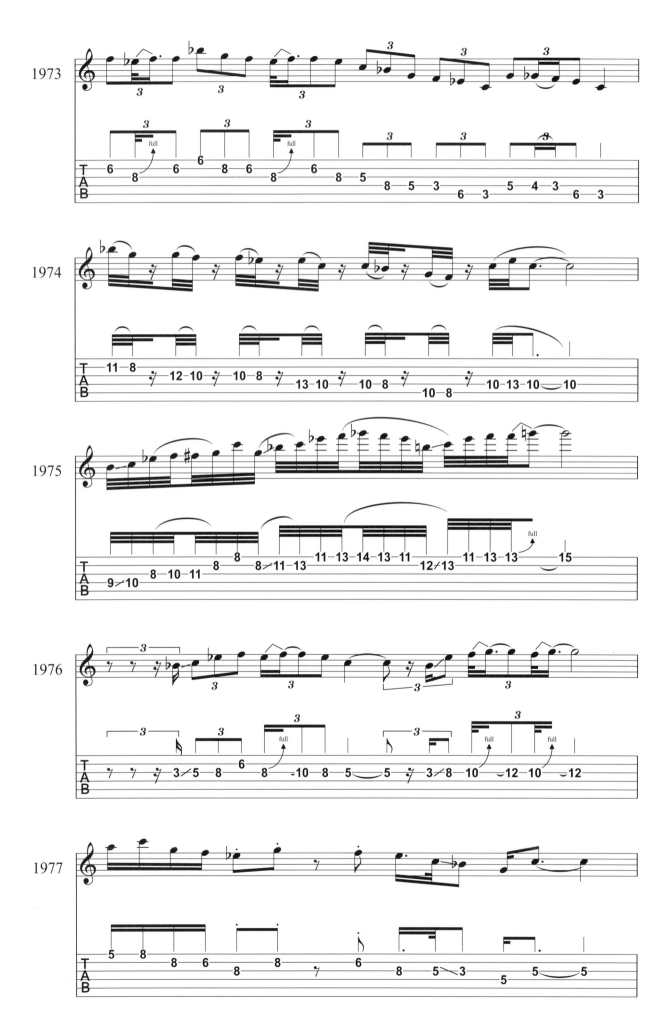

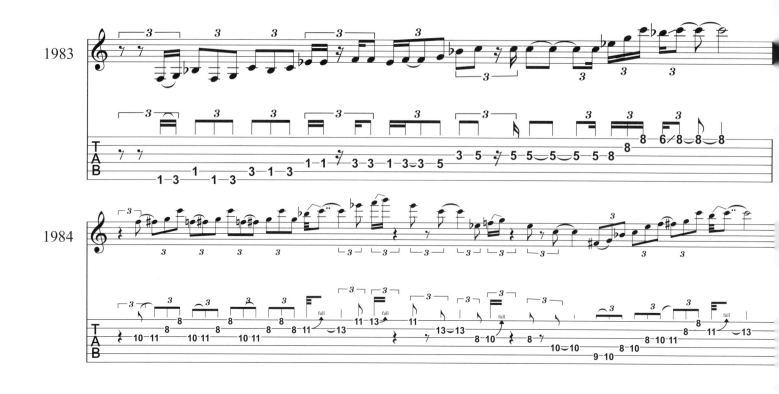

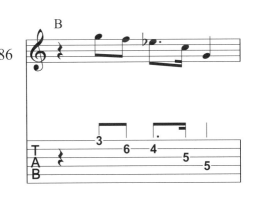

985

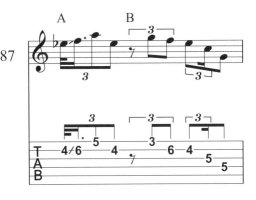

986

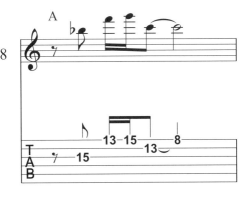

987

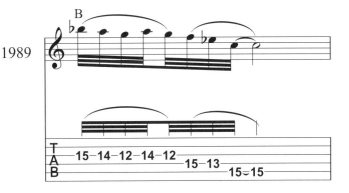

1988

Chapter 36:
Combining Licks

There are two considerations in joining two licks together in the chapter. The first issue is the technique itself. One method is to begin the second lick on the same note that ended the first lick. Another method is to start the second lick one step higher or lower than the note that ended the first lick. The second consideration in joining licks together is how the process is presented in the music. One way is to play the first lick, pause for several beats or more, play the second lick, pause again, then finally play the two licks joined together. Another way of presenting these kinds of licks is to begin with the two licks joined together, as one long lick. As the phrase unfolds, the guitarist can then play the individual licks separately. This allows the listener to examine the material and compare it. While potentially didactic and obvious, it nonetheless is a very effective way of getting the listener more deeply connected with the material in the solo.

1989

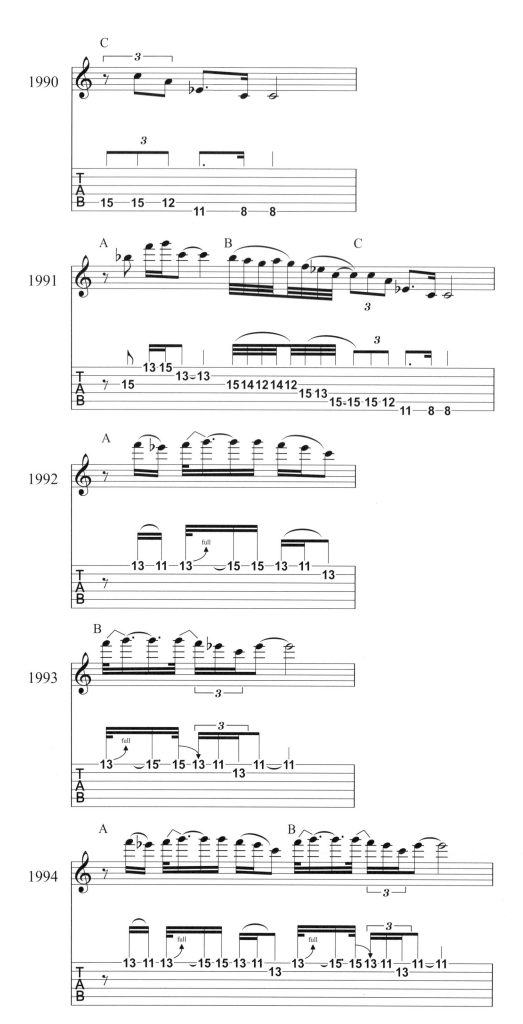

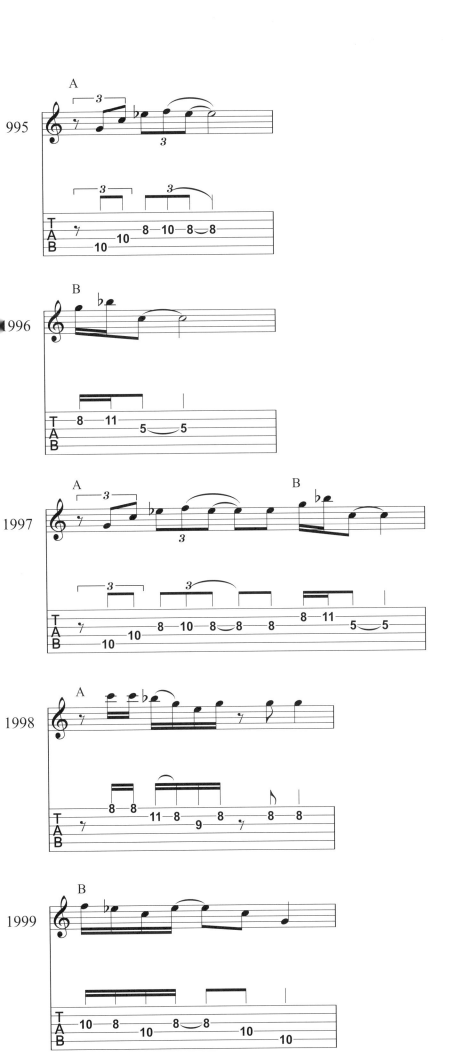

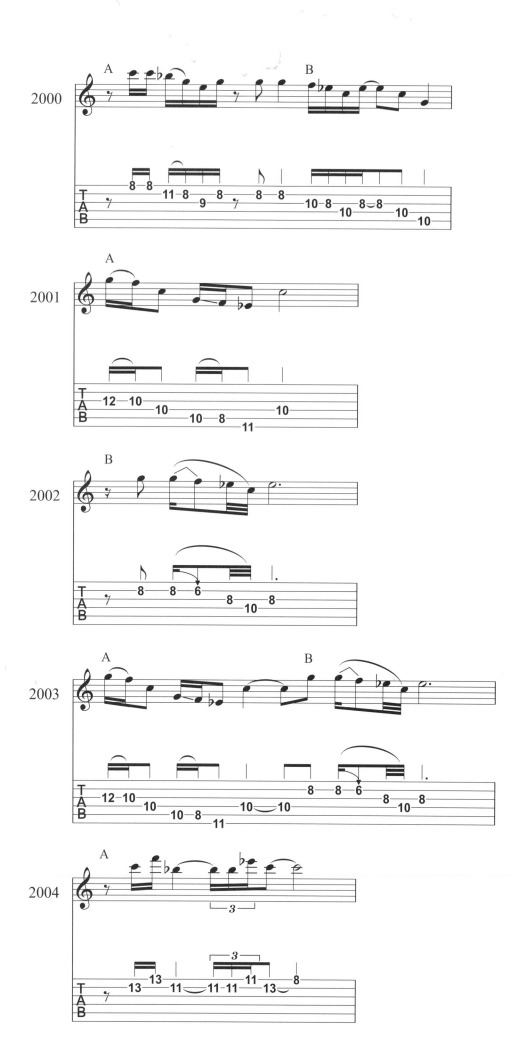

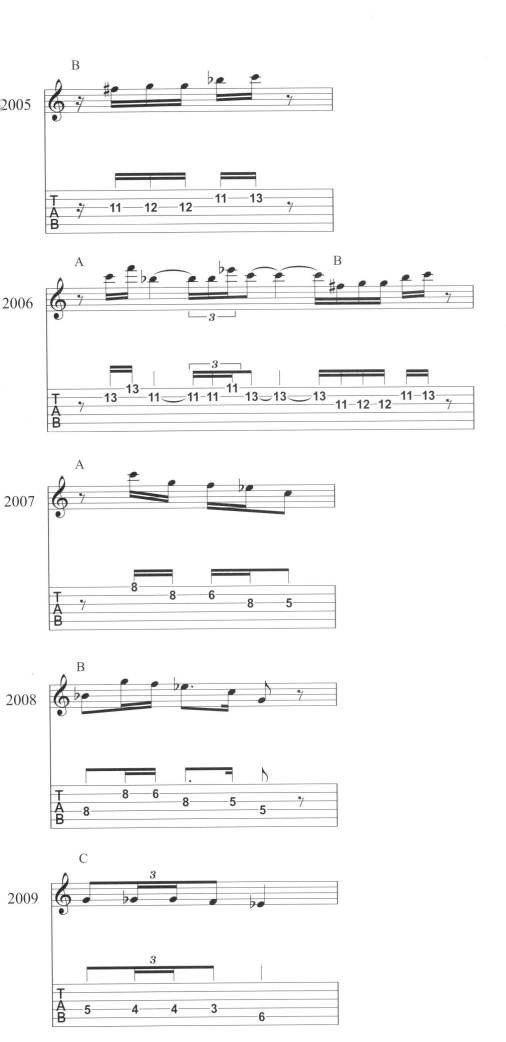

2005

2006

2007

2008

2009

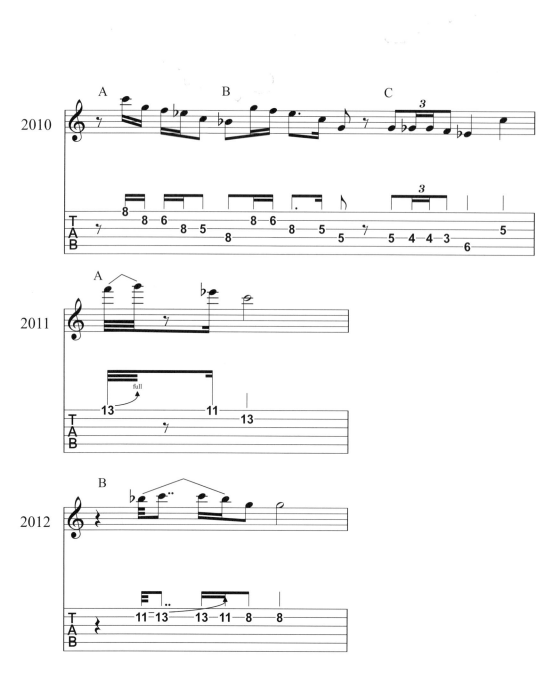

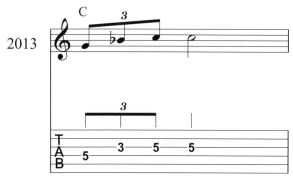

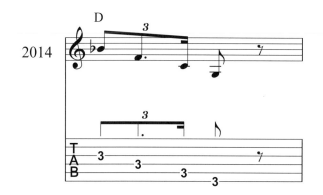

2015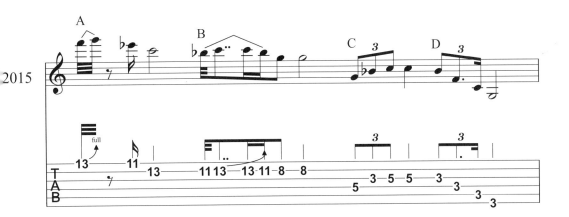

2016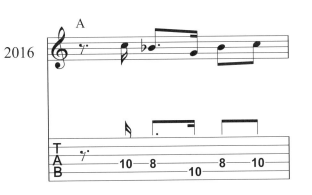

2017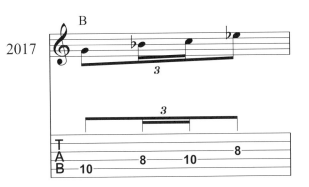

2018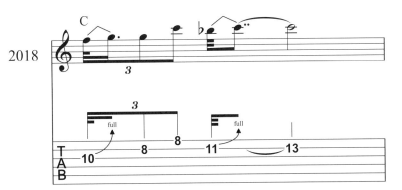

2019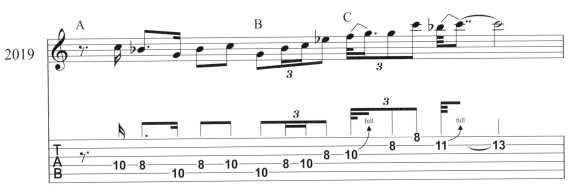

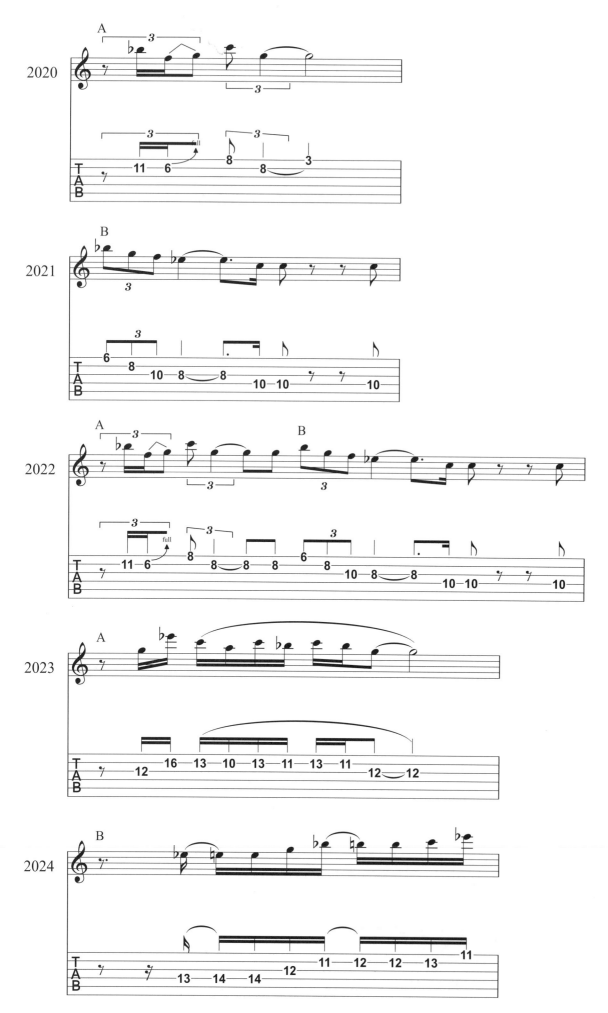

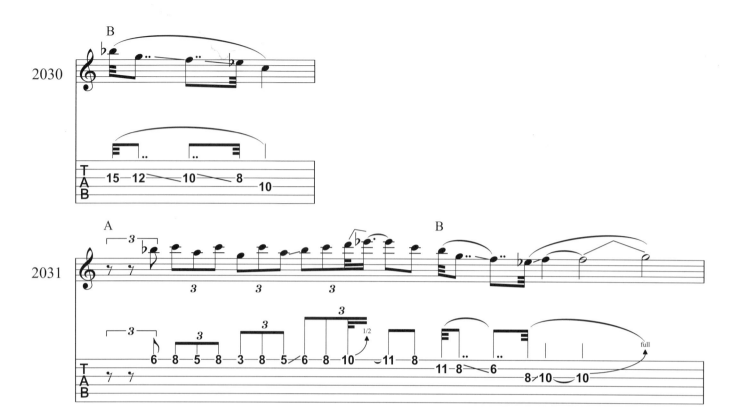

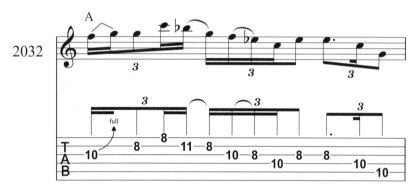

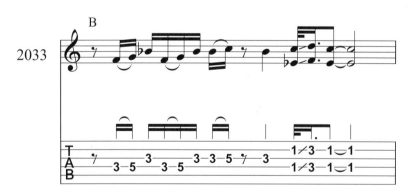

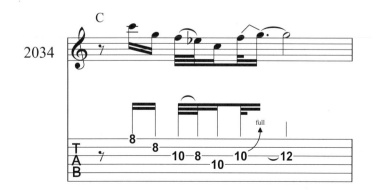

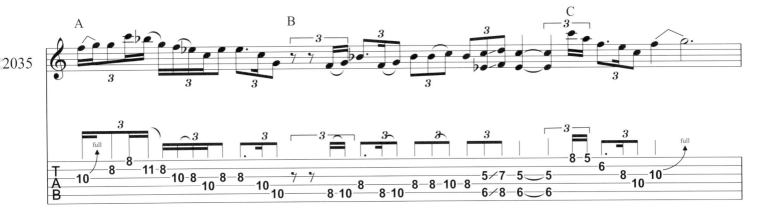

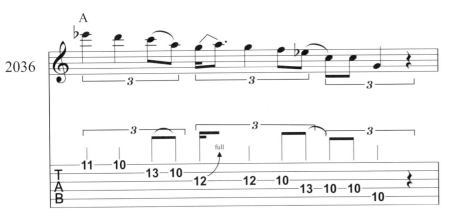

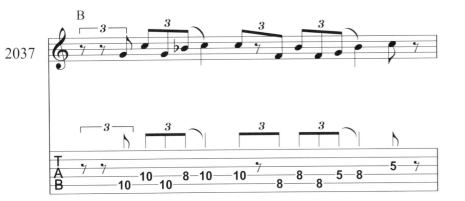

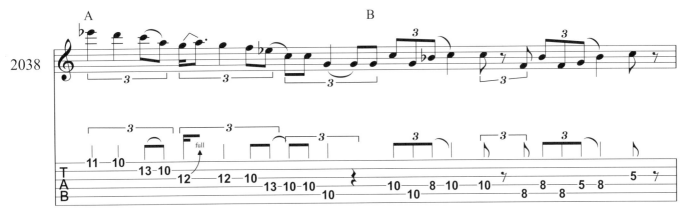

More Great Guitar Books from Centerstream...